A TIME AND PLACE
The Making of an Immigrant

by
Franz X. Beisser, III

ISBN 1-883912-12-1

All illustrations in this book rendered by the author.
Pen and Ink sketches in 1999.

Cover design by author, digitized by Al Beisser.

First Printing December 1999
Second Printing, November 2002

Published by
Bison Printing, Inc.
Bedford, Virginia

REVIEWS

"Franz X Beisser is a proud American. He is also an immigrant and proud to be just that.

With great spirit, proper humility, zero self-pity and prodigious memories, he has compiled more than 130 short stories and anecdotes that span the years in postwar Germany . . .

A Time and Place is more than an autobiography. It is an upbeat testimony that anyone can achieve happiness and success . . .

The strong influences the author describes as being key to the molding of his character bear fruit in the success he has achieved."

–Barbara M. Dickinson, THE ROANOKE TIMES

". . .easy to read . . . you can quit any time you like . . . yet there is a theme to "A Time and Place" that goes beyond anecdotes. Here is a man that lost his father in World War II, endured long series of deprivations as the great conflict wound down, then ended up emigrating to the very country whose soldiers had captured and occupied his home village.

Among the high points of the book for me were stories about how Beisser's mother broke the world record for peeling potatoes (and received a better apartment from the Mayor of Munich as a reward), war stories from his stepfather and an account of Franz's first meeting with American GIs."

–Darrell Laurant, THE NEWS AND ADVANCE

"A warm and witty raconteur, Franz X. Beisser III fills his fast-paced narrative with lively vignettes of growing up in Germany during and after World War II, and starting a new life with his family in America in 1955. The 130 short stories and anecdotes allow the reader to pick it up at will. But once opened, this autobiography is hard to put down.

The young Beisser was a keen and incisive observer, storing up sharply detailed memories, skillfully picturing his family's life as refugees who moved from bomb-shattered Munich to the comparative safety of the small southern Bavarian town of

Griesbach. There the little family made a home above a Gast-haus in a medieval building while his father served his country. His father was lost during the war. Beisser reports how his new stepfather survived ghastly hand-to-hand combat on the Russian front.

This absorbing tale told by an eager and sensitive boy with a fine sense of humor, poignancy, and inspiration leads us through the family's return to city life in Munich, his apprenticeship as a photoengraver, his eventual immigration to America, and how he overcame the uncertainties and anxieties of living in a different culture in a strange country."

–Ravelle Hamilton, THE REVIEW

"The delight of the book is the informal and easy style in which Franz tells his story.

It's the kind of story that holds your interest if for no other reason than how well it is told. The book is also a sincere retelling of one man's engaging journey from boyhood to maturity."

–THE WHITE OAK MAGAZINE

Table of Contents

Book Three

Book Four

FOREWORD

I am proud to be an American. I anxiously waited for five years until I became an American citizen in 1960. The stories in this book are autobiographical, except the ones told to me by my Stepfather who was a soldier for the German army. These WWII stories are his version as I recall them and thus reflect his personal viewpoint rather than mine.

SPECIAL THANKS

Although my wife has heard some of these stories several times over the past 33 years, she always encouraged me to continue with this project. She made many helpful suggestions and corrected words that I had badly butchered. I love her and I thank her.

My two-fingered typing skills afforded my kids many chuckles. They always would say, "Dad is writing his memoirs," grinning from ear to ear. They teased me by saying, "I know you walked to school barefoot in the winter and uphill both ways." But I know they love me and I want to thank them for always being close to me.

I want to thank the good Lord for being a light to my path and for giving me a wife, a family, health and strength and the opportunity to live in the greatest country on earth.

I also want to thank,

Barbara Norton

Karina Inglin

Jim Morrison

There are times one sows–

There are times one tends–

There are times one reaps–

There are times one mends–

There are times one weeps–

In between these times,

One must love

FXB

BOOK ONE

AUTHOR'S NOTE

A flash and a big bang, a cold cellar floor, and a fear of falling from a window– these are the only things I distinctly remember as a three-year-old.

The air raid sirens, the approach and roar of bomber planes, those memories came alive only, when after 30 years I visited the Smithsonian in Washington, DC. Upon entering a wing of the museum that was dedicated to World War II, sounds of bombers and sirens were being played as a background to the exhibit. Such dreadful emotions were aroused in me that I had to leave. I simply could not cope with it.

A picture of me playing in a sand box and one showing soldiers boarding a train completed the time and place that provided me the recall of the events recorded in the first pages of this book.

My father and I on a fishing trip when I was 2 $\frac{1}{2}$ years old.

1943

Südbahnhof, one of several train stations of Munich, was always busy in 1943. The four-story row house we lived in was facing the railyard and also the south and western sun. The rhythmic sounds of the rail cars and steam locomotives became a soothing accompaniment to everyday life. It also evokes a blue and piercing memory, a feeling of sadness, to think my father shipped out to war from that same station.

The window sills were wide, extending outward, overhanging the building's exterior wall. They were surrounded by a wrought iron basket like a cage that enveloped the lower half of the window from side to side. Mom used the sill to grow flowers as well as parsley and chives. You could close the window from the inside and have the miniature garden left to be exposed to rain and sun. I was given my first trembling memories of that time and that place when Mom decided that I needed some fresh air and sun and had me, three years old, sit out on that ledge looking three stories down to the sidewalk below. Seems like sister Dagmar, then just an infant, got to enjoy some sun as well.

The air raids of that time made a dreaded imprint in this little fellow's mind. Often the peace of the moment was shaken by that ever more frequent piercing scream of the siren. It seemed to come through the windows, the walls, the curtains, the ears, the head—straight to the soul. This death blast would come, never respecting whether you were sleeping or just swallowing your first bite of hot cereal. Instantly, Mom, carrying baby sister, and I would, in a state of highest mental and physical agitation, holding on to each other, race down the long flights of stairs to the basement of the tenement. I do not know why, but once down there, I always was looking at that window...one small window up high, probably level with the sidewalk outside, that window that made me tremble so. Mom and us children would be sitting on the damp floor, leaning against a cold wall, looking at that window. There were many other people huddled around the outer walls of that cellar, all mesmerized by one source of light, that window. That light of the moment was not from the sun, since most bombing attacks were at night, nor was it from the street lights, since power was cut off, but from the fires burning. One burning so close it had singed the window curtains in the apartment.

The bursts of orange flashes, accompanied by earth trembling sounds, were a gauge in every one's mind as to how close every bomb was. They were all close, because no railyard was spared. There were never any tears or screams, because fright is not accompanied by tears and cannot be consoled by one's own emotions.

The last etching in my child's soul of that time and place was when the expectation of the worst became reality. A tremendous burst of white light–an earth shattering shock from a hit–the little window exploded amid an enormously hellish flash and was no more. The disintegration of that window formed the final blanket that would put to rest the hell of a three-year old.

Soon after that, the government evacuated most women and children still living in the city. We were allowed to live in a small town in lower Bavaria called Griesbach.

BOOK TWO

AUTHOR'S NOTE

This portion of the book spans a time from age four to ten years old. The events are not necessarily in chronological order. The experiences, though mostly set in pastoral settings, show that even the small turbulences of life can leave an indelible effect on a child.

*Beisser Opa (Grandfather), Franz Xaver Beisser I, and his wife
Katherine on their wedding day. circa 1904*

My parents Friedoline Baumann and Franz Xaver Beisser, II,
on their wedding day Dec. 28, 1935.

A NEW LIFE

The creek pebbles in front of the house felt good on my bare feet as I explored my new surroundings. The quietness was so real you could hear the bees buzzing. The town clock on the church steeple chimed every quarter hour. Listening, I could hear things I had never heard before. Folks were busy doing their daily routine, banging, knocking things, closing doors. There was a bustling that could be heard but not seen. It was all new, a blissful mix of nature and life.

The narrow road to our new place was lined with a picket fence on one side and a fieldstone wall, all covered with vines and moss, on the other. The wide spot in front of the little old stone house was where little sister took her afternoon naps and where grandpa split firewood. It was also the spot from where I explored in all directions. The gravelled wagon road to our place stopped at the wide spot, but the stone wall turned north and became the edge of a pasture. Over this wall hung some of the town's biggest walnut trees. The pasture falling off to the west afforded a little fellow some real chance for exploration. I walked along the cow trots that never went straight up or down the hills but rather followed the contours of the land. Picking daisies for my mom was a delight. Walking on those cow trots a small tyke could just reach up and pluck flowers standing tall above the path. I have forgotten whether I was picking daisies or mushrooms; but while stretching over a wide spot in the path, a big jack rabbit jumped out of a little depression in the grass and practically knocked my arm off as it bounded away. The scare produced an extra dimension in understanding nature as well as a little extra moisture for the grass under my feet.

The town's chimney sweep and his family lived in that little old house, but they willingly shared their cramped quarters. They rented us a small room to which a narrow stairway led almost straight up.

An espalier pear tree clung to the outside wall, sort of

growing around the little window of our room. Mom picked a pair of large pears and put them in a shoe box to ripen until golden yellow. A regular pear tree was in a dale to the side of that little house. I remember the many bees and wasps feeding on the dropped fruit. I, barefoot as usual, picked through the rotten and over-ripe pears, careful not to get stung. We ate the fruit either raw or slightly cooked in a light syrup. Mom called it "Kompot."

EISSTOCKSCHIESSEN

My father came home on furlough for a short while. We would go Eisstockschiessen (like curling) on the community pond. He had a miniature Eisstock made just for me. To get a game going, two teams got together and each team posted at one end of the ice alley that was swept clear of snow. The alley was about 8' wide and 100' long. Each end had a square wooden block that was moveable and it served as the object to aim at. The purpose was similar to horse shoes. The team that slid its Eisstock closest to the "duck" or wooden block added points to its score. The "Eisstock" was a turned block of oak, half the size of a watermelon. Often a lathe was used to cut some grooves and ribs into the wood of the Eisstock to personalize it. A hole was drilled through dead center from the flat bottom to the top of the round. A customized handle with a grip similar a hatchet handle was inserted into the hole. For the proper weight of about five kilo (11 lb.), a

Eisstock

blacksmith created a ring of iron around the bottom, about 3/4" wide and tall. The red hot hoop was placed on the wood, and the whole thing was dropped into cold water. As the hoop cooled off, it forced itself onto the Eisstock. This ring acted like a bumper when the Eisstock was being knocked around during the game. The game required supreme finesse. There were different Eisstock for different ice conditions. The real fanatic would have two or more of them. The first one was for shooting on super slick and smooth ice. On that one, the iron ring would be a little lower than the wood part; so it slid extremely easy with very little effort. The second Eisstock would have the wood portion lower than the ring and was used in conditions when the sliding alley became snowy or covered with refrozen slush. The wood bottom would more easily glide over slightly rough conditions whereas the steel edges would cut into the frozen snow and be slowed up. A spin of the handle during the delivery, much like in bowling, made the Eisstock glide with a hook at the end of its travel, allowing it to sneak around or behind another one and possibly get closer to the "duck". Once the men were hooked on the game, only darkness brought them back home. Home my father must have come because my mother was expecting again. So, the little room in the little house would soon be too small. Mom was much relieved when she found a place more uptown in Griesbach.

Passport photo of my father, 1943

THE NEW PLACE

The new place was truly more in the center of town. The move was only a quarter of a mile, but it was uptown nevertheless. The entrance to our building was right off the market square. Along one side of the square was the only surfaced road in town, and it was of cobblestones. In the center of the town square was a sculpture of a reclining lion on a square marble slab. Since no one bought and sold in the town square any longer, a decorative hedge was planted to form rectangles on the northern and southern half of the square. Row buildings of various shapes and sizes were stuck close together and were all around the square. I remember there was a bakery, a newspaper printer, a bank, a trucking service, a dairy store, a clothing shop, a Gasthaus and restaurant (which was our building). There were various other businesses in which a little boy had no interest. The schoolhouse, which was in the center of buildings on our side, faced the lion.

THE LANDLORD

The Gasthaus was basically a restaurant that offered beer and rooms in years past. It also served as a gathering place for people to play cards and make music. The music often came from a zither. Sometimes there was even umpah-pah style music with dancing. Stories were swapped and acquaintances made. But the Gasthaus that belonged to our landlord was usually not well patronized. Beier Sepp, the owner, always appeared grumpy. He was a short, middle aged man with a big head and a gruff looking face. He wore his dirty hat way down onto his ears, making them stick out. With the brim of his hat pulled down on his forehead, he could avoid making eye contact with the rest of the world. He had a young wife who was somewhat friendly when he was not around. She was taller than he and had fifty pounds on him. Mrs. Beier ran the restaurant, trying to build it up, while Mr. Beier worked long hours in the fields with his horses. In addition, he milked two cows that were stabled at the back of the store. Beier Sepp disliked us and resented our being there. I guess the government made him give up some room for us evacuees whose husband and father was away in the military. I don't think he liked kids in general especially since there were two of us children, and Mom expecting again. Although his wife bore him a son, who was about my age, we hardly saw the kid. It was obvious the parents did not want him to associate with us since we were from the big city and were not really welcome there.

OUR VERY OLD BUILDINGS

The entrance to our dwelling place was not through the restaurant but through a little wooden door which

The great door that led to the apartment over the horse stable.

was cut into two very large wooden doors hanging within a massive stone facade facing the town square. The doors were big enough for a hay wagon to go through. Those big doors covered the entrance to a huge Roman style archway which led into and through the main building. We were given a key to the little door. That key was so heavy and big, I practically had to carry it with two hands. As you entered the door, you were in darkness; and a cool breeze always hit your face. The light you saw was coming from the other end of the arched way, about 50 feet away. The rear stables, which were all connected to the front building, could be accessed after going through this tunnel. This passageway turned into an uncovered alley between the horse stables and the milk cow stables. Over the horses was a second story that had served as quarters for soldiers during medieval times. The walls that supported the halls above were massive. Stone buttresses about every ten feet jutted out at the base and gradually tapered in to meet the flat wall about twelve feet up. All of the arched way and alleyway were lined with large cobblestones. They were so big that a small boy's feet could never run across them for fear of slipping to the side and wrenching an ankle or worse.

UPSTAIRS WHERE WE LIVED

Cut into one side of the arched way were two recessed arched door openings. One led to the kitchen of the Gasthaus, and one led to the upstairs. As you entered, stone steps turned left with every step until you got to a landing with two doors. One led to our front room, the other led to more rooms over the Gasthaus. The farmer's cold storage for dairy products and winter vegetables was below our front room. I had the privilege once of getting a peek into that cave-looking arched room. When the door was opened and the day's light hit the wall, literally thousands of roaches scurried like a wave toward the nearest dark corner. Where we lived, we had no roach problem; I guess they had enough to live on where it was damp and closer to ground level. Upstairs in our front room was a half-round, brass sink or basin hanging on the wall with a water spigot above the center. The front room led to our rooms, the Johnny house, and to the attic.

The attic was strictly off limits, not only for us kids but also for Mom. The stairs were boxed in with boards to keep the cold air from coming down. On one occasion Mom did sneak up to the attic while I stood guard at the door below. Mom came down with an old green bottle that was about a third full of a syrup-like liquid. Whether Mom consumed it or poured it out, I do not know; however, for years after that, the green bottle with a sprinkler added where the cork stopper had been, served as a sprinkling bottle to prepare clothes for ironing.

SOME GOOD SIZED RATS

In the front room under the attic stairway we stored kindling wood which provided an excellent place for rats to build nests. It is a strange thing, but I do not remember ever having mice. I guess the rats must have eaten them. Those grey varmints sure got aggressive when the kindling was being used and their nesting places were disturbed. I remember in particular one large joker that bounded out of the woodpile and darted around the front hall. Mom went after him and clubbed him to death with the broom but not before he had run up the walls in big semi-circles. Mom had me get the dust pan, which was not a dainty one, and put that rat in it. The thing was as wide as the pan with the entire tail hanging over the edge. We then politely pitched him out the window. He landed in front of the stables where Beier had a chance to contemplate its beauty. Mom thought it necessary on one occasion to borrow a friend's German Shepherd dog. We kept him in the front room for a week and supplemented his diet of rats with fresh bowls of water.

INTERESTING ROOMS

To get to our main room or kitchen, one went through the wooden door to the left of the water basin. This long room was facing south and was directly over the horses below. Looking out the window, one could see the tile roof over the milk stable, which was also made of stone. Behind it were various shops and stone buildings with tile roofs. All were attached to the front, or main structures, of neighboring businesses facing the plaza. The main room of our assigned living quarters was about 10' wide by 30' long, with a high ceiling. The room had a small frieze around the top of the walls just below the ceiling. Mom divided the room with a curtain between the two windows.We put our eating table under the one light bulb hanging from the ceiling. The wood burning cookstove had a small firebox, with four eyes on top and an oven. Mom always had a pot of water heating on the stove, as well as her iron that had the wooden handle removed until she had need of the iron. When summers got hot, it got hotter in the kitchen. When winters got cold and the cooking fire died down, we went to bed. From the main room a door led to a similar shaped room but darker. It had one small window, with wrinkled glass, facing north and looking down into the backyard. The backyard, shaded by a big beechnut and a huge horse chestnut tree, faced a side road which led to the plaza. Mom also divided that room with curtains and furniture to make a room to rent. It had its own window and entrance from the front hall. She rented it, most likely at no charge, to a young woman from Sudetenland who had been displaced by war. That young lady became a live-in baby sitter for my two-year old sister and me, and later the twins. soon though, the young lady left to pursue her own life.

Mom and my father were married for five years before I was born. With both working before the war, they had been able to acquire some nice furniture. Mom was especially proud of her bedroom suite.

We loved our lightweight, down covers and the feather

pillows in the summer, as well as our huge feather beds and feather underbeds in the winter. The wood furniture was dark and shiny. A large wardrobe, a mirrored dresser, two beds side by side, and two night stands completed the set.

THE SECRET COMPARTMENT

In the kitchen area, Mom had a good-sized hutch that stored the fine dishes (breakable ones) on top and the pots, pans, and cookie trays on the bottom. On the right side, covered by a little door, was a spice rack. The spice rack itself was hinged and could be swung out allowing for some more storage behind it. Behind the spices was a small, hidden shelf. You could get to its secrets only when you swung the rack all the way out. Mom had hoarded, by advice from Beisser Opa (Grandfather Beisser), all the silver coins she could. Hitler decreed it unlawful for citizens to keep silver coins; hording silver coins might hinder the war effort. After 1945, those coins became very valuable, as paper money was worth absolutely nothing. I expect that several of these coins were wisely traded by Mom to sustain us, maybe to save our lives. To this day, the Beisser family still has some of these coins.

OUR WINDOW

The windows in the main room, which were facing south, were a good size but had no fly screens. Mom constantly hung from the ceiling those sticky, long, brown paper curls to which flies stuck. They were never enough. With the horse and cow dung below, we had a vast host of flies. The most I ever killed with one smack was nine flies. The flies all sat in a circle around a drop of sweets.

The window sills were wide on those old buildings, wide enough to hold trays of nuts and fruits to dry. After the first frost, we gathered small pears which seemed to grow on scrubby trees only along the dusty roads. They were very bitter and not edible during the year; however, after the first good frost, they fell to the ground, turned black, and became very sweet. We dried them on the window sill until they were hard and totally shrivelled up. We called them "Glätzen". During the cold days, Mom reconstituted them by simmering them in hot water. We all loved them. During the summer, we strung up mushrooms and hung them in the window; in the late fall, it was apples.

A window was part of life–where God sent through His warmth that loosened the stiffness of the elderly and chased the pallor away in the children. A window also shielded us somewhat from the elements outside and was often decorated on the inside with wonderful swirls and scrolls of frost that collected and shimmered on the panes.

With a large roof overhang, the windows could stay open most of the summer. Every year a pair of swallows nested along the stucco frieze near the ceiling in the curtained-off part of the main room. That portion had its own window. As to why Mom allowed the swallows to nest in one of our rooms, I can only guess. Thinking back, life was so very simple. Watching the life cycle of a pair of birds and their young probably was like having some cheerful friends around.

SCARY TIMES

My father did not know that Mom was expecting, much less that she would give birth to twin girls. Two were a surprise to Mom as well. The first baby arrived without much trouble. When the pangs of giving life did not subside, Mom was shocked as the midwife told her to get ready for another baby. The second girl was born feet first about twenty minutes after the first. Mom told me that it had turned blue and was not breathing. The baby was revived by a very skilled midwife at the small hospital in Griesbach.

Baumann Opa (Grandfather Baumann) was staying with us. My sister Dagmar and I got to visit Mom in the hospital. The hospital was very crowded those days, and Mom was on a small bed in the hallway. During one of our visits someone noticed that little Dagmar did not look well. Checking her, they found she had a very high fever. They kept her in the hospital and discovered that she was only constipated.

POTTY SCIENCE

After that scary episode, Mom delegated most of the potty science to me, the ever-curious five year old. Of course, we kids used the potty mostly during the night when nature called. Sister used it all the time. In cold weather, we both would use it during the day as well because of the icy wind that whistled up the outhouse shaft. The use of the potty had many other tactical advantages, such as monitoring the daily bowel movements of kids. Constipation was checked so Mom would know when to let up on the feeding of breads, noodles, pancakes, and such. Stewed prunes were always on standby. Of course, there was the constant watch for

The Science Lab

worms, which appeared quite often, and usually had other itching early warning signs as well. The regular dose of medicine for worms was a sugar cube with a drop of turpentine. Sister Dagmar once had a time when she became lethargic and weak. With a doctor's advice and some medicine, little sis passed a potty full of dead tapeworm. The pinkish white, 3 to 5-mm wide worm had come out in sections of 3 to 15-mm long. I remember the rejoicing in the victory over the silent devourer.

Dagmar also accidentally swallowed one of my marbles. After the third or forth stirring of the deposits in the potty with a stick, I found the marble - another occasion for rejoicing.

THE FLYING OUTHOUSE

As I got a little older and bolder, I was allowed to use the grownup's throne room. It was a medieval masterpiece. From the back yard, it looked like a pair of giant bird houses just stuck up there. The "flying outhouse" was actually attached to the outside wall. It was precariously clinging there, high up, with an enclosed wooden shaft extending down fifteen feet to almost the ground. The outhouse was in a corner of the ell-shaped building, facing north. It was a two-seater, partitioned only by a couple of vertical boards. The only decoration in the room and on that partition was a wire hook which I laboriously filled with little square pieces of newspaper. We could enter the Johnny house from our front room. The first seat, after entering this private chamber, was ours to use. The second seat was used by a man who we never got to know. He lived in an apartment over the Gasthaus about fifty feet from ours. We never knew his name or whether he had a wife. We never bothered him when he used his assigned throne, and he never bothered us. We always shied away because he never spoke. This went on for about five years until we moved.

Our half of the throne became a subject of study to

me. The shaft, being in a corner, would catch every breeze, as well as raging winter gusts, and would amplify them up the shaft. My derriere was not enhanced enough to cover the entire opening on that wooden box, so in times of excessive upward drafts, I did not linger. It was always annoying when the lighter liquid came flying back up at you. The wiping became a science not taught by the elders but by the physics of the situation. Usually the first wipe would force you to make the appropriate adjustment. You knew it was no use trying to fight the wind and the laws of nature when the used paper refused to go down into the hole, but would stick to you or float around in the room. Wiping then was simply done with one hand and the used paper collected in the other. When finished, you jumped off the box, pants around the ankles, grabbed the large wooden lid with the round knob in the center, and with a closely timed movement, pitched the handful of used paper down the shaft, quickly closing

The Flying Outhouse in the corner, and bedroom window upper right.

the lid. Now, as I said, the timing had to be very precise. If you slammed the lid down too fast, you would smash your hand on the way out of the hole. Conversely, if you were too slow, with your face now straight over the opening and the draft coming up, you might wind up doing a little dance and ducking step to get away from the airborne little papers.

In less turbulent moments, I would linger on that seat and watch the drama of the great spider in the little window. The glass panes were long gone, so the spider could monitor the comings and goings of every fly. The drama of life and death in that window was great entertainment. I don't think I have ever seen a movie that surpassed it. The Johnny became a sanctuary to me, as it was and always will be to every man: a place to ponder, to think things out, a headquarters for inspiration and long range planning. Now fifty years later, blessed with a family and a business of my own, it is still the only board I ever sat on–the one with a hole cut in it.

Over the years, the pit just below the shaft had gotten full and was now overflowing, oozing along the north wall and beneath our bedroom window. It was a shaded back yard. The murky substance would mostly seep into the ground along that back wall. During the wet season, however, the seepage moved along the entire back wall of the stables, across the rear entrance to the buildings, then turned right onto a sunny area where Mom was allowed to have a garden spot. Ah, the bureaucrats of this day and age could have hyped and regulated over such a situation for a lifetime, but we grew cabbage!

A NICE VISITOR

The curtained-off room next to the kitchen was used mostly for storage. It was also where my twin sisters had slept in their cradle. This cradle was like a large wicker basket, made for twins, with rockers. They slept close to the door leading to our bedroom. Mom always had her babies bundled-up in cold weather. The temperature in that room, as well as our bedroom, often got down to the freezing point and below. Every morning I jumped out of my bed and ran to see the babies. They would flail their arms and be glad to see me.

Mom would have to beg for milk for the twins. Our landlord would not offer any. One night, just before the Americans arrived, the Lord called the first of my baby sisters. Delores was four months old when she died. That morning she was still, ashen gray, with her sister Friedoline beside her just staring a frightened stare. Part of my life had passed away. Five months later, Friedoline became ill and died, delivered from a sparse and scary world. Mom moved the empty cradle over next to the window up against the wall, sort of under the abandoned swallow's nest.

As a waitress, Mom was on call and ready at all times. The few times she worked, she left my sister Dagmar and me alone. On one of those evenings, after I helped Dagmar get to bed, I sat alone at the kitchen table under the light bulb, absorbing the last radiance of warmth from the stove, drawing pictures. An almost imperceptible sound disturbed the stillness of the night. My attention was drawn to the curtained off room. Listening very intently, I knew it was the casement window opening. Perplexed as to how this could happen, I got up and very quietly peeked into the dark room. There, to the right of the window, directly over the empty crib, hovered a very bright shape, a shape like an angel with arms straight out forming a cross. The apparition was bright white with indistinct edges, made no sound, and had no face. Puzzled, I returned to the table to ponder what I had seen. Then, I heard the window again. Getting up the second time, I looked and found the vision gone and the window once again closed tightly. This experience was very real to me, and to this day I do not know the reason or message behind it.

OOPS!

My mother, a firm believer in lots of fresh air even in the coldest of weather, often bundled me up and sent me out to play. Likewise, my sister, never too young for fresh air, was wrapped and tucked in woolens, put in the carriage, and set out to enjoy. I was told not to wander off too far, and to keep an eye on Sis. During cold weather it seemed like it snowed all the time. Anyway, I totally forgot about little sister. Apparently Mom did also. When I finally checked on her, the carriage was full of snow, except around Dagmar's little head were I saw her face as she lay there peacefully taking her nap.

GOING TO BED WAS NOT PUNISHMENT

Mom never had a steady job during those years but was called to waitress (which was her learned trade) mostly on weekends when social events were going on. Those evenings, when I was five and older, with Sis three years younger, we had to fend for ourselves. I usually put sister to bed then returned to the kitchen table, the center of all activities. Again, I'd like to mention the extreme quietness of life in those times. The kitchen clock, with its dome shape, added a constant ticking that soothed and somewhat mesmerized. A little crackling in the stove made the evening complete. When all the fire was gone, I went to bed also. Bed was a heavenly place, a refuge from the cold. On very cold nights when Mom was home, we would pre-heat the foot area of the bed with a warm water bottle. It was oval and solid brass, about as big as a football. This warm friend was kind of flat, with a screw-on cap on top. A little chain soldered to the cap and the bottle kept them from being separated. The water bottle was real shiny, and we could easily slide it around under the featherbed to our desired spots. It was wonderful. Other tricks we used to warm the bed were several clothes irons wrapped in towels, as well as a hot cobble stone or two. I remember almost sneaking up to the bed, reaching in with arms stretched and moving the warming objects around under the covers until heaven was ready. When I jumped into bed in the winter time, I lay between a feather tick under me and a feather bed as thick as a fat man's belly on top of me. The pillow, also stuffed with feathers, was as wide as the bed; and when my head hit it, it would collapse around my ears. In the dead of winter when the stone walls of the building got as cold as the outside, I would pull my knitted hat down over my face with nothing but my nose sticking out. At times the horses below would kick their stalls but mostly the nights were deathly silent. My sister and I would overreact to any noise and crawl into bed even deeper. How many times I remember waking up in the morning when the breath of the night's sleep was frozen and formed a circle of hard crust on the feather bed covering.

The neighboring cemetery had in its midst a funeral chapel. It was home to several large hoot owls which always sounded off in the night and made two little kids wide-eyed and well-behaved, especially when the large owl decided to sit on our lone window sill of the bedroom, look in at us, and hoot loudly, while bobbing its head from left to right. We prayed a lot.

LEAF TOBACCO

The beds all had an addition to the regular mattress. It was called a Keilkissen, "Keil" meaning wedge and "Kissen" a pillow or headrest. This wedge-like mattress was put under the pillow end of the bed. It elevated the upper body somewhat. At one time, in my early memory (1945), my sister slept on a mattress and Keilkissen entirely made of tobacco. Mom had, in some way, obtained a bale of dried leaf tobacco. She took the straw out of the crib mattresses and replaced it with tobacco. She then carefully sewed up the tobacco in oilcloth, such as an old table cloth, to keep the smell down. Finally, she re-covered it with the old material. I knew that something was not right because we conducted the tobacco business in secret. Although the Nazis were no longer in power, the fear of them was still in the hearts of people. Stories of brother turning in brother and son betraying father were everywhere. No one really knew what anybody's political affiliation was. Of course, I did not know such things; all I knew was that I had to keep my mouth shut about the tobacco. It was a product not legally available to the populace as yet; therefore, it travelled only in underground channels as probably many other products of habit did. As it turned out, the tobacco was a life saver. Mom would weigh out small amounts, about five to ten grams, and trade it for a variety of foods. One particular smoker, a chimney sweep by trade, had a great chance to get all kinds of food from customers through bartering for his services. I remember him, black from head to foot, bringing eggs and smoked pork in exchange for a small bag of the desired tobacco. Mom hung the smoked pork, totally black from the smoking process, on a broom handle across the corner of the bedroom, hidden from sight by the corner dresser with its fold-out mirrors on each side. The amount of pork increased as the tobacco decreased. In the summer time the aroma of the meat made us feel very secure and happy. I'm sure Mom sold a lot in larger blocks for money to buy knitting yarn and cloth for sewing.

FRET NOT

Mom's knitting yarn always presented tasks that were part of life. When knitted clothing was outgrown, it was never thrown out but simply unravelled and wound into a ball. New wool (yarn) came in a skein and had to be rolled into a ball ready for knitting. For Mom to keep two kids busy, she had one hold the skein between their hands with arms sticking straight out and the other kid undo and roll up the yarn into a ball. Whether sister was too small, got tired, or just wanted out of this kind of monotonous work, I don't know; but a quarrel often ensued when she either dropped some loops or was not giving me the right tension so I could make a ball that suited Mom. Consequently, many times I wound up putting the skein over the back of a straight chair and then roll the yarn from there.

Rolling the wool was not the only time my sister became fretful. Most often it was my job to comb and braid Dagmar's hair. To get her to sit still was the first challenge. To comb out the tangles in her long hair became a nightmare. With tears rolling, she would vociferously complain and accuse me of purposely hurting her. This would only shortened the fuse of Mom, who was trying to get some other work done. Most likely, I was not good at combing out the knots in her hair. As the racket continued, Mom finally came, huffing and fuming, to take over the task. She made short work of it. Since Dagmar was already screaming, Mom simply grabbed hold of the hair with one hand and with the comb in the other hand gave a few mighty jerks, and the tangle was all out. I don't know which was the worse cure, the one sudden pain, or me picking at her hair for an extended period. Mom answered to a lot of life's problems that way, simply slam bang and you're done.

A WAY TO MOLD A CHILD

Mom did not like to be sassed. Her authority was final and without question. The rule of the land was: kids may be seen but not heard. Mom was a go-getter, and things were getting done. I do not know when I learned to keep my mouth shut, but I sure knew the things that brought out the wrath of Mother. Punishment was sometimes just a smack behind the head, or it was a barehanded salting on the exposed bottom. She molded us to be a help in her everyday life and not prima donnas to be wooed and catered to by her. All had to jibe with the smooth day-to-day working of things. When squabbles began, the plan of action was always swift, with a resulting finality that never let you forget that the same could happen at any time again. Some of the molding she did with a wooden cookspoon, which I, at a very early age, learned to not tempt the wrath thereof. On the other hand, Dagmar, three years younger, also had to go through this testing process. One time, when she was about 4 years old, she could not handle her temptations. She got into my night stand and ate the one piece of chocolate that I was saving for just the right time to enjoy. I felt bad tattling on her, especially after I saw Mom break that wooden spoon on little sister's bare behind; but after all, it was my only piece of candy.

THE CONQUERING FORCES

At the beginning of May in 1945, my little world took a new and somewhat interesting turn. Artillery fire, just a few rounds, were set off outside of town. It was a signal for the mayor to fly a white flag of surrender and to come outside the town limits and give the invading forces the okay to occupy the town without resistance. The word that the occupying forces were coming had arrived weeks earlier. That gave the town folks, business men, and black marketers time to do all kinds of hiding and trading of goods before the Americans arrived. (This is most likely how Mom got her tobacco.) Mom also took some valuables, including our camera and silver coins, placed them in a tin can with a lid, and buried them under a certain tree at the edge of the woods. Although I never learned first hand, the word was that the American soldiers were souvenir happy and would take what they could find.

When the GIs first rolled into town with all their trucks, tanks, Jeeps and other gear, I remember I was sitting inside the hedge that bordered the gardens of the plaza, peeping out, not knowing what to expect. I did notice that the tanks were tearing up our only cobblestoned road on the east side of the plaza. Mom was expecting candy and chewing gum to be thrown from the passing vehicles, but I remember seeing only old worthless German paper money flying in the air. The GIs set up squad tents right in the middle of our town square, along with a first aid station. A few of us curious boys timidly inched our way toward one of the tents to look inside. The sun was bright on that day, so the inside of the tent seemed very dark. Suddenly, as we peeked in, we saw a row of teeth as white as pearls, surrounded by a wonderful smile that was set in a dark face, was walking toward us. It was the first black man I had ever seen. Somewhat startled, I headed out of there toward the big arched door, ducked inside, and shut the door tight behind me. I then pondered what I had just seen.

PADDED GLOVES and "REAL COFFEE!"

The next venture out onto the town square turned out to be even more puzzling. Right in front of our Gasthaus, two men in uniform were throwing a ball back and forth with no apparent aim or purpose. I watched. No one was saying anything, nor did it look like it was very competitive, and no score was kept. What really got to me was that these men, the great American forces, the conquerors of our country, had to wear gloves to catch a simple round ball. What soft hands! What a sissy portrayal of masculinity! Several months later, I found one of these balls stuck in the hedge with the leather popped open, exposing some thin yarn. Upon further inspection I decided to tear off all of the leather outside and give the yarn to Mom. She gave me the job of unravelling and rewinding it for possible re-use. To my surprise, I found a treasure inside–a little dark rubber ball which bounced better than anything else in the whole town.

After a while, everyone got used to the newcomers.

Life and play went back to the usual. The word got out that one could find treasures in those American's trash cans. Once, Mom and I went scavenging after the Americans had dumped their morning coffee grounds. We scooped those still-warm coffee grounds out of the trash can, went home, and re-brewed the best coffee ever. Even us kids got some, with milk and sugar. The so-called coffee that we were used to drinking, was just roasted grain with malt, and lord knows what other stuff was in it to make it go a bit farther.

A CHANGE IN THE AIR

Before the coming of the Americans, people seemed to live more in fear and distrust. Once I heard a pig squeal in the middle of the night. Mom explained that it was being killed, and the family did not want to share it with the government. Sometimes peddlers from another town would walk through the streets, shouting to sell pigeons with their feathers still on, that had been strangled. They carried them inside a sack which hung from their waists.

On the day when all bank savings were declared worthless and everyone was given forty marks per head, things began to open up. The presence of the GIs made us finally relax and realize that the past was over. All was not lost, and life was worth a new beginning.

Some people were caught between the changing world. I recall a day when Mom took us kids, about a mile out of town, to pick the spring sprouts of fir trees. The trees were small enough for us to reach the new shoots. When these shoots were boiled down, a sweet syrup remained. We spread this strange tasting sap on buttered bread or pancakes. For some reason, I bent down to look under the trees and into the woods. I saw four men sitting in a circle about a hundred meters from where we were picking. After Mom saw what I had seen, we swiftly got out of there. Upon returning to town, we reported the sighting to the authorities. Later we found out that these men were infiltrators from the East. They found themselves, after the war, caught without a country and a purpose.

MY FIRST ORANGE

No summer would ever end without a major fall and scrape of my knees. After one such wreck, hobbling home, I was bleeding from both knees, with gravel imbedded in the wounds. Mom went to get the first aid man at the GI post. The young man arrived and was invited into the kitchen. He picked me up and sat me on the kitchen table. After some soft and gentle communication with Mom and me, we finally understood his offer. If I would allow him to clean my wound with iodine and not cry, he would give me an orange. It was a deal! Although I hung onto Mom through the burning that seemed to last an eternity, I did not shed a tear. The young man came back and brought me my first orange. We all shared in it and savored every slice.

HOME REMEDIES

We also had some of our own remedies. For a bee or a wasp sting, we always ran to the nearest stream or damp spot and pulled out a clump of grass. We placed the damp, cool dirt onto the area of the sting. Most of the time it was on the foot somewhere for we usually were barefoot. The coolness of the sod worked like magic, and it was no time before we were up and running again. When we burned our fingers, we simply grabbed our earlobe. Instantly, the burning seemed to leave the finger as the ear seemed to suck up the heat. For an earache, Mom heated a few drops of oil in a spoon on the stove, lay us on our side, and let the warm drops fall into the ear. Then the ear was plugged with some cotton. It usually helped enough to let us fall asleep. Mom must have been convinced by the GIs to give us kids cod liver oil as a supplement. Taking one teaspoonful every day was sure an unpleasant ritual. The only good thing was that we got a sugar cube or a piece of rock candy to overcome the shuddering after swallowing that fishy oil. No self respecting home remedy medicine cabinet was without goose grease. This yellow fat, used for chest rubs, was collected when we had a goose for Christmas. When goose grease was depleted, lard worked just fine. Rock candy was the main ingredient of the cough syrup Mom made. It, along with several onions, was boiled down in water until thick. After this syrup was administered, we often got the hot towel treatment. Goose grease was spread on the chest and then rubbed in from the neck down. The chest was then covered with a hot damp towel, plus wrapped all around in an oilcloth,

Spring of 1945 with remaining twin sister Friedoline

after which we were put to bed. These many layers and warmth would soon loosen the chest congestion. For a dry, hacking cough, Mom boiled a pot of Chamomile tea, put a towel over my head and the pot, and made me breathe the steam coming directly off the pot, until my nose or chest loosened up. There were other sworn-to remedies that Mom stayed away from, such as the fix for a high fever. The word was while the sick person lay in bed, the caretaker simply cracked an egg into a dish, then placed it on the floor, and slid it under the bed directly below the head. People swear that the fever leaves the body, goes into the raw egg, and makes the egg foam-up in the dish.

WE DID NOT HAVE FLEAS

Mom washed sister in a small, galvanized tub set on the kitchen table. She got the first bath, then using the same water, I got the second bath, standing up in the tub on the floor. After being soaped down, Mom poured a teakettle full of warm (sometimes a little too warm) water over my head to wash all the soap off. After my sister and I were in bed, Mom used the same water to wash herself.

Once, we made soap in that tub. I remember bones, fat, and ashes; and we were not to go near it. After a period of soaking, the mixture was boiled. Later, blocks of strong brown soap were cut. I don't know how long all this took, but we must have been some very clean and well behaved kids during the time the tub was used for soap making, for some how we needed no washing.

An early recollection was a time when Mom, Dagmar, and I, as well as a baby in the carriage, were having an outing at the edge of the woods. Mom was combing our hair with a square black comb with very fine teeth. After each stroke she would inspect it. She showed us each louse on it. She placed the louse between her thumbnails to crush it. She let us listen to each small crack as the lice popped. Mom did the same with the eggs of the lice which seemed to me bigger than the louse itself and also would pop louder. She then wiped every squashed critter on the rubber wheel of the carriage which had my remaining twin sister Friedoline in it.

RABBIT STEW

All of us loved fresh air and sunshine. Mom would teach us the various plants and flowers, have us chase after pretty butterflies, and make us beware of thistle, nettles, and bees. A picnic outing was almost a whole day's affair. One of our favorite spots was along the sunny side of a creek bank. Once we had our blanket spread on a little knoll that overlooked the fields, beyond the stream, where a farmer and his men were repairing the fence. Mom noticed them trying to keep the fence in a straight line by directly aiming it at a spot on a property corner mark near us. So, Mom volunteered to help, using her arms to guide them to set their posts in a perfectly straight line. This seemed to help the men, and work progressed quite well all afternoon. Then suddenly the dog they had with them jumped a jack rabbit. The rabbit's running and zig-zagging, and the hound after it, made for quite a show for us kids. After a long chase through the fields, the rabbit made a turn out of desperation directly toward the stream. Instead of doing one more zig, it dove over the deep, washed out edge of the bank, into the stream. The dog ran right after it, taking the hearty plunge also. Under the water they went, the hound emerging with the rabbit in its mouth a few seconds later. The faithful friend, wagging his tail, proudly placed his catch at the farmer's feet. The man picked up the rabbit, walked to the creek's edge, and tossed it to Mom on the other side. With a heartfelt thank you, Mom took the prize and went home with the booty stuffed into our picnic basket. Meat was on the menu that night.

MY BEST FRIEND

In 1946, when I was six years old, I got my first, very own Lederhose. The pants were the pig skin variety, naturally colored, with the usual trap door in front secured by two buttons at the beltline on top. The pig leather at first was kind of stiff. After a period of every-day wear, the Lederhose were still kind of cumbersome but somehow conformed to my body a little better. In my case, my body was not anywhere near the garment. The hose (pants) were so big that they started at the knees and nearly went up under the armpits. Mom made sure that I would not soon outgrow them. The Lederhose became sort of part of me. They were held up by a set of leather suspenders which had a horizontal strip of leather between the straps to keep them from falling off the shoulders. The suspenders were buttoned to the leather pants. Woolen underwear were usually the order of the day, bearable only in the winter when they did not itch. Summer time brought freedom of such encumbrances, and we wore nothing under the pigskin pants. Instead of the usual zipper in front, the lederhose had a buttoned-up trap door that flopped down when the boy had to use the bathroom. Unfortunately, when I, the little boy, had to pee, the dropping of the trap door in front was not really the big problem. It was the spigot, that was yet too small, that just would not reach, no matter how much I pulled, trying to stretch it past the dropped flap. So inevitably most of the pee bounced off the inside and down the pant legs. This was okay because wet leather molded itself to the body and its movements better. Anyway, the pants were not considered broken in until they were black with dirt and grime. Anyone with a "new" pair was considered sort of green–a bit snickered at. Therefore, as quickly as I could, I wiped every dirty thing that needed wiping on the pants. With no pockets in the back, the slick part of the breeches made a great tobog-gan when sliding down a steep hill made of damp mud. No one ever wore a hole in the Lederhose. The pants just got more "broke in." My breeches, when standing at the side of the bed, turned into sort of a get-a-way car parked at the curb outside the bank. All I had to do in the morn-ing was swing my legs around, jump out of bed, and pull them up. The pockets, one on each side in the front, were the ideal place for a little boy's treasures. All of us six years and older carried a pocketknife. Usually, I also car-ried some marbles with me, never all I had, just the ones I could afford to lose.

THE SHARPENING STONE

The pocketknife was big enough to fit solidly into the palm of my hand, so when open, I could get a good cut at a stick or whatever I was whittling or working on. The

It takes two to sharpen a pocket knife

blade had to be super sharp at all times, to a point where sharpening the knife became a daily task. A friend and I would go to a neighbor's yard where, at the side of the road, there was a grinding wheel; a large gray, round stone, about two feet in diameter and three to four inches thick. It lay almost half submerged in a trough of water. An axle went through the center of the grinding stone, being cradled by a socket on each side of the trough, blubbering in gobs of grease as it turned. We would give the stone a spin and immediately pounce onto the pedal with both hands pumping with our arms. The foot pedal had a linkage to a crook in the axle much like the sewing machines of the day. It always took two of us to sharpen a knife. One pumped the pedal any way he saw fit while the other chap was intently honing his treasured possession. Trying to sharpen your knife by yourself was pretty well impossible. Standing on one leg, holding the knife with two hands, and pumping with the other leg, was like standing on your head trying to spit in your shirt pocket. As it were, we would sharpen and sharpen, then test the edge by gingerly scraping the thumb across the blade, sharpen some more, cut one twig, then sharpen some more.

THE GOOD DOCTOR

I remember a time, after such a sharpening session, when we decided to cut some pussy willows for our moms. After climbing to the top of the cemetery wall, we walked along to a spot where the willow bush hung over the wall.

There were patches of lush nettles growing on the outside edge of the wall. We were careful not to bump into each other because no one ever wished to fall into those nettles. Every one I knew was very sensitive to the Brennessel, the burning nettle. Even an imperceptible touch by the leg or arm of the weed would almost immediately result in burning and itching welts. Mom heard that those plants were edible. So, gloves on, we carefully picked us a tender serving. She cooked it up like spinach. We ate it just once because the mere thought of eating such a disliked weed gave us the heebie-jeebies. We never cooked them again.

At spring time most children searched for and picked flowers to please their mothers. There were few men or fathers around, but even the boys knew that Moms liked blossoms. Since pussy willow bushes were taller than we, the one next to the cemetery wall was the only one in town where we could cut a few twigs and not get into trouble. I reached way up to get a branch with an exceptional bunch of shiny silver buds on it. Holding the branch down with one hand, knife in the other, I gave it a whack; and, lo, I cut the tip of my left thumb off. Bleeding like a stuck pig, I ran home. Mom did not say too much, she just sent me to the town doctor. He took the sliced-off tip, sort of hanging to the side, realigned it, cleaned it and bandaged it up. Then the doctor asked to see the weapon that did this deed. My heart sank to my toes, figuring my goose was cooked, and I was going to be disarmed. I reluctantly showed him my knife. He looked at it, opened it, tested its sharpness, and never said a word. He then went to the other end of the room, opened a drawer, and dug around in it a bit. When he came back he returned my knife, placing it into my hand, along with a new knife to keep. I thanked him of course, and feeling like a real man, with pain all gone, I went home. Now, did he think I needed a better knife, or did he think with all that sharpening I was going to grind the old one away and needed to get a new one? I do not know. It has been over fifty years now, and I've never been without a pocketknife since.

WHY SHOES

Along with scarred and banged-up knees came tough, little bare feet. Shoes were worn only in the winter. We never wore boots when we were sleigh riding and doing other things in the snow. Our knitted socks kept us warm only until the snow around our ankles melted. Then our socks and the inside of our shoes became saturated with water. It seems like I always had to quit early–not because I was tired, but because my feet were about to freeze off. It seemed the shoes were always too big or too small. When they were too loose on my feet, Mom had me stand on cardboard, as she traced my feet with a pencil, then cut out the shape to put inside the brogans to fill them out. Often more than one layer was needed along with some wool balls or old rags that were stuffed into the toe area so the feet would not slide forward. The shoes we got were always used. Where they came from was not discussed. As I got older, I wore my mother's old ones. If the sole was worn out, which was often the case when I got the shoes, a piece of stout material was slipped under the cardboard on the inside. As the feet grew and the shoes were still usable, spacers were removed a little at a time.

The Sunday-going-to-church shoes just did not wear out. Once your toes became cramped, you balled them up and walked kind of pigeon-toed until the feet were liberated again. In any case, you did not and could not do much running with shoes on.

SOME APPLES

We always longingly waited for the days to grow longer and the snows to be gone from the well-travelled paths so we could be bare footed once more. Ah, what a welcomed sight and frequent springtime experience, when horse drawn wagons were coming to pass where we were playing. We always craned our necks to see if a generous pile of horse apples had been left behind. To spot such a pile, still steaming with warmth, was a treat just for the taking. We would run and lovingly step into that warmth, sort of kneading the fluffy droppings with our toes. The juice oozed between our feet and toes as we worked to find the last pockets of warm spots. No wonder we had such growth spurts in the spring.

TIME TO BARTER

Mom was always busy. Looking back, I now can see that she was ever ready to work, mend, cook, preserve food or do anything to uphold and feed her family. When I asked Mom, then well in her eighties, if she remembered why I was able to get milk at a farm about a mile outside of town, she simply told me: "I sewed and patched clothes for the farmer, his wife, and their children." Thinking back fifty years or more, I can still see and feel the frequent long walks I took with our one-liter milk can in hand. The tall cap lid, that slid way down into the neck of the container, prevented the milk from spilling while I carried it by the bail handle, swinging it about while walking. The walk was long enough to give a kid a chance to get to know the stillness of time. The pastoral settings were being deeply etched into my soul. I can see the amber shimmers of wheat fields, over which I could barely gaze, as I pondered the beauty of the gentle swaying stirred by the breezes. I did not realize then that God was whispering and molding me. Everything in due time God will reveal. He showed me even then His call to "Be still,

Griesbach. The gravel road that led to the farm that swapped milk for sewing. Also pictured: The tallest tower from which the flag of surrender was flown.

and know that I am God." He was with me walking along those wheat fields as I tasted of the ripening grain. So when I read, thirty years later, of Jesus and his disciples as they walked and ate of the grain, I could relate.

I often made that trek to the farm to get milk. I recall that there was a peach tree on the sunny side of a stone house that I had to pass. The only one I knew about; it was very close to the south wall, and probably the branches were attached to the wall. There was a small picket fence in a semi-circle around it, giving warning that no sample fruit was to be taken. Even Mom was refused when she asked to pick some drops from under the small apple orchard in back of the same house. I guess some people are just totally selfish, or they simply did not like us big city transplants.

THE BAUERNHOF

The farm (Bauernhof), where milk was bartered for sewing, was an interesting place. There was a big table in the kitchen around which all the farm hands sat on benches and chairs. Often the evening meal was fried potatoes and clabbered milk. Big bowls of each were set in the middle of the table within easy reach of the hungry men. With several heaping scoops of potatoes on each plate, the men ate with spoons, alternating from potatoes on the plate to the clabbered milk in the center of the table. The yellow cream collected on top of the milk was always a big hit with the men. With each dip into that bowl, the men hoped for a little cream along with the blueish, congealed milk. The large drawer that stored the bread during the day was in the middle under the table top. Mom warned me not to eat any bread offered from that drawer because she once saw a mouse jump out of it. The Kachelofen, the oven where the large loaves of rye bread were baked, was fired from the kitchen side with the baking ovens above and to the side of the fire box. This massive structure was encased with concave tile (Kachel) and was like a big room divider. The tile were on all exposed sides from floor to ceiling. This was also the central heating system. After the tile got good and hot, it stayed warm all through the day and night. On the side opposite the kitchen, the Kachelofen formed a wall of the den. Against that wall always sat a bench with a table in front of it. This is where the farmer and his wife soothed their aching muscles by leaning on the Kachel. The evening was spent sitting in the den reading or doing chores such as darning socks. The regular cookstove with its four eyes and water tank shared the chimney that went upstairs and then on up through the roof. In the chimney upstairs was the smoking chamber. Long slabs of pork were hung there to be smoked after they had been soaking in brine for a while. Occasionally, we got some of the meat while it was still marinating. It was called Surfleisch. It did not taste as good as fresh meat and not nearly as good as the smoked meat. The Geräuchertes (smoked meat) was totally black with soot. Washing it would not have removed the black. The lean part of the smoked pork was a beautiful dark pink while the fat was pure white. It was tender and tasty, a delight fit for the gods.

The help slept upstairs. Those days in Germany no child was left to wander the streets after completing the years of required schooling. Usually at age 13 or 14, every kid was assigned, by choice or by designation, to an apprenticeship. A lot of children moved out of their parents' house at that time to live under the roof of the master craftsman. The ones appointed to learn farming and all its related skills came to live on the farm. If girls were indentured, and very often there were, they usually slept near or within the family quarters downstairs. The hope was that by doing that, the growing masculine sprouts upstairs had to do their usual courting during the few glimpses they had of the girls at meal time. Many a young man borrowed the nearest ladder to climb up to his sweetheart's window at another farm, and stories abounded of young men breaking legs as a result of falling from ladders. I'm sure many a young lady climbed out of the window to meet with her lover in a spot more romantic and where the moonlight did the serenading. Often the courting male hid in the shadows of the night, threw tiny pebbles at the window of his love's room as a signal. He then waited until she found a way to sneak out to meet him. Illegitimacy was all too common. The girl's life then, as it is still, was severely hampered while the stud went free.

The moon was believed to have powers to whiten sheets hung out over night. It also had the power to lure a sleepwalker to walk forbidden heights and ledges. The moon also had powers to grow a young maiden's bosom when exposed to the fullness of its celestial light.

The farm was very close to being completely self sufficient. From making brooms out of fir boughs to threshing wheat grown in the fields, from making cheese to making applejack, from shoeing the horses to plowing with oxen, the work never ended.

BROWN GOLD

The layout of the house, barns, and stables was time-tested and efficient. Think of a square courtyard with the house along the road side, and the hay barns parallel to the house along the back side, the milking stables and stalls for other animal were positioned at right angles to the house on one end, with the equipment, tools and workshop in a shed along the opposite end. The cows were milked by hand. If there was electricity, it was direct current only. The outhouse was free standing and stood like a statue next to the cobblestone walk which led around the perimeter of the barn yard. The Misthaufen or dung pile, pitchforked from the stables, was the only other dominant fixture. Both the outhouse and the Misthaufen were contributors to the Odel tank. This tank, much like a cistern, would catch all seepage from the two waste stations. The Misthaufen, a mixture of straw, cattle, and horse manure, would age; and its juices, increased by rain and snow, filled the hidden tank below. In early spring, both garden and fields, before being plowed, received the excellent richness of the 'Mist' from the pile. The seepage that collected was pumped into a vat on a wagon and sprayed over the hay fields.

HAY CUTTING

Hay was cut with the scythe. All men folk worked long, muscle-aching hours to cut the many acres by hand. The hay was raked in wind rows with help from the older women. Using large wooden rakes, the workers frequently had to turn the hay to dry it after heavy dew or light rains. Often, tepee-like structures were made out of three or four poles onto which the damp grass was pitchforked. It was left hanging there to dry. These giant haymen stood there in long rows like massive and eerie storybook creatures, especially when the shadows grew long and the daylight dwindled.

The hay harvest was brought to the barn on large

wooden wagons with tall sides that tapered out. It was forked up with pitchforks and then slung up into the wagon where a packer received the forkfuls from four men rhythmically pitching it up. The packer skillfully wove each forked segment until the load resembled a monstrous mushroom fifteen feet tall. On the way to the barn the wagons groaned and listed from one side to the other as the wheels sank into the ruts in the field roads. No hay ever slid off; however, at times all available men had to rush to one side as the tremendous load threatened to capsize. The men jabbed their forks and rakes into the hay and pushed to keep the wagon from tipping over.

Along field roads like these, you often found large wooden crosses driven into the ground. A small board to kneel on was attached to the bottom of the cross. These crosses were erected at the place where some soul had a heart attack or a heat stroke and died. Members of the surviving family prayed there. Some crosses were a bit ornate with carvings of Jesus and other embellishments. Most were covered by a single board A-frame that sort of made the whole thing look like an altar.

THE HAY MOUND

Back at the "Bauernhof", the wagons had to be unloaded. This was accomplished a pitchfork full at a time. The hay was stacked in tall mounds under the roof. Often, any excess hay was stacked the same way out in the open. These outside mounds naturally were fed to the animals first.

I had the fortunate, or maybe unfortunate, experience once to witness the ritual of a clubbing. As you might imagine, many families of unwanted critters made themselves homes under such stacks of edible fodder. As the mound shrank down to merely a foot tall, the critters in it were forced into some highly over-crowded living space. As the hay was fed at last from the edges of the bottom layer, the concentration of crawling varmints was neared a state of panic. At such a time, all available hands–men women and children–were given weapons and told to surround the remaining pile of hay. A couple of men then eased their pitchforks under the edges of the remaining hay and shoved them way in to get the biggest forkful possible. With a synchronized jerk, they yanked the hay out of the way. Mice and rats, young and old, fat and gray, small and large, scurried in a bewildered frenzy in all directions. All the assembled warriors attacked with their brooms, shovels, rakes, sticks and clubs, swinging them in a wild and frenzied exuberance at the exposed menaces. This went on until all the hay was scooped up and all the vermin were clubbed to death or escaped.

SOME LEARNING GOING ON

Of course, the hay barn was "The" place to play. The other boys and I had many wrestling matches, and learned how to fly by jumping off the highest beams into the fluffy cushion. I'm sure the older boys had different playing in the hay in mind.

Once I slid between the hay and the outside wall all the way down to ground level. Since there was nothing to get a hold of, either on the barn boards or the hay, panic set in; and I thought I was doomed. But by wedging my feet and knees against the boards and my back against the hay side, I found I could shimmy up enough where my buddies could grab my hands and pull me up the rest of the way.

We were always warned of pitchforks hidden in the hay and were told gory stories of kids that had gotten speared and killed. At times we'd find a dozen or so eggs where a hen had "stolen her nest out." We did not disturb these nests. Mother hen and a new brood of chicks were a welcome sight.

THE SCYTHE

The mowing scythes were kept in the tool shed. They were long sword-like blades of steel attached to the end of a long, bowed, wooden handle which had two wooden grips attached to it for the hands to hold. During hay or wheat cutting time, the men carried the scythes out to the field on their shoulders very early in the morning. Strong, long arms, a powerful back, and a long scythe could cut a big swath, sometimes six feet or more wide. During a long day of cutting, the razor sharpness of the blade would often get dull. So, the cutter stopped, reached into his back pocket, and pulled out a sharpening stone about eight inches long. With the scythe's handle between his knees and the pointed end of the blade held with his left hand away from his body, the cutter would reach up somewhat above his head, and sharpen the blade. He did this by striking the blade with his rock in rapid four-to-six inch strokes on both sides of the edge. He worked the stone by starting from the inside all the way out to the tip of the blade. Slipping the rock back into his back pocket, he'd get right back to cutting the swaths.

DENGELN

In the evening, usually after dinner, men would recondition the much-sharpened blades of their scythes. A man would sit straddling a wooden bench much like an old shaving horse. On one end it had a small anvil, the size of the blunt end of a splitting wedge. With the scythe blade removed from its handle, the man then struck the cutting edge of the blade, which rested on the anvil, with a ball-peen hammer. The purpose was to thin out the blunted edge into a more tapered one. The edge therefore was also being hardened as well as made slightly wavy in the process. All together it must have made a formidable difference in the way the 'dengeld' edge would cut the next day. This systematic striking of metal against metal resonated into the still evening air, making an interesting counterpart to the crickets and tree frogs.

No one complained about any noise. Noise was usually made because someone worked. It was understood, it was life. The person hearing the sounds was probably not working; therefore, it gave him comfort and gladness that it was the other fellow and not him. Today we have different noises—loud music, loud mufflers, loud TV, traffic, jets, lawn mowers, parties, and rackets in general. Today, you can see a honeybee two feet away but cannot hear it; those days you could hear a bee thirty feet away even if you did not see it.

SCHOOL AND THE LIKE

The four-room schoolhouse faced the town square. One door led into it, and the playground was the town square. There were no fire drills, no fire exits, no intercom, or air conditioning. It was a two story structure with two rooms on each floor. The stairs, the hall, and the bath rooms were in the middle. The toilet had a copper trough for the boys, plus a throne. The girls had their private chambers. The use of the bathroom was closely monitored so no one would lose time in the classroom. There was a time to stand, and a time to sit, a time to speak, and a time to be quiet, a time to play, and a time to learn, and a time to answer nature's call as determined by the teacher. Two of the rooms faced the square and two the rear of the building. To each side were businesses or other structures also facing the town square. There was plenty of light coming through the windows. It lit up the blackboard on the teacher's end of the room. The teacher taught all subjects. Pupils never knowing when they were going from math to science and never a break in between. The school day was from 8 to 5. By the end of the first grade, we could write sentences in cursive.

Each boy usually brought a hard roll for lunch, and these rolls often became the objects for a contest. Several of us boys would sit on the rolls with our well worn Lederhose, from morning 'till noon, then compare whose roll had gotten the flattest.

THE SLATE BOARD

The large blackboard on the wall and the small ones we brought to school daily in our little Rucksacks (back pack) were actual slate. Our small slate boards, on which we learned to write, had wooden frames around them. In our backpacks we also carried a wooden ruler and a Griffi, which was a little square rock with a pointed end. We were taught to scribe lines on our board using the ruler to measure the correct spacing between the lines. After learning how to measure, we learned how to write. I remember making my first letters. We learned by drawing walking canes upright and upside down as well as circles and half circles. They were scratched with the pointed end of the rock onto our slate board. We used the lines as writing guides to stay horizontal with words as well as vertical with the letters. At the end of each lesson and after inspection by the teacher, we erased the little slates with a damp rag that hung by a string from the wooden frames. This type of repetitive learning for all subjects was done on that board for a long time. Paper and pencil were scarce, and were used only for writings to be kept.

GIVE ME SOME SPACE

I, the city kid, was not without battles. The year 1946 was no different than 1000 years ago or now. Each character had to establish his or her territory among peers. I was subjected to taunting, verbal abuse, and some physical aggression by these country boys. Their aim was to see how far they could push me, the city boy, and how much fun they could have by doing it. On one occasion, I remember being bopped by an older boy after he wrestled me to the ground. A dozen or more kids watched the commotion as we squirmed around in the dust right in front of the school. The tussle was not over until I established a position on top of the aggressor and returned some of the same medicine he had dished out. The disturbance during lunch break never made it to the teacher. All was fine returning to the classroom. I gained a little respect that day, but it did not last too long. In the next confrontation, I was determined not to wind up on the ground. About a half dozen hecklers surrounded me itching to get something started. I sensed a fight was inevitable, so I just clenched my fists and started swinging in a wide circle striking anything in reach. When a hole in the group of fellows appeared, I quickly darted through and headed for home before I got the short end of the stick.

CAT AND MOUSE

One day I must have daydreamed away part of my allotted play time and apparently did not use the bathroom time for what it was meant. A good bit into the afternoon's teaching, I raised my hand and asked for permission to use the toilet; it was denied. Shortly after I asked again; denied once more. A bit later, I frantically asked again, brimming with excess and absolutely no capacity left,—denied. In desperation I made a mad dash to the door leading to the copper trough of relief. The teacher shouted with a loud impassionate yell "get him." Upon that command, several of the boys sitting near the door jumped from their seats and wrestled me down. I was made to sit down again and listen to the lesson. Soon after, I eased myself toward the front edge of the chair and quietly relieved the pressure. The warmth ran down my bare legs, funneled by the Lederhose onto the floor. A few kids knew what went on but kept quiet. The floor was of oiled, wood blocks. The dust that had accumulated over the years between the cracks made an excellent sponge. So, within minutes I felt much better, and the floor showed little evidence. The cat and mouse game was over. Who won? I do not know.

A TRIP TO THE MILL

The rationing of food started before I can remember. I did not know what was going on; therefore, I did not really care, being just a child. The one thing I do remember, that by collecting bread coupons, the little tag you could buy bread with, you could, when you got enough of them together, go to the mill and trade them in for flour. So one day, Mom and we set out early to make the trek to the mill. We pulled our wagon, a four-wheeled cart with a draw bar. It was a pretty far distance to the mill. Dagmar, being too small to walk much, always got to sit in the wagon and be pulled everywhere we went. The town of Griesbach was on a hill. The gristmill, naturally on some body of water, was several miles from town and down a valley. When we got to the mill, I saw several old buildings made of stone and some wooden ones. The miller greeted us and then took us to a small room where Mom made her trade of stamps for a huge sack of flour. Every thing was white. The floor, the furniture, the table and even the man were white all over. I thought, how interesting. The chimney sweep has a black hat, the miller a white one. One wore a black outfit and the other all white. The flue sweeper had a face that was black with the red of his irritated eyes peeking out while the miller's face was white with bright eyeballs poking through. What is it about black soot that makes us feel dirty, yet white seems clean? Both are just a covering, probably each being perfectly clean on its own.

The homebound trip was something else. First of all, it seemed to be uphill all the way. And most likely it was. Sister had to do some walking and also some pushing, which did not set too well with that little thing. The ruts in the road were often diagonal and always led the wagon into the ditch. It took a lot of pulling by Mom and a lot of heaving by me to make those wheels get out of one rut and over and through the next one. That fifty kilo sack of dead weight turned from a blessing to a burden with a purpose. Mom always brought along some homemade stuff to eat, a sweet roll and a bottle of water. Lots of times she would doctor up the water with a spike of vinegar and a bit of sugar to give us some flavor and maybe cut the thirst a little better. Finally we'd get to town, rolling in like the conquering GIs, and all the struggle was worth it once more.

THANK GOD FOR BREAD

I do not know why the Lord made weevils. Maybe He wanted to create moths so they can eat holes in our woolens. So maybe the Moms of the world could teach their little boys and girls to mend sweaters and holes in socks. Or maybe God just made weevils so we would have to sift each scoop of flour to get it fluffy and soft and be rewarded with a small handful of weevils and weevil hulls. The flour sifter was like a round cake pan with a fine fly screen on the bottom. I got to use it often holding it in one hand and banging it against the other wrist. Each knock released a small sprinkle of soft white flour that Mom quickly worked into the dough she had going in a large designated dough bowl.

There were times when Mom sent me to the bakery to get Seierl, the starter dough to make bread; but most of the time Mom made yeast breads and rolls. She'd crumble up the block yeast with her fingers, and many times she'd give us kids a small chunk to eat. The dough was worked with her hands and with a long wooden spoon which was also the disciplinarian. After resting the dough a while, she commenced beating it with that spoon once more, cradling the bowl in her left arm, then rigorously inserting the spoon into one end of the mass, lifting it up and out, creating air pockets to form inside the dough. She would let me beat it some, with her holding the bowl to the table and me standing on a chair. It was an honor in a sense to think that Mother thought I was grown enough to beat the dough. After the mass was rising in the bowl, covered with linen cloth, Mom would get her Nudel board. It was a two by three foot piece of wooden board with a lip on one side that wrapped over the edge of the table and kept it from moving when she rolled out her dough. She sprinkled flour on the board and then spread it around with her hand to make sure the dough did not stick. With the big wooden spoon, she dipped a dozen or more portions of risen dough onto the Nudel board, covering them with the linen cloth, to let them rise a little more. The next step was either into the pot, the skillet, the pan, or the hot grease.

The same dough-flour, yeast, water and salt–using milk and an egg only when we had it–was the basis for all the various foods we mostly called Nudels. When Mom cracked an egg and dumped the insides into the bowl, she always then stuck her finger into the shell, to remove the little egg white that was stuck inside. She'd work that finger till absolutely all of the egg was removed. To this day I still do this the way Mother did it fifty years ago.

There were Rohrnudels, round yeast rolls baked in a greased roasting pan. A variation of these had raisins added to the dough. Some were stuffed with stewed plums, raisins and butter, or apples with cinnamon and sugar. In all cases, there were always some of these to eat; the brown crust on the bottom was the best.

Then there were Schmalznudels. The same dough was used, but it was worked with the fingers into doughnut shape with the center almost transparent. It was then deep fried in hot Schmalz which was plain lard. We just changed the name to Pfannennudel, using much less grease when we slowly browned them in the iron skillet.

Then there were Dampfnudels, the same amount of dough, scooped from the main lump with a spoon and rolled into a ball in the palm. They were placed into a tall soup pot, in which a dollop of lard was melted. With the lid on the pot we baked them slowly, not directly over the hot spot on the stove, but sort of in the corner, rotating the pot gingerly for even heat. You did not open the pot until the end of baking so the Nudels would not collapse. The dough rose in that covered pot, stayed very soft, and was milky white when done. We'd make a meal out of those, with warm vanilla sauce, cherishing the browned bottoms, eating them last for dessert.

There was Zopf, the same dough worked into three long strands, then braided into a long loaf. Often Mom enhanced the taste and looks of it by adding raisins to the dough and brushing melted butter with cinnamon and sugar on the strips before braiding them together.

A festive sweet bread was called a Stollen, a little sweeter dough than the Zopf, with some lard worked in. Mom added what ever was available, like candied citrus peels, but always chopped walnuts that we had gathered, plenty of raisins with the usual butter, cinnamon and sugar. The Stollen was bigger than the other breads because it had to last through the Christmas holidays. Mom carefully rolled and folded the dough with these succulent additions into a long shape, placing it onto a greased roasting pan, then bent into a giant horseshoe. No perishable ingredients were used like milk. The Stollen was baked in the oven on low heat. I got to help by adding little sticks to the fire until the Christmas treat was all done and brown. Yum-yum, heaven came down and glory filled our souls.

Then there were Suppennudel. Using the same flour, water, salt and eggs, (no yeast) Mom made bunches of it. After the dough was stirred, the Nudel board was sprinkled with flour. Working out the dough with a rolling pin was a tricky job. Mom picked up the rolled dough repeatedly with her hands, hanging it over her left hand and arm, while she added more flour to the board to keep the dough from sticking. She'd roll it again and again, until the desired thinness and consistency was achieved. We hung those hand towel looking pieces of dough over the back of the kitchen chairs. By the time all the chairs had their drapery, the first one was dried enough to be rolled up and cut into strips of about one centimeter wide. The trick was, they had to be dry enough to roll and cut, and not stick together, but not so dry as to crack and break up. The freshly cut strips were placed on cookie pans to thoroughly dry, then put away for soup time, which was often.

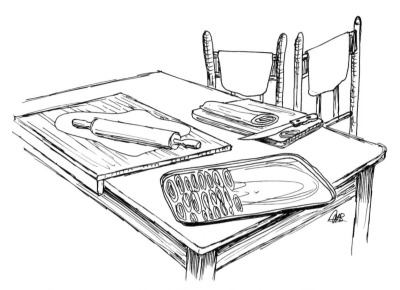

Making soup noodles. Roll'em out, hang'em up, slice'em up and dry'em out.

And there also were Pfannenkuchen, or pancakes, nothing fancy, just flour, milk, and salt stirred together. Sometimes when we felt rich, we added an egg to the dough. Mixed thin, they'd easily cover the bottom of a greased skillet. We browned them good on both sides and ate them with sugar and cinnamon sprinkled on top. Often we put some butter on as well, rolled them up, and ate them with our fingers. Any leftover plain pancakes we rolled up and cut up into soup noodles. A good variation of this pancake was the addition of fresh, chopped apples. To get us kids to eat more, Mom made designs with the runny dough. She'd call them elephants. She did so because there were always legs, ears, tail, and trunk to eat up, which was a lot of fun for us.

To tell you what we ate for long stretches at a time, I have got to add Mehlmuserl. It was nothing more than white gravy made with milk or water after the flour and lard were heated in the skillet. The liquid was stirred until it was a bit thick. We then spread it to cover our plate to cool,–you guessed it,–covered with cinnamon and sugar. This was mostly fed to babies until they were old enough to chew. But baby food or not, we had it often for a meal and were encouraged by Mother to lick our plates so nothing was wasted. As for crumbs of bread on the table, we licked our finger so it was wet and then picked up all the crumbs with it and ate them.

A coarser form of wheat flour was called Gries, or farina, which was cooked to make a hot cereal and eaten for dinner, sprinkled, of course, with cinnamon and sugar. The left over Griesmuserl was spread on our wooden cutting board to cool and set up. The next day after it got somewhat hard, it was sliced into squares and browned on both sides in a skillet. The second round was better than the first.

The meat dishes, or should I say the dishes that had some meat in them, were complemented mostly with rye bread bought at the bakery. Oh boy, some of the bread bought in the mid-forties had a variety of chunks in it. We often tried to analyze those lumps, some hard, some softer, some as big as a sugar cube and some just small hard bites. The things we concluded were sure additions were potatoes and chestnuts. We swore the bread also contained acorns or beachnuts at times. In any case, it filled the belly. If any type of bread got old and dried out, Mom made bread crumbs; or if purchased bread was getting old, she made bread soup. We fried the chunks of bread until golden brown, then roasted onions with salt and pepper, stirred them together, and added hot beef bone broth in a soup bowl.

Potatoes, like bread, were also a mainstay. They were easy to grow, easy to keep, and almost impossible to mess up when cooked. Of course, mashed potatoes were my favorite. Fried spuds were great with other fried foods, as were boiled potatoes especially when you needed to sopup gravy from a pork roast. The crowning jewel of potatoes was, and always will be, the potato dumpling. Dumplings were hard to make. We grated potatoes into a large bowl using a hand held grater that had four sides to it. This kitchen gadget was also used to slice cucumbers, grate carrots, and cut slivers off a chunk of cheese. After grating a half dozen potatoes, Mom took a big dipper and scooped some of the mash into a linen cloth. The corners of the cloth were held in one hand while she wrung out the wet lump with the other, letting the juice run back into the bowl. The semi-dried grated potatoes were put in a mixing bowl where Mom added a couple of grated onions and the dregs of the potato juice which was pure white starch. After adding salt and a little flour, she mixed it all up. With her hands she formed round balls of the mix and gently dropped them into simmering water. For a special treat, we'd take some of the mix and fry it golden brown in a skillet. These Reiberdatschi (hash browns) went well with pickled red cabbage.

SOUPS

During the latter half of the forties and up to 1955, the year we came to America, any piece of meat bought at the butcher had to be sold with 10% bones. It did not matter whether the meat you purchased had bone already in it. You still had to take additional bones and pay the price that the cut of meat cost. You could either save the bones to make soap, which was impractical because we never had any refrigeration, or you could make soup all the time. It was certainly more appealing to us kids to eat soup every day than stay squeaky clean using up all that soap. So, soup it was. If the hot soup had some yellow puddles of fat swimming on top, it was declared as being very good and able to wake up the dead. The bones were boiled with celery greens, onions, parsley, peppercorns and salt, which gave the soup the distinct flavor that we learned to love.

Most soups were eaten with home baked breads. Roasted onion soup was good; so was the leek soup, which was made with a white sauce base. Yeast soup was really good. We stirred lard and flour in a skillet until it turned golden brown then added the yeast and water or broth to make the base of the soup. In a separate bowl, we whipped up an egg, added flour to stretch it, then poured it into the boiling soup. When we added some salt and pepper, sprinkled in chopped chives (Schnittlauch) or green onion blades, we had a hit.

Also very good was Griesnockerlsuppe. It was my favorite. Mom stirred up farina, an egg, lard and salt and thoroughly mixed them until they were the consistency of mashed potatoes. With a teaspoon, she'd scoop out the mixture and drop the little dumplings into the hot broth. They were cooked until the farina was cooked all through.

Potato soup was made from leftover boiled potatoes and often was complemented by cooking with it some carrots and chopped soup greens which consisted of parsley, parsley roots, and celery leaves. With the potato soup in front of you in the soup bowl, you took a good pinch of marjoram, placed it on one palm of your hand, and with the other crushed it up and let it fall on top of the soup. What aroma, I still do it and enjoy it very much. In all instances, we sprinkled chopped chives, during the growing season, on dishes just before eating.

Canned tomatoes made a good soup when thickened with flour. Often when making the soup base, Mom cooked a little meat with it, which we'd eat hot or cold with freshly grated horseradish. Most of the time, the bits of meat were scraped off the bone. Gristle and all was chopped up and added to leftover bread dumplings and onions, then fried up in a skillet. Ground meat was always just pork which we made into little patties after adding lots of homemade bread crumbs and/or chunks of stale bread, chopped onions, oatmeal, parsley, salt and pepper. An egg often was the only thing that held this delicious concoction together while it fried to a crunchy brown in a skillet. A Sunday treat - you bet.

Do not think we ate nothing but odd foods. We had lots of other dishes on occasion and when in season. Some things we never had nor heard of were peanut butter, corn, broccoli, steak, hot dogs, chicken, grapefruit, watermelon, and popcorn. Of course I would not trade any of the above for Limburger cheese and onions on rye bread, or hot liver loaf with spinach and homefries, or bratwurst with sweet mustard on a fresh hard roll, or boiled blood sausage with sauerkraut and potatoes fried with onions and lots of caraway seeds.

PIG HEAVEN

The pig was to the Bavarian people what a large block of marble was to Michelangelo. He could see a work of art in the block; so could my country people use and create from the hog some of the most unique meals and concoctions. The only things we did not use or eat were the hoofs, the intestines, and the eye balls. A slab of skin, with bristle still on the one side, was used to grease pans and to ease a sunburn on the shoulders. The pig was the source of meat. We ate the snout, the tongue, the ears, the lungs, the heart, the kidneys, the brains, the sweetbread, the liver, the feet, the knuckles, the belly, the tail–everything but the goodies such as the hams, tenderloins, and chops, which we could seldom afford.

Sultz, a favorite eaten cold, after the aspic gelatinized, is delicious. To prepare, take the snouts, ears, knuckles, and shin bones (the marrow in the bones and the skin make a good stock that turns into jelly), add vinegar, salt, a little sugar, peppercorns, bay leaf, onions, a couple of carrots and water to cover. Boil this feast for a good two hours until the meat comes loose from the bone. Divide the contents into several soup bowls. Put in each bowl one pig's knuckle or shin with meat on it, and add parts of the ear and snout. Pour hot broth all over until all is covered. Then garnish with a boiled carrot or two, add half of a hard boiled egg and parsley sprigs to the dish before fully cooled; and you'll have a beautiful, good tasting dish. Serve with buttered rye bread. The closest thing to this dish is the American soul food called souse.

The kidneys and lungs, though separate dishes, were marinated and cooked the same way. The kidneys however were pre-soaked in salt water to remove some of their strong taste. The meats were marinated in a brine for about 36-48 hours. This was done by adding vinegar, salt, onions, peppercorns and a bay leaf to water sufficient in quantity to cover the meat. After soaking, the meat was cooked for at least an hour in the brine. When done, the stock was strained to remove the peppercorns and such, and a flour-based white thickener was added to make gravy. When preparing lungs, cut them into 1/2 centimeter strips before serving with the gravy poured over them. The kidneys are cut into bigger chunks and also served with the same white gravy. The heart, tongue, and beef roast called Sauerbraten can be prepared in like manner. All of the above dishes are served with Semmelknödel (bread dumplings) and hot German potato salad.

Fresh sowbelly, mostly pure fat, is simply cooked with sauerkraut for an hour or more. Served with bread dumplings and fried potatoes seasoned with onions, salt, pepper, and caraway seeds, it sure is a poor man's feast.

The brains are soaked in saltwater to remove blood or bone chips. This delicacy is then chopped with knife and fork in a large bowl, to wich are added several eggs to your liking, fresh, chopped parsley, salt and pepper. Stir to mix. Slowly cook in a skillet with butter; cook longer than eggs alone, to assure the pork is cooked. Chopped onions may also be added, but they tend to overpower the mild flavor of the dish. Brains are good served with potatoes boiled in salt water and savoy cabbage chopped and creamed.

MUSHROOMS

There were three kinds of mushrooms we'd hunt. Steinpiltz is a rather large mushroom which only Mom recognized and was allowed to gather. I guess it looked a lot like several poisonous ones, and she did not want us kids to possibly handle one of them. The other two were all right for us to hunt and pick. The Reherl, a little yellow mushroom, almost looked like cauliflower sections when it popped through the mossy shaded patches. It seemed they were always on a slope where wind and rain had cleared an area for them. The other was the Wiesenchampignon or the pasture mushroom. It was easy to find and identify because of its white top and a pink comb-like membrane underneath, sitting on a plump white stalk.

Only the Reherl was not peeled, but the tops and stems of the others would peel easily before they were sliced to cook or dry on a string. A serving of fresh mushrooms with chopped parsley was a delicacy and a special treat. Mushrooms were also added to gravies and soups. Some times we would take the pork rind, which was always handy, and quickly grease a spot right on top of the hot stove where we would fry a mushroom.

A CARE PACKAGE

Mom's brother Max came to America during the Great Depression. He kept periodic correspondence with her. During the hardest years of the postwar period, Uncle Max sent us a small package at Christmas time. I remember a few of the things in those care packages. Chewing gum was one, and goods such as boxed rice were another. I recall Mom would carefully inspect to see if the packaging had been tampered with. She was looking for smuggled cigarettes. My uncle very cleverly suspended with tape or glue one or two packs inside the box of rice. He then carefully returned the rice to the box totally surrounding the cache. The box always was meticulously reglued to its factory condition. All this was done so the customs' inspectors, who inspected every package coming into the country, would not find the illegal cigarettes. Mom was looking for such concealed goods from the moment we opened the package. A couple of packs of cigarettes before the GIs came were a tremendous commodity to trade for other much needed things.

Of course none of us could read English. In one of the care packages we found a block of butter or something like spreadable cheese the size of a brick, boxed with a small plastic capsule of dark red liquid. We could only trust uncle Max and assume it was meant to be eaten. The capsule was discarded; we could not figure out its use. Only now I do know that it was food coloring to be mixed with the margarine.

NICKOLAUS AND HIS KNECHT (Helper)

Practically every day of the Catholic calendar was designated to a saint. The saint's name was honored that day; and if you had been given the same name, you celebrated your name day. December 6th was Saint Nickolaus' name day. The activities of honoring St. Nick were a bit unusual. It was closely related to what we now-a-days call Christmas in the USA. Both the German and sadly the American celebration has nothing to do, to a great many people, with Christ and His birthday.

Linoleum block print of St. Nick with switch in hand, doing double duty for Knecht Rupprecht.

Saint Nick was dressed in a red coat with white cuffs. He wore a tall hat like the pope wears during certain festivities. He walked with a tall staff in one hand and had a long white beard. In the old country, St. Nickolaus was never connected with Christmas at all; but he had a sack over his shoulders with goodies in it. When he came to visit on the evening of the 6th, he asked the parents for a report on the behavior of the children during the previous year. If you were deserving, maybe along with a little lecture, you would get some cookies, apples, nuts or rock candy. (Men wearing their St. Nick outfits were gathered in the local Gasthauses waiting to be hired out by the parents to visit their kids). However, for the kids who really needed a bit of reprimand, St. Nick's helper, Knecht Rupprecht, would come along. He was the one that doled out the punishment. Oh, he was an ugly, bent over, mean-looking creature. His hair was dark and scraggly. He had dark shadows under his beady eyes and a deep frown extending down from each side of his mouth. He wore a sackcloth mantle over his shoulders and had a crude rope tied around his waist. A long thick chain, which he dragged on the ground behind him, introduced him as the coming of doom. He would snort and grunt and make an eerie noise as he came along the front walkway or up the steps to pay a visit.

I recall one night when we were visiting the home of a friend who had two daughters in their middle teens. We heard a terrifying commotion as Knecht Rupprecht approached the closed front door. St. Nick was with him and had to restrain his Knecht from totally going mad and breaking down the door. We little kids just shivered and vowed never to do anything wrong again as long as we lived. After a brief report from the girl's mom, the Knecht was stomping and smacking the wooden switch onto the floor, chasing the giggling girls around the house and into the bedroom. The calamity was soon over, and the girls had gotten their reward. I, however, could not understand the disrespect these girls had for an individual of such authority.

I also remember on one such night when a young boy a little older than me, still having respect for "authority", was given a good caning, and then stuffed into Knecht Rupprecht's sack. The boy was carried into the night several hundred yards from his house. After being shaken out of the sack into the snow on the ground, he was given additional stern warnings, then told to find his way back home. I bet he had to change his clothes from the inside out after that ordeal.

THE WREATH OF FLOWERS

As I grew up, being a good kid was connected with going to heaven when you died. This was made apparent to me when I was six years old by a nun who demonstrated to me how to get to heaven. She suggested that I take a dinner plate, put it upside down on a piece of paper, and with a pencil outline the plate to form a circle. She then explained that when I did a good deed, such as bringing in firewood, washing the dishes, searching out the owner of a found item, I was allowed to draw a tiny flower on the edge of that circle. Then after doing good again, I could draw the next flower on the inside of the circle, and with another deed the next flower close to the other. Upon completing this wreath of flowers, the nun assured me I would get to go to heaven. Well, it took me close to two years to complete that wreath of flowers. It was not until I was 35 years old that I finally realized what a futile effort it was. The intentions and training were good, but the complete mockery of God became apparent when I found out that God cannot be bought by my own efforts. The point I had finally learned was whether it be money or good deeds, God is much too holy to be bartering with for His favor. He is the One who formed and created me and certainly is not in the business of making deals with me. The way to heaven I found is Ephesians 2:8-9 and John 14:6.

OUR LITTLE WISH LIST

A week or so before Christmas, Dagmar and I would write an invitation to the Christ child to come and visit our house on Christmas eve. The little letter also included a wish list. We kept it real short because we never got many things other than some cookies and fruit. It was just not right to be a hog and ask for too much. The note was then stuck between the window and the sash so the Christ angel could pick it up as he flew by outside. The longer the letter stayed stuck in that window, the better behaved we became. There was always that chance the angel would remember some bad deed and pass us by. In my imagination, looking through the window into the night, I actually saw, very briefly, an angel fly by. He did not come close and take the letter, but I prayed he would come back; and he did. The letters always vanished.

GANSJUNG

Several times we had a goose for Christmas. It was always a freshly butchered one. Though I never witnessed the act, the head was cut off and immediately the blood was drained into a pot and reserved. The goose then was dipped into scalding hot water after which all the feathers were plucked off. That I did help do. The innards were carefully removed, the feet cleaned, and they were put into the pot of goose blood. The neck was cut off and put into the pot. The gizzard was turned inside out, cleaned, and was put into the pot. The heart, split in half, and along with the fresh liver were fried on the spot to make a lipsmacking snack. Now, that pot of blood with its additions was destined to become the New Year's Eve meal. All we had to do was add a good cup of vinegar, salt, bay leaves, a couple of sliced onions, some celery leaves, fresh carrots, parsley, and lots of peppercorns. This concoction was left to marinate until that appointed day when all was brought to a boil and left to simmer 'till done. Flour thickener was then added to give the sauce body. The feast was complemented with Semmelknödel, which are hardroll dumplings, cabbage, and some root vegetable. The meal was called Gansjung, young goose, a perfect extension and finale of the holiday season. Good luck and happy New Year!

THE CHRISTMAS GOOSE

The Christmas goose was stuffed and baked. Stuffing was made of stale, chopped hardrolls, onions, celery, parsley, a couple of eggs, some sage, salt and pepper mixed together with scalded milk to get a loose, moist mixture. Mom made lots of gravy with every meat dish; and the Christmas goose was certainly no exception. Gravy always could stretch a meal. Each time we had a goose, there were always plenty of other trimmings with it. Of course, the rendered goose grease was like gold. Some of that fat was skimmed off the gravy. When it cooled, it was golden yellow, sort of granular, and easy to spread on rye bread with a little salt. A bit of that yellow gold was saved for medicinal purposes. Hot goose grease rubbed on the chest, then covered with hot damp towels, was a sure bet to loosen a winter cough. Story has it, that the reason the Christmas goose was so good and fat was, that it had been force fed. This was simply done by putting the goose up in tight quarters and systematically forcing the goose to eat much more than normal. The head was held, the beak pried open, then the food was poured in and stuffed down the throat with the handle of a wooden spoon. Not a pretty picture, but it rendered a lot of gold.

THE MAGIC OF CHRISTMAS

December 24 started and proceeded just like any other day. But we knew this was the big day. There was no sign of Christmas anywhere, no decorations. We helped Mom bake various kinds of cookies. There were nuts to crack and pans to grease. Dagmar and I knew that sometime before the end of the day, the Christ child would come. Around four in the afternoon, Mom put us to bed. She told us if the Christkindle is going to come, it would not want to be seen. It only took a moment for it to come and be gone again, but the timing had to be perfect. So we went to bed, full of excitement and expectations.

We lay perfectly still. Whether sister went to sleep, I do not know. As for me, I was too wound up to do much sleeping. I listened, dreamed and imagined, trying to put things in order. I was a thinking little fellow, always wondering why things worked in certain and often unexpected ways. Around 8 o'clock Mom woke us up. As we entered into the kitchen, also our living area, the whole world suddenly was a glowing splendor. The regular light bulb was turned off, and in the corner stood a tall Christmas tree, all trimmed with real lighted candles, many glistening ornaments and lots of tinsel. The candles, each with a little drip bowl under it to catch the dripping wax, were clipped to the branches of the fir tree. The ornaments were of blown glass, very fragile, and sprinkled with many sparkling tiny crystals. The tinsel was placed lovingly onto every branch and hung straight down. They quivered slightly from the warmth of the candles and every breath we took. Our little family stood there in front of that tree, with the candles burning, holding on to each other, as we sang Silent Night, Holy Night. After the song, Mom held us up, alternating one of us at a time, to blow out the candles. To this day I love to smell a candle's smoke after it has been snuffed. When the light was turned back on, only then did we search under the tree for presents. The presents were mostly woolen clothes knitted by Mom. One year I also got a drafting ruler, 10 cm long, another year a stamp collecting album. Once I got a compass set with a fountain pen and coloring pencils and paper to draw on. After the opening of the presents, we'd sit around the rest of the evening, eating cookies and drinking Glühwein, which is glowing wine, made from a cheap red wine or grape juice mixed half and half with hot tea. It was simmered with orange peels, cloves, cinnamon sticks and sugar. Just before midnight, if we did not go to midnight mass, we would eat Weisswurst (a white sausage) dipped in sweet mustard, along with warm potato salad and hard rolls with butter. The goose was tackled the next day. The meat, gravy, stuffing, and dumplings easily lasted until New Year's eve. That was the evening for the Gansjung.

A BROKEN TRUST

The young lady from Sudetenland named Friedl left shortly after the twins died. Mom rented out the curtained off room to a man who was to become also a watch-over-us person when Mom worked or visited. The man was not too friendly with us children, but he was around when needed.

One morning when Mom had gone to see her Tante Maria in Simbach, the man kind of quietly and orderly searched everything in our living quarters. As an innocent kid, it never crossed my mind that he was up to no good and actually was in the process of robbing us. He stuffed his and our suitcase full, gave me some good excuse why he had to go, and left. Mom came home that day, realized that we had been taken, and promptly walked to tell the police. The fellow was caught several days later wearing my father's coat. We got most of the stolen stuff back although he had sold some things. After that episode, I don't remember my mother ever renting that room again. It turned out to be good because when either grandpa came to visit he had a place to sleep.

THE TRUCK RIDE

News of the impending arrival of a carnival came, and the town folks were abuzz. The carnival was to set up in the nearby town of Karpfham, which had a train station that served the entire area. On a cold dreary day, a lot of us kids were huddled around a pot-bellied wood stove that stood on the back of an open truck. I remember the stove being stoked with wood and stuff to feed the fire, but the truck just would not start. The poor man was cranking that handle in the front of that truck until he was blue in the face. He'd jump up on the back of the truck, run to the stove which was in the corner in back of the cab, mess with the fire some, jump back down, and crank that handle again. Finally the truck started and to the carnival we went. I do not remember anything about the rides because I most likely did not have money to ride any. I do remember the carnival crew sliding back the side doors of their railcars, exposing the living quarters of a traveling group of Lilliputians. Everything was so small. The midgets talked, joked, and put on a show in general. It was fun. But that truck ride was the experience of the year. In fact, that truck, running on burning wood gases, was to me a normal thing, since I was too young to remember when diesel oil was around to run the trucks. I know that some cars also had their trunk covers removed and had a stove mounted in the trunk to generate the gases to keep running. There were no cars in our town, but such contraptions show that man's engineering is greatest in times of need.

THE IRON HORSE

One other memorable ride was the one we took on a train to visit Tante Maria in Simbach. We walked the five kilometers to the train station, then, with great expectation, listened for and then watched the big iron horse come rolling in, all huffing and puffing and squeaking to a halt. I remember I had to be lifted up to the first iron step which led up and into the railcar. Only people of means were getting to ride in this style. That day, we were people of means. Whistles blew, first from the conductor, then from the big steam engine itself. With groaning and snorting and lots of loud puffing the big machine slowly pulled our train away. Naturally, I had to go to the bathroom while in motion. Some things a young man had to check out if he is going to tell all his friends back home about this exciting adventure. Mom took me by the hand and led me to the end door of our passenger car. All the while the car was rocking back and forth. We had to grab seats and metal pipe handles to hang on to keep from being slammed into a corner by the rocking mammoth. Opening the door at the end, we stepped out onto a rickety catwalk leading to the other railcar, which had a toilet in it. I remember, as we stepped across that small catwalk, the strong way the cars were connected and the loud noise they made as they banged from side to side and the noise of all those iron wheels clacking in rhythm. Looking down, I saw the railroad ties whizzing by with dizzying speed–enough to scare a fellow into having to really use the bathroom. The chamber that I had sought was, to somewhat overstate it, basic. With several handles to hold on, whether sitting or standing, you could look straight down the chute onto the rail ties flying by. I thought I was going to be sucked into that shaft which was certainly big enough to swallow me. Mom left me to walk back by myself. Crossing that small walk again, I felt much more confident than before, now that I had conquered the noise, the rocking, and the shaft.

Every window on our passenger car was shut. That gave me a reason to open ours. With my head stuck out, I soon found out that the air was not all that fresh coming from the locomotive. To cap off my nosiness, I got a flying cinder in my eye. With my head back inside, now knowing why all the windows were shut, Mom took her white handkerchief and with its corner fished out the black cinder. The rest of the ride, I was just like a peacock glowing in the new adventure.

NEW IDEAS

In the mid-forties, a circus passed through town offering rides on a camel. Mom dug up the fifty pennies it took to get a ride around the town square. They lifted us way up and over to straddle the camel between its humps. Sister sat in front, and I was jammed in tight behind her. With a man leading the beast, we started out. The motion from left to right with every step almost made me sick long before we had to get off. The ride was not much fun, our little legs were spread way out, and holding on was hard. We had become terribly afraid that we would fall off this tall strange animal. To this day, that ride was the farthest I have been carried by any living creature.

Another example of the beginning of a new entrepreneurial spirit in post war Germany was when a flat bed trailer, pulled by a truck, came to town to display a large, dead, whale. For a dime you could get up close and be given a little lesson on the make-up and feeding habits of these large animals. I remember learning that this particular whale was not the meat eating kind but rather opened its mouth while swimming in the sea to catch and trap thousands of small creatures, straining out the water through its gills, then swallowing the catch. Thinking back, what would possess a person to haul a dead beast, weighing many tons, four hundred miles inland traveling from town to town, over poor and dusty country roads, in the heat of the summer, to make a few dimes. Maybe he used wood for fuel also?

Mom got a chance to show off her salesmanship when she took the opportunity to sell beer and soda, which we called Gracherl, at the soccer game. Some big event must have been planned for she expected hundreds of people. She borrowed an extra wash tub, and along with ours, used them to hold the block ice. This ice was sawed from the pond during the cold months then stored in a pit covered with mounds of straw to keep frozen. Blocks were hewn from the mass and sold for purposes such as keeping drinks cold. You know, this was all new to me, and I felt quite privileged to be part of this enterprise. After we hauled the tubs and ice in our wooden wagon to the soccer field, we went to the creek to get water to add to the tubs. This was the same creek and spot where we caught our minnows. We also used our wagon to haul the cases of bottled beer and lemon soda, the table, and some drinking glasses. A cigar box with money and change was our cash register and was closely guarded by me. We charged double our cost. Business became quite brisk at half time with me handing the bottles from under the table to Mom. The experienced hands of Mom worked frantically to stay ahead of the demand. Clean glasses were now only as clean as the creek water after being quickly rinsed in the tubs. The afternoon was a big success thanks to the Lord's providing a hot and sunny day. Now, all of the gear had to be hauled back uptown. With the empty bottles loaded on the little wagon and money in Mom's pocket, the trip back to the brewery, and then home, was a joy. Our faces were wreathed in smiles.

GATHERING WOOD

There was never enough wood for warming, just enough for cooking.

Gathering was always a challenge, but especially in the winter. The knitting skill of my mother, who made woolen hats, ear muffs, mittens, socks, underwear, sweaters, and long johns which we wore indoors and out, was really a life saver.

The wagon we used to collect most of our wood was about four feet long, with slatted sides tapered out at the top. The four wheels were wrought of wood and banded with an iron ring just like the large farm wagons. The rear wheels were larger than the front ones. The front axle, which swiveled with the drawbar, was pulled by hand.

I've seen bigger and stronger boys get to go down hill, sitting in their wagon, and steering the pull bar between their stretched out legs. Mom would never allow me to do that. The ruts and gullies in the roads were too deep, and a wreck would have been disastrous. Understandably, the biggest reason was, we could ill afford to lose or disable that little wagon.

We took our wagon along when picking berries or hunting dropped apples and pears. Of course, pine cones and small sticks of wood, with which we started most of our fires, were horded whenever we found them along the

Wagon out of East Germany. Very similar to what we had. (Purchased at an antique shop in Savannah, Georgia.)

way. The government let people cut or break off any dead branches up the tree trunks as far as one could reach. So, Mom, standing on a foot-tall wagon bed, would get a few more sticks than someone just on ground level.

All wood forests were managed and planted. The trees were planted in rows, and the forest floor was spotless. We had to pull our wagon a far distance before we even could find the first stick or pine cone to burn. After a long day at it, however, we usually came home with a heaping wagon full of sticks and branches. The longest of these always dragged the dirt behind the wagon as we made our way around the forest and country roads.

The government allowed the people to cut any dead tree up to 8cm in diameter if there were any to be found. On occasions, we lucked out. I guess it was like striking gold during the California rush. Since all the woods and its cutting were controlled, stacked cubic meter measures of wood were often found on the forest's floor. These professionally produced piles, all with logs much thicker than 8cm, were called a stere. Seeing these stacks sometimes presented too much of a temptation not to steal a log or two. This my mother did at times. Now the trick was to get these logs home. Forest rangers or inspectors roamed the country side and were always about because of that very problem. They had one drawback— they were riding on what we called a Hennaschrecker (a chicken scarer), a mode of transportation that simply was a bicycle converted into a meek motorcycle. A small engine, like a chain saw's, was mounted in front of the handlebars. A chain leading to a sprocket on the front wheel provided the drive mechanism. When the terrain demanded it, the forester also pedaled the bicycle to help make it up the hills. Those vehicles were very noisy and could be heard a kilometer away.

The task of camouflaging those stolen logs was a challenge for Mom, but she turned it into a real science. Since the wagon was totally open all around, except the floor of it, the thinnest, most dense, dried dead twigs had to be stuffed all around the outside of the stolen logs. You had to keep in mind when stealing these logs that it was necessary to load them near a gully or some thicket usually by a branch of water. If the inspector happened to come through, there was a place to either throw the logs, or, if the disguising was not quite complete, pull the whole wagon out of sight. All three of us then would hide by running deep into the woods. The other choice was to hope the camouflaging was good enough to fool the ranger. In that case, he would get off his 'wheels' and, using a long stick, poke all around the wagon looking for evidence of the stolen goods. All he had to do was look at me and see how frightened I was. My heart quit beating, and I must have been as white as a ghost. Whether it was a guardian angel, a blind inspector, or an inspector that had a soft spot in his heart, whatever, we were never rep-

Hauling home a load of sticks.

rimanded or brought before the authorities for sneaking home some of those logs that would last long enough in the cookstove to bake a cake. After a long day and many anxieties, the wagon was finally fully loaded. Piled high and tied down, little sis sitting on top, we'd make our way home slowly with the branches dragging behind wiping out our tracks.

Now, you could not display obviously-stolen logs in the wood pile in the back yard. So, upon getting home, we had to sneak the logs up the stairs and hide them under the bed. When Baumann Opa came to visit, he would saw up the logs. He knew how those logs got there. Baumann Opa, being a religious man, would just look at Mom with his bright blue eyes in a cold stare. He'd then take a clenched hand and rub his forehead in small slow circles, glaring at Mom as if to say–you beset and crazy woman. Seeing our need, he'd give in, cutting them all to fire box length and splitting them with an ax.

To work on the wood, four items were necessary–a homemade saw buck, a buck saw, a hand ax, and a chopping block. The chopping block was a wooden stump that had been cut close to the ground and therefore was fatter on the bottom for more stability. This chop block had developed a character of its own from the many choppings it endured. A block lasted a life time. It was never burned and became part of the family. Generally very little had to be split. The twigs were chopped to foot lengths, tied into bundles with boughs from a fir tree, and then stored upstairs in the front hall.

Baumann Opa, who cut up our firewood and chopped our twigs.

As for the ill gotten logs, all anyone had to do was listen in the middle of the night when we threw those logs out of the bedroom window–just enough of them for Baumann Opa to cut up the next morning. The logs had to be pitched out far enough into the darkness to clear the perpetual seepage from the building's open cesspool which would have swallowed them up. I can still hear the thuds in the night as the logs landed on top of one another. Surely some of the neighbors knew what was going on, but no one ever said a word.

THE SNOWMAN WITH A NECK

Sister and I had three Opas (grandfathers). Baumann Opa was Mom's father. When he visited, he was all business. He cut up most of the wood that needed sawing, watched us kids somewhat, and sort of kept a lid on any excessive joviality. Beisser Opa and his former wife had two sons, one my father Franz and his brother Alfons. (During the 1940's, my sister and I never met Felsner Opa, who

Beisser Opa,
passport photo at age 92.

lived in Munich with his wife who formerly was married to Beisser Opa.) When Beisser Opa came to visit, very little work got done. There was just a lot of kidding around, story telling, and card playing going on. When I was six, Beisser Opa was 76 years old. Although his learned trade was a butcher, he had not worked as one in over 50 years. All that Beisser Opa did for a living was play cards and engage in other forms of gambling. Needless to say, he

Wooden sled, very similar to what we pulled.

was not rich; but he had savvy. When he visited, he always drank a glass of wine and ate one clove of garlic a day. He also did knee bends and stretches and walked every day. Beisser Opa was fun to be around. He often took some 'pre-cut' paper with him on his walks in case nature called. The times I got to walk with him, he'd point out those certain markings which always had a small flag stuck in them, made out of a twig that was split on top with his pocketknife with a leaf wedged in. These were a warning to him and me not to step too close.

When cold weather came, it was determined to stay a while. It seemed like each snowfall would lay around waiting for another. Building snowmen and fortresses with tunnels and sled runs with jumps was never a problem. Maybe we were just small tykes or the snow was plenty, I don't know –probably a little of both. The sled tracks had to be packed down after each new snowfall. The tracks had to be ready for that perfect Schlittenfahrt (sled ride). They were fun times, but my lack of boots kept me from staying outside too long. One crisp wintry day, when Beisser Opa was visiting, he and I went for a walk. I wanted to show him how good I was at building a snowman. He let me build it; and when I was done, he criticized it, saying it needed a neck. Well, after some arguing, I knocked its head off, stuck a tall neck on it, then a new head. The snowman now was absolutely ugly. Opa laughed heartily. But, I got so upset I ran home alone, tears flowing.

MY TWO BEAUTIES

To get to sit and draw pictures has always been a pleasure even at a very early age. One Summer, I got a chance to herd, or should I say watch, two milk cows. I was happy to get the opportunity to do some serious drawing. The offer was made; I took the job. The pay was a quart of milk a day.

When I picked up my two b-b-beauties, as I should have called them, they were always ready and willing to walk from the stable behind the milk parlor on the town square all the way out of town to the green pasture. The two cows were hitched together with a simple harness, with a short lead rope hanging between their heads. I remember my eyeballs were the exact height of their wet and dripping nostrils. So, walking a step ahead of them kept me dry, and it also gave me a guarantee I was not stepped on.

The dairy man had shown me the perimeter of the field, which was on the sunny side of a gentle hill, bordered by a swampy bog on the lower edge. The fence was a one or at best a two-strand wire strung between and along some short posts and half rotten boards.

Looking back, I can see now why the two beauties had to be watched. It was either pay the shepherd a quart of milk or fix the fence. Those cows would have been all over the country.

It did not take long for a youngster to get fidgety sitting on a rock, with nothing to lean back against, in the middle of a four acre field. Basking under a full sun all day, eating a stale lunch, sipping water with a little vinegar and sugar in it, was not all that exciting. As for the drawing part, well, that sounded good in theory; but how often can you draw the same hill and few trees that I looked at all day?

Thank God there never was a worry about snakes. I never heard about ticks either. The mosquitoes were few, and they never did zap you in the heat of the day anyway. Poison oak we did not know about, and I knew how to stay away from the nettles that gave a burning itch.

My job was to watch the cows and keep them inside the assigned area. What I did not know was that after they had their fill of grass, they would seek shade. Looking back, this makes a whole lot of sense. But then, that was not part of the orders I had. The only shade was on forbidden ground, on the other side of the marshy area over the one strand of wire. The cows sort of eased on over there and laid down. No, no, up I jumped, sloshing through the swamp, circling around behind the beauties, shooing them back onto the assigned area under the noon day sun. Well, you know what followed. As soon as I sat down again, the cows ambled back into the shade. This circus kept up all afternoon, every day, all summer. After all, a German kid takes orders, follows orders, does not change orders, nor ask questions about orders. I was going to earn my pay–only after doing the work.

When the sun was at a certain spot, it was time to start bringing the beauties back home. I never did find out why they were so well behaved when it was time to go to the barn and just the opposite when they were not supposed to use the other man's shade. With a couple of shouts of "Kuh-li-geh," they'd come waddling toward me. Looking up at their large heads and horns always frightened me a little when I harnessed them together no matter how often I did it. I always thought they might hold a grudge for running them out from under the trees. Thank God for their lack of vindictiveness. Those two cows seemed always happy and never once did they buck or try to run me down. After I snapped them together and attached the rope, we leisurely strolled back to town.

My pay was prompt, and I was the man of the house.

BERRY PICKING

Wild strawberries grew in patches. These seldom yielded enough for preserving, so we ate them on the spot. A day or so later, we usually remembered and visited the patch again to get another handful. Some people had huge gooseberry bushes. They would share their bounty if you had the will power to tangle with the thorns on the branches. Mom had a liking for gooseberry jam, so we picked enough to make several jars of the tart preserves.

Currants were easier to pick although those bushes had thorns as well. But if you wanted some, you had to have your own bushes. Currants grew in little clumps of red pea-sized berries. The white variety was the same in tartness and in taste. Some people even had a black variety that tasted similar to elderberries. Though all these berries were good, the various wild berries were the ones that we and the town folks went after.

Huckleberries, (wild blueberries) grew close to the ground. So, we, the shorter folks, had no excuse not to do our share of picking. We hung a tin cup by running a belt or a string through the handle of the cup on our belly so we could pick with both hands. I was always driven by some unknown motivation to eat at most just one berry so I could wholly concentrate on filling my cup. When the cup was full, I poured it into a quart-size milk can that had a bail handle and a deep lid that prevented the berries from spilling out should the can fall over. Sister Dagmar was not participating in our survival skills. She picked berries alright, but three into the cup and twelve into her mouth. She quit picking all together when she got full. We stayed busy all day. It was really hard to fill our milk can with those little tiny berries. What was most irritating, after we walked a long way to a known berry spot, was to find out that some one had just picked it clean. At times we even saw evidence that some of the patches were raked. Raking was a commercial way that combed the plants from underneath, removing all berries of a certain size, even some that were still green. As young as sis and I were, we both agreed with Mom that such a seemingly wasteful method of picking was beneath us.

Blackberries were picked by us as well as by others but were not as desirable as the red raspberry that grew wild in patches of overwhelming profusion. With red raspberries, you had to look at every berry picked because many had a little white worm in them. It seemed the riper the berry, the more likely it had a worm in it. The picking was a bit harder for us kids because the plants grew much taller then we were. However, the cup, hanging from our belt or on the suspenders on my Lederhose, would fill up much faster. One episode put a damper on an otherwise perfect picking day. I, barefoot as always, slipped under a tree root and was immediately bombarded by dozens of mad yellow jackets. I was stung mostly on one leg from toes to the bottom of my breeches. By the time we got home, my leg looked like a round log with little fat toes sticking out. I do not remember what the antidote was, but I lived. The lesson was to look where you stepped when in the woods; shoes were for wearing to church.

To preserve the berries we picked, Mom generally pro-

Straining berries to make jelly.

longed the evening cooking fire and brought the berries to a boil. She moved them over to the side of the stove to let them simmer a while. I was then allowed to skim off the foam as it simmered down. The foam was considered impure and was thought to cause mold to grow. When jelly was made from the fruit, Mom turned a kitchen chair upside down and rested it on our eating table. The four legs sticking up into the air provided a natural setup to tie and hang a linen cloth. In the middle of the four legs, she sat a bowl. The berry juice was then poured into the cloth which served as a strainer sack. The pure juices would at first run through the linen into the bowl then continue to drip until the next morning. The next day after supper, the juice was reheated, sugar added, cooked and skimmed once more. After the jars were filled, they were sealed with melted beeswax on top of the jellied juice, then covered with a piece of cloth tied by a string to the jar. Preserves of blueberries, raspberries, and zwetschgen, a plum also grown to dry as prunes, were sealed the same way.

THE WHISPERINGS OF GOD

My Lederhose were a friend to me, but my gathering trousers were closer than a brother. These pants were sewn by Mom. They were longer than shorts and hung a good bit below the knees. The length was for one reason only: to provide and also accommodate the extra deep pockets. These pockets were so deep I had to bend over to reach to the bottom of them. The gathering pants were also kind of baggy; so when the pockets were filled, they had room to expand.

Late in the year when the air had a new crispness in it, the time was getting near to gather nuts. Hazelnuts grew on large bushes, and not many of them were considered public property. However walnuts, the English or Carpathian kinds, grew into massive trees; and I knew of several around the outskirts of town. So did many other townspeople. At first just a few pods would pop open, and the nut would drop. Gathering was sparse, and the red squirrels were busy hoarding them as well. As the next several weeks passed, timing became paramount to being able to gather enough for the upcoming Christmas baking season. A feverish excitement mounted in my soul as the nuts matured and started to fall by the hundreds. We made sure the bedroom window stayed open so I could listen and read the signs even when it rained at night. In the back yard was a massive horse chestnut tree that still had its browning fall foliage on. It rustled at the slightest breeze blowing through it. That was the whispering voice that told me when there was a strong enough wind that would loosen and drop the nuts. Then as always, the Lord in His ultimate wisdom picked the right days. At times, after an evening of calm, first some drops of rain would fall around midnight. After a while, the wind would stir a little, then later during the night little stronger gusts would quickly arouse me to complete alertness. As I listened and heard these rushing sounds, my heart knew that the Almighty was tenderly shaking the trees just for

Making use of my special gathering pants.

me. Long before dawn, I'd get up, step into my special packing pants, and sneak out of the house. I, alone, then walked in quiet excitement to my favorite spots. Barefooted, in total darkness, I gingerly stepped with great anticipation under the trees. Slowly I walked around on the damp, cold, fallen leaves, feeling with my toes for the desired gift. The effort was always richly rewarded. I felt like God was smiling at me. He certainly talked to me in whispering kindness as His breezes would loosen a few more of the fruit. I could hear them hit the ground. I would judge how far they had rolled; and always to my sheer delight, my toes would find them. On mornings like these it was easy to fill my pockets to the brim. With pockets packed full and some more in my fists, I hurriedly walked home, giddy with happiness. Oh, there were times when my pockets were not full, but my heart was always full.

The quietness and the utmost communion during those early hours, at such an early age, etched an everlasting impression in me of our Creator and the peace He offers, which passes all understanding. To this day, the rain, the wind, and the whispering pines around my house remind me that He is still there. I now have one of these walnut trees growing in my yard–50 years after those childhood days. I again, with my shoes off, search for the fallen fruit, but this time –out of thankfulness and nostalgia,–not need.

HAMSTERN

The day was just beautiful, bright and brisk. Mom had packed my Rucksack. In it was a paper bag for flour, a padded box for eggs, a metal can for lard, and some loose paper to wrap other goodies. I was ready to go "Hamstern". Although we always gathered and brought home what was edible and in season, this time, whether it was out of need or just to give me some additional freedom to help me grow up, I don't know, but I went bumming, big time.

I set out early in the morning, heading north. There were no roads, just wagon trails. My aim was to go from farm to farm and ask for food to take home for sister and Mom. At first I did not know how to ask or explain what I wanted, so every farmer's wife I visited thought that I was hungry. I got so full that by lunch time I could not eat another thing. I started to stuff Schmalznudels and other baked goods into the Rucksack. I learned I had to be more direct in my approach. The day went along beautifully. I picked some apples along the way and enjoyed the wonders of nature. Most farms had a white picket fence around a little flower garden in front of the farmhouse. Often I was greeted by a dog, some friendly, and others were just showing off their watchdog skills.

Every time it was the farmer's wife who would invite me in and pull a little history out of me. The saga about being driven out of the city by the bombs made them quite understanding, and my lard can and other containers started to fill up. It was the women I usually got to talk to. Generally the men were not around the house during the day; their lunch was taken to them by the indentured girls. One farm was an exception. I remember on that afternoon four men were busy at the barn. The barn had a large doorway at each end of it. When standing in that breezeway, I felt the wind blowing through it pretty good. This was the perfect setup for threshing. The men had spread on the ground, at the end of one of the large barn openings, a tarp, made of burlap, about two meters square. One of the men scattered a couple of pitchforks full of harvested wheat on the tarp, then all four encircled the pile and commenced to flail the grain. Each flail, about as long as a baseball bat and about six to eight centimeters in diameter, was attached to a short stout handle by a good-sized, leather strap. The men, in rhythmic succession, flailed at the grain heads in perfectly timed intervals going around and around. In just a short time, the flailing stopped; one picked the straw off the tarp. Then all four grabbed a corner of the tarp and winnowed the newly threshed grain by slinging it into the air. The breeze, praise God, then took the chaff and it floated away. This was done several times until nothing but grain was left on the tarp. Lovingly it was scooped into a sack, and the cycle began all over again.

The trek I made that day–I do not know how many miles–was all new to me. We had never been on these farm roads before, and neither Mom nor I had ever met any of these people. I did not know where I was all day long. I guess I was basically lost. One thing I figured out was, that if I kept the sun in front and to the right all day while I was walking, I would come out somewhere south of town. That I did. I quite suddenly came out on the road that led to the train station where we had walked before.

The tricks I brought home that day were not so shabby. There were 6 eggs, a can full of lard, and butter. The flour sack was not quite full. Also, there were various breads and rolls, some apples, and a few select pine cones, which we always needed to start our fire.

HARDENED SOLES

Summer time was when you got your bare feet in shape. Nothing was hard enough to hurt the bottoms. We took great pride in the toughness of our soles and tested them by showing off. On new gravel, we'd spin out, doing a stationary run and seeing how far we could throw the rocks backward with our feet. Another boy thing that was kind of fun, was the dirt a slide. Sliding down on our backsides of the Lederhose was fun, but taking a running jump and sliding down the almost vertical track on your bare feet was tough. For sure, after a good rain, the wet mud really added to the speed of going down; but climbing back up was a bit slower. We even dared each other to walk on shattered glass.

OUR PERCH

Each of us had a favorite tree for climbing. Mine was a fir. The Aborigines had nothing on us as far as speed was concerned. We got to the top of our trees in mere seconds. With a small running start and a leap, we'd grab the lowest branch and in the same motion sling one leg over the adjoining branch. Then, one quick pull up and our arms reached for the next tier of branches. Up and up we went until the trunk of the tree was like a sapling, covered with needles and pitch. The twigs I stood on kept sagging, and often I'd slip off. Although the top of the tree would bend severely, none of us ever fell out of our roost. With the sticky sap all over us, we showed the other fellows what really hanging out was all about.

THE MINNOWS WOULD NOT EAT

Playing in the stream was fun. Our favorite spot was the one running behind the town's soccer field. The same creek, just a little upstream, was dammed up to create a good-sized pond that was also the town's public bathing spot. The pond had a shallow wading pool with a level, concrete bottom. This provided a nice area to bring the

Setting a trap to catch minnows.

children to play in the summer. Over the years, the bottom of that level spot had gotten covered with mud. This made for quite some murky water when a bunch of kids got to wallowing in it. Well, it was cooler in the water than sitting in the heat.

In the branch below were minnows to catch. On occasion you could catch one barehanded by running it into a shallow corner, but most of the time we used a large white handkerchief. We'd hollow out a low spot in the water, then stretch the cloth out, pinning it to the stream's bottom with a few rocks on the corners. We then squatted on each side of the branch with hands ready at the water's edge, waiting quietly and motionless until several minnows came to rest in the hollow spot on the kerchief. With a sudden snap of the corners, we pulled up the cloth. Most of the minnows would dart out, but often we caught one or two. The prized catch was quickly added to the jar filled with water.

At full speed, we then carried our cache uptown where my friend had a bathtub in his house. We filled the tub half full of water and then dumped our catch in it. Now time came to hunt for food for those fish. If we were to see them grow to any edible size, we had to feed them. Well, down to the branch we went again to catch some morsels in the fish's natural habitat. Worms, snails, bugs, flies, grasshoppers, and leeches were good to start with. The leeches were kind of hard to get. They were stuck on slippery algae under the water that ran over the dam. Those critters were kind of orange-red with a jagged sucking cup on the end of them. They would rather quickly stick themselves to your body if you let them. Well, the food we gathered for the minnows was enough to grow some good sized fish. All we had to do was dump the jar full of creepy things into the bathtub.

While the project was still on our minds, we'd check on the minnows before the day was done. But after a few days, we found that most of the food had died in the tub or merely crawled out to greener pastures. A week or so later the report was that the minnows also had croaked. This gets me to wondering, with my now Americanized brain, why did that family have a tub when no one used it for over a week? As to the extent of our own washing, most days Mom just washed us with a coarse rag swiftly around the face and behind the ears. We had to wash our feet with a cursory inspection by Mom to make sure the rust was washed off.

THE SNAIL RACE

In damp, dark places, where the rain washed the ground bare, we had snail races. Big snails that carried their houses on their backs were thought to be the real racehorses. We would get the track ready by scratching starting and finishing lines as well as lanes into the dirt guiding them to the goal. We also made chutes behind the starting line out of sticks to guide the snail into the correct direction. Then we searched for snails. We looked for big fat ones with their houses seemingly too small for them. We figured they did not have to carry the extra weight. Well, the race started when the snails were placed with their head facing toward the finish line. Of course, when you picked up the critter, the head and tail disappeared into the house. So, you had to be aware which end was where and not place your racer with the south end facing north onto the starting line. Good thing it was cool under those trees because it took quite a spell for the snail's body to expand and reappear. Slowly the slimy glob got bigger with the eyes coming out of the body first as two bumps, then expanding outward like two little sticks with a distinct dark eye at the end of each. The race had officially started. Yelling and cheering on your own did not work; you just scared the snail back into its shell. So you left it alone. The snail usually just sat there, checking out the new environment, becoming oriented. Well, after a minute or so had passed and not a sliver of a movement toward the finish line had been made, the snails finally began to slither leaving a thin trail of clear slime. With eyes as good as theirs, stuck way out there on those little stems, one would think they could see better. After all we had the finish line and the side lines clearly marked. Yet they were determined to cut to the left or right or even try to turn around. Once the race began we were not allowed to pick up our racers and face them in the right direction. However, we would place a

Snail race . . . 0-10 inches in 58 minutes.

stick to one side or the other if the snail started to veer off the track. Every time we did that, the dumb critter would retract into its shell, then take its good old time coming back out, look around, and then slothfully continue.

I never won a snail race, nor did anyone else. After an

hour's worth of racing, the racers, having traveled hardly eight or ten inches, were certainly not worn out, but the trainers were. So we went on to more exciting things.

WALKING A FROG

A frog is a frog is a frog. We thought that all frogs were great leapers. We would goad them with homemade sharpened sticks to do some mighty jumping. The biggest jumps that never failed to surprise us were always by the

Walking a frog.

green frogs, straight into the creek or pond. However, the brown frogs were kind of lethargic, and we never could figure out what was wrong with them. When you goosed them, they would hop or scamper a bit but never with much enthusiasm. So, when walking a frog from point A to point B, it exasperated us when those creatures just quit altogether and closed their eyes. Therefore, judgment was passed by one of the boys that all frogs shall jump. Even that daffy one, the one we were coaching and coaxing now, was going to be champion jumper.

We found an old, long board, under which we placed, in the center, a good sized rock, making a low seesaw. We placed one of the uncooperating toads on the end of the board touching the ground with the other end up in the air about a foot. The oldest boy then took a running jump onto the board's end, slammed it to the ground, and sent the poor, tired frog heavenbound. If altitude did not kill him first, the ground surely did. A great cheer went up, a champion jump, but something told me that this game was not for me.

A GAME OF MARBLES

Shooting marbles was my game. A level area on the ground, not growing any grass, was an ideal place to shoot a game of marbles. We wiped and patted the ground smooth with our hands and bare feet, and also removed any rocks or pebbles that might impede the game. An area of about two meters in diameter was usually sufficient for a smooth shooting area. In the center, a very shallow depression was dug a half inch deep and as wide as a dessert plate. The dip in the middle of the playing area was designed for the marble to spin right back out when shot just a bit too hard. The game started with a predetermined quantity of marbles on each side, usually ten. After placing our ammo on the outer rim of the circle, we would putt (shoot), with crooked index finger, the marbles toward the center hole. If you got one to stay in the hole, you removed it to keep. However, if the marble rolled back out or stopped short of the depression, you could easily lose that marble to the other boy being it was so close to the dip. You can see that placing your ten marbles on the playing field was big strategy. Once all the rollers were on the ground, you took turns putting with the index finger. Usually the competitors picked the marble closest to the dip in the middle to try to make it stay in the hole. You lost your turn after the one you were shooting failed to reach or rolled back out of the cup. Every time you got one to stay in the cup, it was put in your pocket so as not to hinder the next shot from possibly rolling out again.

My finger used to stay quite crusty and stained from shooting those little round prizes. During summer time, my booty was the envy of many of the boys. That made trading marbles for other goods a nice way to collect some of the valued necessities a boy usually had need of, and other boys often carried, in their pants pockets. I already had a pocket knife, so, some of the things I wanted were copper wire for the manufacture of medieval weapons, bits of leather for a slingshot, a small whetrock to sharpen my knife away from the community grindstone, the balls out of a ball bearing, a magnet, some fishing line or even something American, like a piece of chewing gum. In the words of Bill Watterson's Calvin: "The days were just packed."

WHAT ABOUT CIGARETTES

Many men rolled their own cigarettes long before the GIs came. Few smoked cigars, I guess you could not get them readily. Many smoked pipes. The elders of the town had their long hanging meerschaum pipes; the younger men much smaller and sportier ones. Cigar stubs were finished in a pipe. Nobody chewed tobacco or dipped the stuff like they do in the United States.

Snuff was actually sniffed up the nose. When the need for a dip came, Beisser Opa would, with greatly exaggerated and somewhat elegant motion, reach for his silver snuff box. He always kept it in his coat pocket. After tapping it with his knuckles, knocking off any snuff that may have stuck to the lid, he'd flip it open. With the precision of an orchestra conductor, he took out a pinch between his thumb and two fingers, then flipped the lid closed again with his pinkie finger. Carefully, he'd return his treasured, little box back into his breast pocket. All this was done before the pinch was ever placed on the backside of his left hand. Then,with great expectation the hand was slowly raised to his nostrils. One good snort up one nostril took about half the dip, the other nostril like-wise getting the rest of it.

Opa Beisser's silver snuff box.

Since a kid could not get hold of any real tobacco, we made our own smoking tools and hunted stuff to smoke. We began by making our own pipes. Corn cobs were out since no one had ever seen or eaten any corn. Where we lived bamboo or reeds did not grow, but elderberry bushes did. The elderberry branches had a pithy center that could be reamed out. The bowl of the pipe we made from the thick part of the bush reaming it out with our pocket knives. Only the portion of the annual leaf growth was used for the stem of the pipe. We cleared the pithy stuff from the pipe stem with a wire that we stuck through, then pushed back and forth to increase the hollowness. We then drilled a hole in the side of the bowl with our knife and stuck the two parts together. The tobacco sub-stitute we decided on, after experimenting with various dried leaves, was that of the horse chestnut. None of the stuff we smoked tasted good. Some smelled a bit better than others. When we tried to inhale some of it, it made our eyeballs almost pop out. Smoke we did—with spit and tears just flying. The closest thing in form to cigarettes or thin cigars was what we called Judenstrick or Jewish rope. It was the dried vine of the wild grape. A similar vine here in the States is the Virginia creeper. The vine grew on banks and in gullies. It was thick, climbing up the trees, and often totally covering small bushes. Its hollow underside made a perfect secret hide-a-way for us. We had one particular spot were we had to crawl on our bellies to reach it. Once inside, it was dark and damp but very private. To a secret fort like that, you allowed only your closest buddies, the ones that could keep their mouths shut. Of course, if any clandestine operation was to be done that would have warranted a whipping from our parents, it was done in the vine fort. Smoking was one of these things. The walls and the domed ceiling of the hidden den were made of dead vine, all of it good to smoke. All we had to do was to reach out with our pocket knives and cut us a smoke. The section between knots in the vine made the perfect cigarillo. It was porous, and air could be sucked through it. All we had to do was light up and sit back. The dry vine stayed lit with a little stub of ashes on the end, just like a real cigarette. We sat around exhibiting various stances and techniques to hold the weed, trying to be as grown up as possible, feeling quite in control. The trouble was, after one or two smokes, the bitterness of the vine seemed to dry up the saliva glands. Your mouth became parched, and the tongue swelled up. After the taste buds were killed, you crawled out into the day. If anyone saw us hanging around the water pump, coughing, spitting, they sure could figure out what we had been up to.

So, then the GIs came to town, flipping their cigarette butts all over and creating in us an urge to do some real smoking. We boys were in butt heaven.

We were not the only ones to sheepishly pick up the discarded butts. I believe the older boys and even some grownups were in the hunt and gather mode as well. With four of us boys collecting butts, we soon had a small tin can full of tobacco. Since none of us were allowed to be caught with this taboo substance, we decided to bury the can in our secret hide-a-way. We set a date, most likely on a non-school day, for the great Bavarian Smoke In. A week or two later, the day of all days had arrived. All the practicing we did was finally going to be tested. The occasion was going to elevate us into the world of manhood. I remember sitting in a circle in our secret den, each one of us prepared, with either pipe or roll-your-own paper. Matches were on hand and ready to start the grand experience. The tin can was unearthed, the lid carefully pried open, all eager eyes were focused on that little box of treasure. The lid popped off as all of us stared at a strange, fuzzy haze of light blue and green. Our much heralded stash had totally molded. I have never longed for another smoke since that day.

TIME OUT

Even as a young boy I enjoyed having time to myself. I'd often go, with paper and pencil, and sit at some quaint or picturesque spot to draw streams and hills with trees, or old houses, and flowers.

Mom always insisted that my hair stay kind of long, which I did not like, but so it was. To get a burr cut was out of the question; it was what we thought to be a sign of backwardness. To keep the hair out of my eyes–heaven forbid I might become cross eyed–Mom stuck a bobby pin in my hair to hold it back. In addition to being a city slicker, the bobby pin provided further ammunition for the country boys to pick on me. I had to get thick skinned or die.

I never disliked school; on the contrary, I did all I could to learn–always raising my hand to answer the teacher's questions, doing my homework promptly, and doing drawings with additional studies for extra credit. This also miffed a lot of the country boys. So, being alone at times gave me much satisfaction.

In the springtime, the blessings of new promises of life excited my mom, and we shared these feelings as a family. Early in the year, I'd cut apple tree branches with their buds still closed. Mom placed them in a vase and set them by the window to catch the warmth of the sun. The apple twigs would come to life and bloom in wonderful and delicate profusion, gracing our home and gratifying our souls. Pussy willows added to our delight; and later on, the lilac bloomed in huge bunches–some in white, some in pale purple, and also some in deep wine red. All sent out a fragrance that watered the joy we had in our little family. Some flowers came early and were so few that I never wanted to pick them. I figured that maybe the Lord put them in these secret spots to grace a little corner of His world. Ah, but the tiny deep blue violets were plentiful, and I was sure He wanted me to pick some and take them home. I'd pick a bunch of them, holding them in my left hand with the blooms sticking out and spilling all over to cover my little fist. The aroma of those violets was wonderfully sweet. Mom had a special small, dark-blue, squat vase just for them. The fragrance easily filled the room. After coming to America, it was a big disappointment to find out that violets had no smell. Other wild flowers included lots of daisies and a flower that was called Schlüsselblume. It was shaped like an old door key with a bright yellow beard.

EVERYONE'S GAME

My knees seemed to stay pretty battered and torn. Soon after a scab formed, it got knocked off again, resulting in blood running down my shins. Soccer was the reason. We kicked anything around that would roll or slide and did not hurt our toes too much. So when someone had a real ball, that was the time for a real game.

The town's soccer field was a pretty good one, but the goal was much too big for a kid my size to cover. The length of the field was too long, and it meant too much running and not enough contact. Often the big people had the field occupied. So, we went to our favorite cow pasture

Young Franz as soccer goal keeper in the real goal, about 1947.

and set up our own field. The goals were set wide enough for a little goalie to manage. The goal posts were not the hard, wood variety of the real ones. We simply stacked a half dozen dried cow flops on top of each other. If you dove to stop a ball and knocked it over, you dusted yourself off, found a few new ones, and restacked what was left. I do not want to make a big deal out of it; but, where there are dry cow piles, there also are wet ones. To set up a field for play, we would pick a level spot and pay no attention to the little monuments that may be scattered around. Nobody did any tiptoeing around when the game got serious. Every player kept his eye on the moving ball and not on the parked objects in the field. Quite often one's bare feet would slip out from under, not because the grass was wet. As the goalie on the winning team, I was aware of one large and tender dropping just waiting to be disturbed near my right goal post. The action so far had not worked its way in that direction. With the score just one goal up, a goalie becomes extra keen to protect his team's lead. Whatever it takes, the ball must not go between the goal posts. Well, as the game progressed, the dribbling and the hacking with the feet worked itself into the corner to the right of me. The opposition in control worked the ball closer and closer. I moved out to cut off the angle of a shot that I knew would come. It did. And I reacted. A headlong dive to stop the ball. The game was won, congratulations all around; but no one would help me clean out my right ear.

WEAPONS OF WAR

It beats me how we knew about and played cowboys and Indians. I've got to say, we knew very little about cowboys and imagined a lot about Indians. Their weapons were the challenge. We made blowguns out of elderberry shoots. We found them where the soil was good and the moisture was plenty; even then their length rarely exceeded 20 inches. For ammo, we stuffed green elderberries into our cheeks, thus, always ready for a shot. Bows and arrows were all made with our pocket knives. We whittled an extra sharp point on the arrows, cut a notch for the string on the other end, and decorated it with various chicken feathers. A spear, much taller than myself, complemented my weaponry. Of course, it had a blade-like sharp point honed down with my knife. The shaft of the spear was ornately decorated. This I did while the wood and its bark were still green, carving scrolls, squares, and diamonds into the bark with my knife. By removing every other one of the design's sections, the slick white wood was exposed underneath. The throwing grip was a little behind center. The wood on the tail end was split with the knife, and large feathers were inserted and tied securely. Since our pocketknives were not considered weapons, we also whittled large daggers or Jim Bowie knifes out of sticks or of split, stove wood.

The real menace in our arsenal was not a primitive reproduction but an up-to-date modern slingshot. This weapon we made with great care because the competition in engineering and accuracy was formidable. It was hard to cut two identical strips of rubber out of an old bicycle inner tube. If one side was thinner or longer, making it weaker than the other one, it sure did not shoot straight. The leather tongue of an old shoe made a great pocket for the rock. But, how to attach the rubber strips to it was a problem. It was worked out by trial and error. Knots that came undone made the rubber strip smack your hand, especially after pulling back hard to make a long shot. Even worse was getting hit by the rock itself. Meanwhile, the search for the special fork of a limb, that would make a perfect V-shaped slingshot handle was an ongoing one. If the V was too sharp, it did not afford a wide enough passage for the rock to be shot. If you pulled the sling back not exactly at a ninety degree angle, you wound up with a few bruises from the misguided rock. If you tied the rubber guides too high up on the V, where it was wider, then the handle of the slingshot was too far down and the accuracy was diminished. It taught us that our wrists were not strong enough to hold steady the extended leverage. We never used any of these war implements on each other. We knew someone could get badly hurt. The competition was in the accuracy to the targets or distance of the missile. Whether we knew it or not, all was a valuable learning process which today's video arcades probably do not teach.

TO WHISTLE

To whistle a tune was really in style those days but young boys are not interested in tunes. Whistling to get someone's attention or to give a signal while we were playing war games was part of our means of communicating. The art of our kind of whistling was passed down by the older boys. To make those shrill, loud whistles, first you stick two fingers of each hand into your mouth, holding the rolled up tongue, then blow as hard as possible. If, after many tries, a sound was achieved, you learned to whistle with just two fingers. Of course, when trotting in the woods with spear in one hand and the bow with some arrows in the other, it was inconvenient to throw the weapons to the ground just to answer a call. The next step was to learn to whistle with one hand by using the thumb and forefinger. Through all these steps and exercises and many hours of practice, to achieve a certain volume, you finally learned to whistle without any fingers. With a deep lung full of air and the lips, tongue, and teeth positioned properly, I still, to this day, can make an ear piercing whistle that can be heard for more than half of a mile. I'm sorry I never showed my sons Franz, Alfons, and Christopher how to whistle; well, they are never to old to learn.

As kids, we also made wooden whistles or what you might call a single-note, miniature flute. To make one, you start with a four to five inch long piece of green sapling or twig from a maple. Other fresh cut, small branches from various trees will also work. About two inches in from one end, you cut a ring around the bark. One inch in from the other end, you cut a notch for the sound to come out. Then you put that half of the stick in your mouth making sure there is plenty of saliva on it. Start removing the bark from that section. You do this with your pocket knife open, holding the knife by the blade, tapping lightly with the handle all around the bark, while keeping it soaked with spittle. This was a task done in early spring or summer; when, we never had on long pants. Our bare legs were a good cushion and indicator whether we were tapping the wood properly.

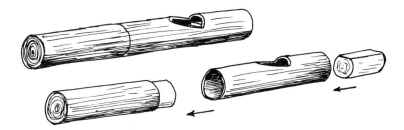

How to make a wooden whistle that would whistle.

Tapping too hard would split the bark and the project would have to be aborted. Holding the two inch end, lay the piece across the leg just above the knee, we kept tapping and rotating, adding spittle for additional moisture to the bark. The tapping, along with the moisture, softened and eventually loosened the bark from the inner core. Equal attention had to be given to the bark all around the core. When you finally gave that little twist to remove the bark from its stem, it came loose in one piece. Done correctly, it simply slipped off like a sock. Now we cut the one inch part off the bare stick (up to the notch). We shaped that cut-off piece by removing about a third of the wood lengthwise, creating an air passage when reassembled. After that, the little piece was slipped back into the hollowed bark, with the air passage lined up with the notch. We increased the tone chamber by cutting off a little of the exposed stem that was still on the stick. After we reassembled the whistle, we were ready to try it out. Depending on how long a stub we left on, we could adjust the pitch of the sound by sliding the still wet bark slightly in or out.

NEVER BORED

The thorny, horse chestnut hulls were murder on bare feet. Oh, but the chestnuts inside of them inspired many a boy's and girl's imaginations. Horse chestnuts were mostly round with a shiny shell. Some grew large, some small, some lopsided, and some almost perfectly round. Along with acorns and their neat little caps, a boy can make a variety of toys. By drilling holes with my knife and sticking the various shapes together with small sticks of wood, I was on a roll. Adding arms and legs, I made many horses, dogs, men, and soldiers. I built houses and stables out of sticks and bark, rocks and mud.

Praise the Lord for the imagination of a child, a mind unencumbered and unmanaged by giant corporations and their subliminal campaigns to create in it the desire to buy their advertised newest sensations.

To make motorized crawling toys, I used the wooden thread spool Mom saved for us in her sewing box. Using the spools as a pair of wheels, I cut notches on the outer edges for traction; then I tacked a small nail on one side next to the center hole. After doubling up a rubber band, I fed it through the center hole in the spool and hooked it on the nail. On the other side of the hole, I looped the end of the rubber band on a six inch stick which was used to wind-up the rubber band. After it was twisted tight, I just sat it down; and the torque of the wound up rubber band provided the power to make the thing crawl around. Those little Panzers also pulled a load if need be. All I did was loop a loose string around the center portion of the spool and tie it to whatever I wanted to drag around. When the thing stopped, all I had to do was wind it up again. Some times the tension of the rubber band was more than the weight of the whole contraption. In that case the little toy raised up on its side or even flipped over. I'd lengthen the stick, or wind the thing up just a little less, that usually solved the problem. Again, the simple physics of a twisted rubber band can challenge a child's mind that is not saturated by video bombardments.

The most prized possession I ever received as a toy and one that I still have, is a small motor boat made of painted and decorated tin. This was a toy the whole family enjoyed. The interesting part and key to the toy was a small water tank from which two exhaust tubes lead to the rear of the boat. This tank was under and inside the boat and really not visible from the outside. We had to prime the tubes and tank with water before setting it in our washtub full of water. A holding device, a small bowl of wax with a wick in the center, was lit then slid under the tank inside that little boat. After a short while, the water started boiling in that tiny tank above the flame.

My favorite toy. The self propelled boat, about eight inches long, with its own energy source, the candle.

The bubbling, gurgling, heated water soon propelled the hot water out of one of the small pipes while sucking in cold replacement water through the other pipe.—pretty basic science. The motor boat went around and around in the tub until the candle burned down or I got tired of watching it, whichever came first.

With a pond now on our small farm in Virginia. And the oldest grandchild reaching four years of age, you know I'm going to get that old boat out and float it on some real water.

A REAL CHRISTENING

First Communion was a big deal in every young person's life. I was about six years old. I know Mom had a hard time getting the money together to buy a large, rather ornately carved candle that I would carry at the processional service up the center aisle of the church. The candle with its added white ribbon and drip cap was about two feet tall. It sure seemed huge to me. I guess the significance of the whole religious ritual was the celebration and the awareness of a young person's beginning the age of accountability. From that day forth, you could go to confession, tell your misdeeds to a priest, do your multi-prayer penance, and go to communion.

All that was good because it made me a better boy, a boy more aware of other peoples' feelings and needs. The impetus for doing better was either the fear of having to tell the priest or saying a multitude of Lord's Prayers and Hail Marys. Whichever it was, I can't remember. I got to wear a white shirt and a dark colored suit that day. Where that suit came from, I don't know. Mom hemmed up the sleeves and pant legs and made other modifications that later could be reversed. All starched-up and ironed, fingernails cleaned, hair spiffied-up, and shoes shined, I went to church.

After the big church service, lunch time must have been a little late. This was why I had some extra time to look at a new baby calf before I went home. Sepperl, the young son of Mr. Beir, wanted me to step through a door that led to the stall of the milk cows. This was not the place where the cows ate out of a manger. I had visited that part of the stall before and even got to touch the cows, scratching them above their noses. He wanted me to step in a small door that led to the rear of the beasts. Obviously, that was where the new calf was so it could get to its mama for a drink. I knew it was dark in there, and there was more than just straw on the floor. I sure did not want to mess up the fine get-up I was sporting. So I asked Sepperl to bring the calf out into the open. Well, he looped a rope around its neck and coaxed it to the door. That is where the calf stopped. Apparently, it was not yet accustomed to being in the sunlight. Stepping outside onto the cobblestoned wagon yard, Sepperl began to yank on the rope trying to budge the young critter. However, it was determined not to step down out of that doorway into the

The calf wins.

open. Well, the rope was long enough to get another pair of hands on it, so I gave him a hand. Both of us kept the pressure on with feet braced against the wall and doorsill, but the calf kept its head down and stayed stiff legged. While we were braced for the duration, the calf all of a sudden jumped toward us sending us sprawling. I stumbled backward, unable to right myself, then I hit a wheelbarrow. I had seen that wheelbarrow before and smelled it often. It was encrusted with years of manure that had been pitchforked into it when cleaning out the cow barn. That day, you guessed it, it was not dry but tenderly soft and wet. When I quit stumbling, I was sprawled out in the wheelbarrow as if soaking in a tub.

Well, the starched shirt and the ironed pant creases lasted long enough to get through Holy Communion plus a christening.

GOING WITH THE TIMES

Wartime is hard on people whether on the winning or losing side. Personal sacrifices are asked by the government, but most sacrifices and heartaches are endured by the people, in subtle and quiet ways. War torn Germany was no different. Most men, from the old to the very young, had been drafted to serve in the armed forces. This included not only husbands, fathers, brothers, and grandfathers, but also most doctors and nurses. Medical and surgical personnel to serve the populace were scarce, as were the medicines, medical supplies, and food. My twin sisters could have been alive today were it not for times and situations like these. I can but shudder thinking what my mother went through.

Around that time, before and after my twin sisters were born, I had become very ill. My mother tells me very little, just that I was sick for a long time. I became weak and vulnerable, catching one childhood disease right after the other. One was whooping cough, as well as measles and a fever that left me with a heart mur-

mur and an enlarged heart. For years I was left vulnerable after that series of illnesses. I guess in today's terms I would have been called a sickly or frail little fellow. My tonsils would swell shut at the slightest cold wind hitting them. I wore a scarf at all times during cold and wet weather. Mom gave me plenty of hot liquids, such as soup or camomile tea, and made me gargle with salt water. The same with my ears; they seemed to throb with stabbing pain so often that my headgear always included ear muffs in cold weather. Even in times when the seasons changed, I wore cotton in my ears. To ease the pain, Mom heated a few drops of oil in a teaspoon on the kitchen stove and carefully dripped them into the ear that was hurting.

Dagmar was not immune to these ills and certainly not immune from the times. She was tough. She fought her battles with no lingering ills.

The medical people at that time gave Mom, and later the school authorities, strict orders that I was not to participate in strenuous athletic activities. The International Red Cross was made aware of my situation along with that of thousands of other children in the country. They put me into a group of set-apart kids and gave me a chance to experience life in a new light.

OFF TO CAMP

It is strange, but I can't remember much about the first time I went to camp, except for one brief incident. I remember I was one of several children walking on a bright warm day along a white picket fence over which hung shrubs and flowers. At the end of the fence was a small gate with a girl stationed there to help us kids through. When I got to her—my heart stopped. She was so pretty. A gentle voice came from her round face. Shining hair woven into thick braids adorned her head. Large, dark, comforting eyes pierced my heart. She patted my shoulder and welcomed me. I was in love.

THE NEXT CAMP

When I was six years old, the Red Cross took a few others and me to a retreat in the Bohemian Woods, where we joined kids already there. We got off the bus and were chaperoned through the town. There I saw her, a startling, dark skinned woman with long black hair, dressed in black, sitting on the front steps of her row house. As we walked by, she offered me a piece of chocolate. I was shocked because I knew I was staring at her. I refused the candy. Even if I had taken it, I would not have eaten it. Later I was told she was a gypsy. During my stay that summer, distinct experiences come to mind.

Not long after I got to camp, I had a dream. Sleeping on the top bunk in a room full of boys, I sat up crying out in my dream. The lights came on; I realized where I was and that I had been dreaming. To my utter amazement and shock, I was sitting in a pool of unpleasant matter. I was so embarrassed. I tried to explain that I was dreaming. Frightened that I was going to be punished, I trembled as a woman lifted me up and carried me away. But she was gentle. She was not angry with me. She bathed me, changed my bed, and tucked me in again. I was going to like it there.

One of the rooms we were allowed to play in was probably a dining hall. The floors, the walls, and the window sills, all were covered in ceramic tile. The walls were a light green tile. Nothing earth shattering took place there except we learned to annoy each other. There were kids who were easily irritated, and kids who dished it out. It turned out that the girls would shriek and hold their ears when we, the boys, scratched the tile and the grout in between them with something sharp. Ah, the girls sure were different, and agitate them we did.

Afternoon naps were taken in a large hall with tall ceilings and lots of windows. The boys and girls had their own little iron frame beds, and we all napped in the same hall. The boys' beds were lined up against and along the inner wall facing the windows. The girls' beds were in one row along the window wall and facing toward the boys. We were not allowed to talk, only rest. The boys were restless. The world was too alive, too interesting, and too much to experience.

We found out that those chimneys along our wall each had a cleanout box near the floor. Apparently during the winter months they had coal heaters in that big room. Investigating what was behind those little iron doors was a mission of high interest. We found them to be full of fine soot, perfectly black and hard to get off the skin. All this discovery was taking place while we were "napping."

There were as many girls in that hall as there were boys. Since there was no talking allowed, the girls were resigned to truly rest; and some went to sleep.

We, on the other side, had a plan. It took a day or so to work out the details. Each boy was assigned a girl located strategically opposite his bed. The older boys conspired and made the decision that this very afternoon each boy was to kiss his designated girl. Nap time came. It was a bright day some thirty minutes into the rest period. Most girls had settled down and were dozing lying in the warm sun that filled the room. We faked likewise. When the chaperone finally walked out of the room, we went to work. Carefully we opened the chimney trap doors which were spaced one about every three beds. We dipped our hands in and brought forth a dab of soot. The soot was passed to left and right so every boy had some. The girls were resting peacefully. As previously planned, each one of us took the soot and carefully smeared it all around our mouth.

All was quiet waiting for the signal. Our hearts were pounding, and we were hardly able to contain our giggles. Then, in one accord, we bounded out of our beds, darted across the center aisle, and pounced on the girls, not along side of them, but fully flying on top of them. As they turned their heads up to see what was going on, we each gave them a good long smooch. There were shrieks and squeals from the girls; but as quickly as the boys came, they also retreated to their respective beds.

When the chaperone came in, all the girls were sitting up not really knowing what had happened. I will never forget the sight. All the young ladies had black smudges around their lips and face proving that none of the young boys had chickened out. The boys acted very sheepishly. None of us were actually caught in the act. All of us were obviously guilty. No reprimand was ever issued. The conquest was a success,–thank God for boys and girls.

THE CATHOLIC CAMP

The next year at camp we were taken care of by nuns. Again, the place where we slept was different from where we napped. This was the camp where our temperature was taken under the arm and not the more intrusive way to which we were accustomed. We had an outbreak of mumps in our bedroom. Seems like the five of us boys were quarantined in our room for a while.

During that time, I learned that flatulence was universally funny. Naturally, each of us in that room wanted to be the funniest. Contests to determine the winner were regularly held. There were players, and there were scorekeepers. Score was kept in goals during a given time much like a soccer tournament. Much twisting and grunting was going on. The scorekeeper had to have proper discernment between a real goal and one fabricated by other means. Accidents did happen which resulted in frequent trips to the biffy. I learned during these educational times that the desired noise can quite accurately be duplicated by placing a cupped hand under the armpit, then suddenly pressing the arm inward thus releasing the sound. Well, that was a magnificent achievement for us five boys. We practiced until we had the perfect five-piece wind ensemble. We expanded our wisdom and even came up with a ten piece orchestra. Spitting in our palms to get them damp, we would lie on our backs, place one cupped hand under each of our knees, then begin to pedal with our legs like riding a bicycle. This filled the room with triumphant music that fed our uproarious laughter and giggles. Thank God for the mumps.

The nuns wore long, full, black dresses with a large white apron in the front. Their wimple or head cover was a wide, white, wing-like creation with a cone shaped part in black that fit the head. To us that was what a nun was supposed to look like. Anything else was not a nun. I knew where their living quarters were because that was the area where we got our earlobes pricked so they could test our blood. One day wandering in that area for what reason I do not remember, I saw the door cracked open to the room of my favorite nun. I walked over and stuck my head in to say hello. A quick movement and cover-up by the nun did not prevent me from seeing a completely shaved head. From that day on, in my mind, my favorite nun was a bald woman.

The napping hall was large. All the beds faced to look out the many windows all around. My bunk was next to an older boy. He talked and tried to explain the facts of life to me. Although my tender ears did hear, my mind did not comprehend it all. The one thing that I could under-stand was the life of the birds. Why, it was happening just outside these windows. Several birdhouses were mounted on poles at perfect eye level to see as we lay there to rest. There I watched the building of a nest in one of these houses. I could see the twigs and strings and feathers that were dragged into it by those busy little birds. I then imagined the eggs being laid and the male and female taking turns incubating them. In due time, the little ones hatched. I could hear them chirping when mother and father provided the food. Then finally I saw them fly from their nest. Now that I could understand.

A MORE DARING CAMP

As I grew older, the adventures at camp grew a bit more offbeat and daring. Looking back, they did lack, as one would expect, in maturity and sophistication.

One hot day, the camp staff and we set out for the lake. It was a long, long hike. Finally we veered off the dirt road and headed through the woods with the promise that we would soon find the lake. Sure enough, the land dropped off, and we saw a large lake before us. It was called Starnberger See. The lady staff member took the girls a little farther along the shore to be out of seeing and hearing of the boys. None of us had any bathing trunks, but we all had on underwear. After all, away from home you dare not look poor; you wore your stuff that had your monogram lovingly stitched in by your mother. The boys started to strip down to their skivvies as soon as the O.K. was given. Shirts and pants hung from every tree limb. Into the lake, we waded. The water was crystal clear with a pebbled bottom about fifty feet out and still only three feet deep.

The frolicking and horsing around went on for quite some time when some boy at the other end of the cove discovered an undesirable object floating among the fellows. One said it was real but would not inspect it closely. Most were hoping it was just a piece of bark. Since the thing was determined to float right into the middle where most of us played, some boys decided it needed to sink. An old, weathered board was found among the decaying branches and stumps along the shore. One brave boy snuck up to the floating matter and started to beat it with that board. You guessed it, it did not sink. It multiplied. The whistle blew, and it was time to go back. No one lingered in that water. It was actually, a perfect way to round up a bunch of boys out of a swimming hole. During the walk home, the speculation continued, but no one ever owned-up to that certain contribution. And life went on.

For a kid who was not supposed to have any physical exercise, I sure got plenty. Jumping was my favorite activity. Almost every day, we hiked to the forest to play. In the woods, there were plenty of those soft pine needles to cushion the fall while we romped around horseplaying and wrestling. We shimmied up skinny saplings that grew along the creek bank, then rode them to the ground, landing in soft mossy patches. I remember one particular great tree that had fallen. The roots had come out of the ground leaving a large pit of fresh, sandy soil exposed. We found out that by running along the trunk of that tree, using the roots as a spring board, we could fly high and far through the air and land in the soft dirt. It was sheer ecstasy.

During those days in the woods, we did a lot of exploring and played hide and search the way the Indians surely would have done it. We learned to sneak up to the other warrior's camp and eavesdrop on their plans. The real test of our skills was to be proven one day when one of the boys came to our huddle and nervously announced that he had, while practicing his Indian skills, accidentally snuck up on two lovers. We did not believe him, but it sounded like something that was worth investigating.

The boy led us to an area of the forest that had only Christmas tree-size trees. The grove of fir trees was thick with most bottom branches intertwined and still touching the ground. We spread out so if one of us was spotted by the couple, not all of us would get our heads knocked off. After all, we were on a spying mission to witness an act that was supposed to be totally private.

Here I was, by myself, crawling like a snake under the bottom most branches. Inch by inch I made my way closer to a spot that had been pointed out to us. It was dark under there, but I could see a clearing, an area of brightness. That was surely the spot. I moved on. The closer I got the more I knew I was tempting the devil himself. I became frightened, but the intrigue edged me on. Or was it the devil?

About ten feet from the clearing I could see the lovers laying on the ground. But to learn something new, I had to move a bit closer. It was truly a lovely spot for a courting couple to rendezvous. The little oasis in the woods was on a little rise covered with thick moss and wispy grasses. The opening was no bigger than a small room. It was apparent to me that this spot was perfect for lovers and probably was not being used for the first time by them.

This time, the other boys and I had the goods on them, close-up and personal. With heart pounding and mind spinning, I slowly crawled away again. On our way back to the camp, we walked past the spied-upon couple who were then sitting on a bench beside the road. I venture to say that they knew that some of our group had discovered them. One of us must have made some noise sneaking up that close. I also guess that by looking at the guilty boys, the lovers could tell from our faces who the culprits were; or maybe they were just sitting there, with smiles on their faces, waiting for us pests to get out of the woods. The older boys pumped us for every small detail of what we had witnessed. The teaching did not all come from the visual experience but also from the explanation of the questions asked by the older boys.

ONE LAST SUMMER CAMP

Some of us stood behind the goal line just to the right of the net. The older boys were having a fierce soccer game. The adrenaline and the cheering frenzy by the bystanders was hitting the upper levels. I had my left arm in a sling. When a hard kicked ball missed the goal and struck me right on that left arm; the pain was so severe that I fainted.

Just the day before, the camp officials sent me to see a doctor in the nearby town because of a badly infected and painful large boil on my upper arm. At the doctor's house there was no waiting, no forms to fill out, or money to pay. I just walked in, and right away the doctor examined me and made me sit down on a stool with my arm on the counter. He then placed a tin cookie tray under my arm. After carefully cleaning an area around the carbuncle, he took a scalpel and, while I watched, cut through the flesh into that monster full of infection. An evil poison erupted out of the gash. The good doctor then positioned my arm over the tray so it would drain unto it. I sat there a long time watching the yellow and white pus, mingled with streaks of blood, ooze out of my arm. Finally, he gingerly dressed the gaping hole, padded it with absorbing swabs and gauze, put the arm in a sling, and said to come back every day until he told me otherwise. Well, that shot with the soccer ball probably was the extra squeeze I needed to drain that wound.

Every day I walked to see the doctor. It took me all morning even with the short cut I took over hills and streams, through some woodsy patches and a grain field. I remember the grainfield had recently been cut, and the stubbles left on the ground were sharp and mean even on my toughened bare feet. I walked across that field by sliding my feet along, with my toes acting like a comb, folding over the grain stubble so my feet could step on them. As a result of that short cut, I approached the town from a slightly different side. The reward was a grove of hazelnut bushes that I had to pass. There were plenty of hazelnuts on the trees and just about ripe. I cracked these filberts with my teeth, gorging on them daily.

The sling was a problem when I needed two arms. We played whack the tetherball except it was not a ball, just a medium sized potato with chicken feathers stuck into one end of it. There was only one tennis racket; so you had to knock the spud into the air, then chase it around to whack it again, before it hit the ground. I, however, had to throw the ball up, bend down and get the racket lying in the grass, look up and find the ball, and knock it back up into the air before it landed in the grass. The interest in that little exercise did not last too long especially since a major sports competition was announced.

No one told me not to compete. Some instructions must have fallen through the cracks. For the first time in my life, I was actually allowed to compete–sling and all. So, at eleven years of age, I got in line to do the long jump, a piece of cake –3.87m; the high jump, a piece of cake –1.25m; the triple jump, a piece of cake –7.70m. I ran the 60 meter dash in 10 seconds and took second place. A smaller boy beat all of us. He was quick. The fifth event was the throwing of a hardball, a small ball that fit nicely into my hand. It was dark brown and covered with leather pieces sewn together with thin leather strips. Arching way back with that one loose arm extended, I heaved that ball with all I had –47m. It was enough to get first place also. When the competition was over, total points counted, they named me over all winner. At an assembly later that evening, I received my honorarium. I was handed a homemade certificate along with some sought after goodies. I distinctly remember getting a stick of gum and an olive-drab can the size of a tuna fish can. Recently I found an old scrap book with the correct distances as well as the rest of the prizes. In addition to the can and the chewing gum, I received a bar of chocolate, a small summer sausage, a pack of caramels, one piece of hard candy, and an apple. Not too shabby for a frail youngster with one arm in a sling. Weeks later, back home with every family member present, we opened that dark green can. It was delicious bread pudding with raisins in it. Praise God for GI rations.

No matter how wise and grown up I considered my self to be, there still were times when I needed discipline. It was understood that when you were at summer retreat the supervisors had every right, to use whatever means necessary, to keep the chaps under control. Aside from grabbing us by the short ends of the hair behind the ears, the supervisors found more ingenious ways to make us look foolish and punished us. One way to make a boy look foolish was to give him a mark that showed that he was out of line. The mark resulted from what I would call the "door butt." One of the camp counselors would punish a boy by having him rub his forehead from as high up as he was tall, all the way down to the floor, along the surface of a wooden door. This would make the boy's forehead chatter and bounce along the wood causing an ugly red and sometimes slightly bloody spot in the middle of his forehead. It left, for everyone to see, the mark of the misbehaved.

Another form of punishment that surely dated back to the medieval days is the one I was subjected to one night. All of us boys slept in the same large hall on single beds. After being told to get into bed, we were allowed to talk and swap stories with a neighbor for a few more minutes. However, the second the light was turned off, all had to be immediately quiet. My bed was near the front and close to the light switch. When the lights went off that night, I was in the middle of a sentence of some tale I was telling and still talking during the first second after dark. That was enough to be called out and led away. I remember having to walk up one flight of stairs that had wrought iron rails. Once up there, I was told to wait in the hall while the man in charge stepped into a room. He returned shortly with a split piece of firewood. He laid it on the floor out there in the hall and told me to kneel on it. Very adamantly he told me not to get off or make any loud noises for half an hour. He made sure that the sharp edge of the log was up and that my bare knees were squarely on it. He ordered me not to rear back onto my haunches; and if he caught me doing so or getting off the log in any way, he'd make me stay on it for an additional 30 minutes.

There was no way to ease the pain that was now unrelenting. At first I thought I could just tough it out with the only solace being that I truly despised that man. But all the wishing that he would fall over dead became to be a mockery by him when I heard a lady friend in the room with him. I was kneeling there, facing that partially open door, with sounds of pleasure and giggles coming to my ears. I was beaten. Seconds felt like minutes, and minutes like hours. Suddenly he came to the door checking up on me with a smirk on his lips. I must have been a pleasing sight to him, kneeling there, looking up with quiet tears streaming down my cheeks from the unbearable pain. He said nothing to me and went back into the room. Frightened anew, the feeling that I must obey his orders were stabbed even deeper into my heart. I dare not get caught trying to do anything to ease my suffering. My heart was destroyed, my mind full of questions. How much time had elapsed since this horror began? Did he keep track of time? Will he remember me out here in the hall quietly agonizing away into the night? Does anybody love me? Will this ever end?

THE CHURCH AND THE KID

Religion was a subject matter. It was taught in school one or two hours a week by a priest. Biblical stories and their accompanying natural phenomena were made into great lessons but were hardly of a spiritual nature.

The going to church part was a thing that you did on

Sunday. You sat through a lot of reading of Latin and got to listen to heavenly voices coming from somewhere in the rear and up in the balcony of the church. There was plenty of bobbing up and down from sitting to standing to kneeling. I'm sure it was full of meaning to a pious parishioner; as for me, I never did get the hang of it. I simply watched the folks in front of me, then did what they did. At Easter time, we took to church a basket of food that included a loaf of bread, eggs, and some smoked side meat. On that given day, every basket was blessed by the priest and then was taken back home. At home, we ate a little of the blessed food every day until it was gone. Before cutting any loaf of bread at home, we always made three symbolic crosses on the bottom side of the loaf with the point of the bread knife.

Reverence for God was a feeling that the culture of the times inscribed into peoples' hearts. As a child, you would never run while in church; neither would you cross the center aisle without a quick bow and kneel facing the altar before you walked on. A youngster would be quiet at all times during service with just a whisper of words in case of an emergency. At times there was standing room only, so a kid might have to look at the back of someone's coat for an hour and be quiet to boot. The churches were not heated nor were they ever locked. Not even a thief would think of tempting God. God's house was a sanctuary for prayer and worship and maybe sometimes to get out of the rain.

Every church in my part of the country had a bell tower with at least one bell in it. It was rung to call the people together; a beckoning sound that made your heart rejoice. The main church in Griesbach had several bells of various sizes making a pleasant mix of chimes when rung. I do not know who normally rang the bells, but one day I was there early enough to witness the bell ringing. The largest bell, the one weighing a couple of tons, had to get in motion several minutes earlier then the smaller ones. There were ropes coming through brass lined holes in the tall ceiling at the bottom of the bell tower. They all had a knot tied at the end of each. Some man was pulling on the rope of the big one, but there was no sound. He asked me to give him a hand and help pull. Together we pulled and pulled. The knot on the rope came down a little farther with each pull. Finally, we heard the first dong. Meanwhile, more men and a couple of older boys had also started to pull on the ropes of the smaller bells. They all were chiming now and mixing in with the big one. I was urged to continue to pull as hard as I could so that our big bell would not skip a dong. I gave it all I had; it was hard work and in the process worked up a little sweat. What a wonderful sound went out through the country side calling people to worship the Giver of life. After a while, the man I was ringing with quit pulling. He told me to make the bell quit ringing, and that all I had to do was hang on to the knot on that rope. Well, at first I thought the monster about a hundred feet up was not going to be quiet. I was being yanked up and down by that tremendous, swinging weight. Enjoying the free ride so much, I just hung on and continued to swing long after the bell quit ringing. I wished I could have done that every Sunday, but it was never to be again.

Church steeple with the large bells, as seen from the town square and the building in which we lived.

BOOK THREE

AUTHOR'S NOTE

This portion of the book finds the little boy transformed, at a very rapid pace, from boy to man. The stories appear in approximately the correct order, continuing from age ten until the time of immigration at almost age fifteen.

Frauen Kirche, the symbol of Munich.
Visible also are the row houses and their attic windows
similar to what we lived in.
(Pre-World War II photo)

Das Rathaus with the famous Glockenspiel.
(Pre-World War II photo)

A NEW PLACE

In 1950, Mom got a chance to move the family back to Munich. I guess she needed steady work. With both of her children in school, looking ahead, she probably knew that the available education of a small country town would not be to our best advantage. As for finding a technically skilled apprenticeship program for me, the opportunities were practically nil.

We moved early during the summer break, which only lasted about six weeks, giving Mom a chance to enroll us in our new school. The movers came from Munich to Griesbach to load our stuff and move it back to Munich. The only place in the city Mom could get to rent was an attic apartment, on the fifth floor, overlooking the rail yard of the main train station of Munich.

Landsberger Strasse was a good-sized road. Trolley cars traversed down the middle of the street in both directions. The road had plenty of room for truck and car traffic as well as a bicycle path and sidewalk on both sides. The movers were parked outside our building. Mom had me stationed there to see that nothing was broken and also to watch that no one stole anything. I found out later that this really irritated one of the men, especially when I told Mom that one of the legs from a piece of furniture had fallen off as they were sliding it around. I did not know then that I was going to call that man "Dad" before the year was out.

The new dwelling was 110 steps off the ground floor. On the way up, on each landing there were two doors opposite each other, each leading to an apartment. Ours, being an attic apartment, was by itself. Our lofty abode was a very small two-room place with a tiny hallway which had a sink and spigot hanging on the wall. From this little entrance hall, you entered on the left the kitchen, which had a wood cookstove, and to the right, the bedroom. Each room had a dormer window, with the ceiling angled to follow the pitch of the roof. There was attic space to the left and right of our apartment. One side was off limits. It was where the other tenants stored their seldom-used possessions in assigned cubicles made of wooden slats. The other side of the attic was for us to use. A clothesline hung in that dark and somewhat spooky attic. The heat generated by the black tin roof sure dried the sheets in a hurry. A vent window was on each end of the attic space to let some of the heat escape. Like I said, it was a great place for drying clothes; but we didn't dare touch anything. Over the years, the floor, the ceiling, and other structural beams were all covered with a layer of fine soot.

Although our new living space was much smaller than in the country, the toilet facilities were much improved. In the corner of our attic sat a commode that actually had water piped to it. There was no tank full of water for flushing, just a spigot that the user turned on and off. For us, this was high class although it was always dark in that corner. The single, dim light bulb hanging in the middle of the attic space did very little since everything was covered with decades of black soot.

THE NEW VIEW

The dormer windows were somewhat small. The windows projected out a little so the roof of the building was just below the sills. The roof was black; whether it was painted or just dirty from the rail yard across the road, I do not know. A row of wrought iron snow and ice stops, like a short fence, ran along the edge of the roof, the length of the building just below our windows. This rack kept small avalanches from tearing off the gutters as well as saving someone's life seventy feet below. The windows were back far enough from the front of the building to let me see only the far side of the road below.

Across the street were many piles of rubble with lots of short walls still standing, left over from the bombing during the war. Some of the taller walls left after the air attacks were knocked down, probably to keep people from getting hurt. The rubble piles laying around were mostly worn smooth from people walking over them. Over the years, the inhabitants had looked for copper wire, gutters, or flashing to sell or wood with which to build shelves or simply to burn in their cookstoves. Unless it was buried deep, all usable material had by now been recouped. Not a brick was un-turned. Foot paths were meandering around and over the piles that led to peoples' still habitable dwelling places. The view from a window that high up was awesome to me. It was better than anything I had when I was perched high in my favorite tree in Griesbach.

Beyond the rubble were the rail tracks. There were many of them. I remember counting them one day as I walked across the bridge that spanned them all. There were 110 tracks, as many as the stairs to my home. The center dozen or so were for passenger trains coming into and out of the station. This main train station of Munich was a Sackbahnhof, a depot where all tracks terminated. The locomotives had to be switched back to be hooked up at the other end to pull the train back out of the station. The rest of the tracks were being used to arrange rail cars into freight trains. At all times, five or six smaller locomotives pushed and pulled box cars around, switching them onto other tracks to make up new trains. A lot of the switching of rail cars was done by gravity. A locomotive pulled the car, or several strung together, up a small incline about five hundred feet long. Then yard men manually worked levers along the tracks, directing the cars from one track to another as they came rolling down the slight incline. Those freight cars always had enough speed to smash into the partially made-up train already on the selected track. With great smacking sounds of metal against metal, new freight trains were being assembled. This constant round-the-clock, banging and slamming, along with the huffing and short bursts of puffing of the locomotives, made quite a symphony we had to get used to. What a drastic change from the pastoral quiet to the sound of commerce and life of the big city. All this newness gave me a sense of being part of something that offered well being and a future.

A boy of ten, with plenty of curiosity, is sure to find all moving machines fascinating. I was no exception. From my new perch on the fifth floor I was able to tell most makes of automobiles even from a distance. Also at night, the shape and positioning of the headlights enabled me to distinguish between an American make and a Volkswagen. I did not know anyone who owned a car. Most folks went to work on their bicycles. Some, though, had mopeds, like motorized scooters; others had regular motorcycles such as a NSU or even a BMW. A cross between a small car and a motorcycle was a contraption that I found interesting. It was a two-seater scooter, with one seat behind the other, covered with a removable dome. When it rained or snowed, the dome was popped onto two hinges on the side. After the riders got in, they flipped the plastic lid over their heads, snapped it shut, then plugged in the single windshield wiper, and away they went.

From my window, I observed a lot of interesting things. I saw rear-end pile-ups and bicycle wrecks, and once I saw a wheel rolling down the middle of the road. As it turned out, the left rear wheel had come off an American Jeep. To my amazement, the wheel had passed the Jeep on the driver's side while the vehicle kept on going on the other three wheels as if nothing had happened.

SIGNS OF THE PAST

Munich in 1950 was still very much wounded from the bombing. I guess all the authorities could do, since the end of the war, was rebuild the infrastructure. Roads, trolleys, electricity, and water had for the most part been restored. As I walked to school or elsewhere, there were many places along the sidewalk with small stacks of bricks. This was to warn the passersby that, at anytime, some loose debris might fall out of holes in the building. Shells that had exploded nearby often knocked holes in the surrounding structures. These buildings were still usable; but, they did shed some occasional bricks. You learned to walk along the curb, not along the walls. The row buildings, most being three to five stories tall, often had common walls. So, when one house was destroyed by the bombing, the jagged remains on the still standing building were grotesquely haunting and looked downright cruel. One often could see the floor levels, outlines of rooms painted different colors, on the wall of the adjacent building still standing.

Small craters in the buildings and sidewalks were everywhere; however, the cobblestone roads seemed fairly well preserved.

NEW GRANDPARENTS

Felsner Opa worshiped his wife. He was a bit younger than she and at all times wanted the best for her. Oma, my father's mother, was a big lady, a little portly, and always wearing an apron around the house. She had black hair and dark sparkling eyes. I remember those eyes as they danced with joy when she saw us, her grandchildren, for the first time since infants. She and her husband Ludwig were always glad to see us. Now, Mom was not one to park her kids in someone else's house, so our visits, often by ourselves, were not all that frequent. We lived only a five minute walk from Oma's second floor apartment. The visits were always a hit. She was a trained hotel cook; and needless to say, her victuals were something else.

Felsner Oma was well known to all the merchants with whom she had dealings. The butcher raised his eyebrow when he saw her coming. She only bought meat when the next cut off the hanging carcass suited her. She'd enter the store two or three times during the day to see how close the cut of meat was to the portion she wanted to buy, likewise with the dairy store. She would only buy milk when the milk in the milk can was at the proper level. Milk came directly from the farm. It was dipped out of large, fifty-liter cans. The dipper measured out one liter at a time. She'd stick her head in the store, crane her neck to see the milk level, then turn around and walk back out. When the container was full, the milk was too stirred-up; and the cream had not fully come to the top yet. When the milk level was too low, most of the cream had been dipped off; and she was not going to waste her money on blue milk. Knowing the traffic in and out of the store, she'd judge when about a half dozen liters were sold out of a fresh can, then, and only then, did she buy her milk. The dairy man had better give her a full dip after she cautioned him not to stir with that dipper before she got hers. She baked with some of the extra cream, and her desserts often had real whipped cream on top.

Oma always had real butter in her ice box. The ice box was a wooden cupboard, a two by three foot cube sitting on four legs. It was the first one I ever saw. It was made of thick oak and held together with iron straps around and at the corners. The interior was lined with tin. At my house, we had no such luxury. Our margarine held up in the attic apartment's heat pretty well; but, when Mom splurged on real butter, we had to keep the faucet dripping on it to keep it from totally melting. Real butter became rancid fast. Rancid or not, we always ate all of it. At Felsner Oma's place we were always being fed. The buttered rye bread with homemade strawberry jam was unforgettable. Her soups tasted better than mother's, probably because she used less water when boiling her bones. There were plenty of "eyes,"–liquefied fat–floating on top. Also, her eggs in the soup were not stretched with flour like Mom had to do when times were rough. I remember her large old grandfather clock in the bedroom. The mesmerizing chimes were soft and rich, as were the pendulum, chains, and inlays, for they were solid gold. The large window sills in her house were just stuffed with potted plants and flowers. Hers was a real pleasant place to visit, but neither my sister nor I ever spent the night there. I can still see Felsner Opa take the old coffee grinder, sit down, put it between his knees, and grind fresh coffee. He was a big boned man with large hands and feet and sported a square little mustache. He sort of shuffled a little on his toes as he walked, probably because he had to hold his felt slippers on, which he wore as he went on nearby errands. He was a kind man.

One hot day he bought me a cone of fruit flavored, shaved ice on our way to their garden spot. The cold treat was about the size of a golf ball sitting in a cone shaped paper holder. I did not know anything could be as good and cold as snow in the heat of the summer.

THE GARDEN SPOT

In those years Munich was the same, as far as being technologically developed, as in the late thirties. It had vacant land areas interspersed between sections of the city. I guess in much earlier times these were the areas of farmland that separated the surrounding towns during medieval times. As the towns were gobbled up by the sprawling city these open spaces became smaller and fewer.

About five hundred meters from the Felsner's apartment was a patch of land, a city block, the size of a shopping mall parking lot. This area was totally enclosed by a four-foot tall, tightly-spaced picket fence. Inside that area, elderly, long time residents of the city were given the privilege of having a garden spot. Each assigned spot, about twenty-five feet wide, had its own little gate to enter through the picket fence. These areas were kept immaculately trimmed and were truly little spots of heaven. There were no individual fences between the plots, people simply knew where their rows of vegetables ended and their neighbor's began. When you entered Oma and Opa's spot, immediately to the left along the fence, pole beans were growing. In front of them, was a strawberry patch about five by ten feet in area. A small path separated the strawberries from the currant bushes. There also were a bunch of rhubarb plants and the leaves of a healthy horseradish. Chives and parsley rounded out the perennials. The rest of the garden, except for flowers and the area where the garden house stood, was devoted to annual crops. Each garden plot had its own source of water. In Oma and Opa's case, the water was piped to an old bathtub, sitting in the open, in the middle of the garden. We young ones got to play in that tub on hot days. Of course, we did not mind the algae on the sides and a little muddy sludge on the bottom.

Opa turned over the vegetable beds with a shovel in the spring. Oma planted and sowed. Opa hoed and chopped the weeds, and Oma watered. The watering was done with a galvanized watering can that had a sprinkler on the end of the spout. In the back of the garden house stood a large wooden barrel that caught the rain water as it ran off the small roof. Oma always brought her vegetable waste to the garden to nurture her compost pile. The egg shells, however, were thrown into the water barrel which was covered with a thick wooden lid, except for a hole where the rain water entered. Rain water and egg shells were not all that went into that barrel. Oma would, after herds of sheep grazed the Octoberfest grounds, go and collect sheep manure. Using her bare hands, she filled up two pails. This precious commodity was also added to her cherished, liquid fertilizer barrel for winning results. Before watering her plants, Oma went to the barrel, uncovered it, and then stirred the rich brew with a long stout stick. Very deliberately, she then took a long handled dipper and measured out two dips into her watering can. With the liquid gold in the can, she walked to the bathtub full of water and forced the can in until it filled. Then it was time to feed the plants. All this was medicine to the plants as well as to the two aging folks.

When either one got tired or too hot, they sat down on a wooden bench inside the garden house. They sat there resting their arms on a wide shelf that also served as a table. I always remember them looking out over their garden and thanking God for what He had given them. Some times they'd eat a little bread with some of the fresh, small, red radishes or carrots just pulled. Oh my! They were so sweet and juicy. The garden house had enough room in the back to store all the implements to do their gardening. The front room, about three feet deep and six feet wide, was open except for the two sides which were covered with crisscrossed slats, enough to let the breezes through. On the south side of the little shelter was the starter bed, a simple box with rich dirt in which all of Oma's seedlings were raised. It was covered with an old window secured with hinges on the back side. Oma propped up the glass lid to prevent the young plants from cooking during the heat of the day. Every evening the old window was lowered over the box to keep the warmth of the day in and possibly the frost out.

One year Opa dug up a little plot especially for me. He showed me how to plant and work the soil. Oma grinned as she watched me, her dark eyes just twinkling. She somewhat drooled a little at the corners of her mouth when she smiled and always had her black hair wrapped into a knot sitting on the back of her head.

The rear of their garden plot was bordered with a few small trees and bushes. One of these was an old elderberry bush that had grown tall and strong enough to support a climbing, eleven-year-old boy. In late spring, the elderberry blooms. The bloom, pure white, is a cluster of hundreds of little white blossoms. It looks like a plate full of snowflakes huddling together to form a delicate looking lace doily. All the tiny blooms were held together by a network of small stems that streamed together to form one stem.

A most delightful dessert was offered by these clusters of blooms. We'd cut those clusters at the stem, take them to Oma's house, and she'd prepare one of my favorites. Mixing one egg, milk, flour and salt, she'd make a pancake batter. Holding the clusters by the stem, she'd dip them into the batter. With hot grease ready in an iron skillet, she'd then deep fried them until golden brown.

After they cooled a bit, we'd dip them into a mixture of cinnamon and sugar. What a treat–you should try it.

A shady perch in the overgrown elderberry bush provided some respite from the heat, as well as a good spot to watch the garden grow. Also from there, in the early summer, I'd shoot green elderberries through a short blowgun. The rest of the time, I did what kids do, dream and while the days away.

LOVE GOES THROUGH THE STOMACH

Not long after we had moved to Munich, this man who moved us, the one who carried all our belongings to the attic apartment, came to visit Mom. He was young, goodlooking, and solid of muscle. He came carrying a package. After we all introduced ourselves, or should I say we mumbled a few awkward words, Mom unwrapped the package. The gift, a big cut of fresh meat, was an instant hit; and the man, with that certain smile on his face, melted all fear and doubt from my heart.–His name was Alfons Pfisterhammer. We got to know him that day as we all chipped in preparing the feast of the year. Hey, pork roast with the fat on top, diced and crunchy brown, lots of gravy, Kartoffelknödel (potato dumplings), and sauerkraut, there is nothing that can top that. This man loved to eat and eat a lot. Mom loved to cook for him, and he loved it. He told us about fighting in the war and being imprisoned in England until 1947. He told us his girlfriend worked in a butcher shop and that he lived in a one-room apartment. His only possessions, other than his few clothes, were an aluminum soup spoon and a coffee mug. His soft blue eyes had a comforting appeal that went straight to my heart. He was starved not only for home cooking but also for a mate and a family. I think he was looking for someone who would help him chart a course for his life.

DAD OR WHAT?

Mom, was a waitress, and she generally worked on weekends. On days off, she sold maps of the city to tourists. The hot spot was in front of the Glockenspiel in the heart of the city. Mr. Pfisterhammer soon was taking care of and entertaining us when he was off on weekends. He played table games with us on rainy days, helped get supper started, and told war stories. Often he took us for a walk, or we would sit in the Biergarten so he could watch and get to speak an occasional word with Mom. At times we'd get on a trolley and head for the

*Mom selling city maps.
Early '50s.*

Hauptbahnhof, the main train station. There we got to see the hustle and bustle of people scurrying around, some in a dead heat to catch a train, others were more "laid back", reclining while getting their shoes shined. "Heisse Maroni, Hot Maroni," a peddler cried out. I do not know what a maroni is; from the looks they were roasted chestnuts. For fifty Pfennig (pennies), Mr. P. took us to a theater at the train station. There were no movies showing, just a sequence of newsreels and other points of interest from around the world. In those days, that was the greatest thing I every did. We sat as long as we cared to in that theater viewing the same information over and over again. Each set lasted about a half hour. Sister and I practically had to be physically hauled out of there when it was time to go home.

He even took us to the science and technology museum. He showed great interest and spent much time with us explaining the needs and functions of the many inventions and machinery on display. Some days he bought us a wiener with sweet mustard and a Semmel (small hardroll). He and I whittled stuff together as we sat on park benches. People strolled by and often started a conversation with us. Dagmar would call him Father, and I'd call him Uncle Alfons; or I would call him Mr. Pfisterhammer, and sister would call him Dad. Folks raised their eyebrows, but we just could not come up with the proper name to call him. He was twenty-nine years old. We certainly could have been his children; but courtesy told me to call him mister and my heart wanted to call him Dad.

DECEMBER 28

The first six months back in Munich went well. Mom's marriage to my father was officially annulled since seven years had elapsed. No word ever came about my father, who had been declared missing in action and now was declared legally dead.

The nice man who had entered our life spent more and more time with us. I remember him even getting to partake in one of our family "things;"–the counting of the tips. When Mom came home from a day at the beer garden, she took off a small apron that acted as a money pouch. She wore this little pouch under her Dirndl apron. All day long as she received tips, she collected them in that black apron pouch. We would all sit on the bed as Mom emptied her bounty on the white sheet. All of us were given a chance to pick up only certain coins out of the pile. Coins ranged from pennies to the five Mark denomination. I do not think there ever was one of those 'fivers' in the pile, but the person that got to fish out all the pennies sure had a lot to pile in stacks of tens.

As the months went on, it was obvious that Mom and her new friend really made a good couple. My sister and I had grown very fond of him, and he was so easy to be with. He wanted a stable home, and we needed him.

The wedding, just a few days after Christmas, was

Wedding photo of Mom and Dad. Dec. 28, 1950.

simple. The most memorable part was the ride in the carriage. We all got to ride in it, drawn by two white horses, as it took us to and from church.

Dad earlier had won a case of wine on a bet. He had carried a box of bolts weighing two-hundred kilos (about 420 lb.) on his back. When his truck was unable to back up to the dock, he simply had his helper tip the box from the truck unto his back. He then carried it about a hundred feet to the loading dock. Well, the wine added a little festivity to the wedding and also helped ring in the New Year of 1951.

ON THE WAY TO SCHOOL

The school in our district was bombed out, so we had to walk to Schwanthaler Schule, which was about three-quarters of a mile away. This was a long walk that provided plenty of opportunity to see new things, experience life, and, naturally, get in trouble. The least likely way to get in trouble was to stay occupied. One way to do that was to kick an object, a piece of wood or a small rock, from home to school and back home without ever picking it up. Kicking it along the sidewalk was easy but crossing

Watercolor of a street vendor in Munich 1953, by Franz in eighth grade.

the street and trolley tracks was a trick. When I got to a curb, I simply squeezed the object with both shoes or grabbed it with the toes, and hopped back up onto the sidewalk. Once I got to school, I parked my companion in a corner so it would be there for the trip back home.

In the mornings when we went to school, street ven-

dors were already at their stations in and around the side streets. The large, two-wheeled, wooden carts had been pushed by the peddlers to their desired locations and set up at the edge of the road. Once the people of a neighborhood became accustomed to a certain vendor and his fruits or produce, that cart in that spot became part of the every day life. The vendor did not move on hoping for a greener pasture; often, he'd sell for a lifetime from that same spot. Every morning the flat area on top of the cart, about one by two meters, was packed with produce, fruits, and other victuals in season. Some of the fruits were obviously imported from a warmer climate. Mom bought fruits and vegetables for cooking and baking; oranges she bought only for the Christmas season. Bananas were a real treat; to make them last, we often cut them into slices to put in pancake batter to make banana pancakes.

I never got a whole banana to eat all by myself. I asked the street vendor what one would cost me; he quoted ten Pfennig. Well, I did not have ten pennies, but I had the better part of five. He, however, did not want to trade for that. A couple of days went by when I spotted a penny that had fallen through a grate in the sidewalk. I ran home and got my magnet. No high-tech minded young chap was without one. With a long string attached to it, I slowly lowered it down to the penny. Since the penny was coined during Hitler's time, it was pure iron and jumped right onto the magnet. The next day, I approached the vendor again. By this time, more of his bananas had turned black, and I hoped he would reconsider the previous offer. He did. Five pennies bought one black banana. What a deal. I could not believe my good fortune to get to eat one whole banana. It was so sweet. Even the inside of the peel was good, which I scraped off with my teeth.

All of us knew about the old black man. He always sat on the stoop of the door to his tenement. His skin was as black as wet ashes, and his hair was very curly and pure white. I forgot his name, but he knew all of us. He called us by name and always was ready to tell us a story or two. He said he came from Africa, a place called the Cameroons, before the first war. He spoke our dialect perfectly. I liked the man.

As I walked to school, I witnessed lots of things. I even saw two people get killed. One poor man was changing a flat tire on his truck when a car, which was about to pass his parked vehicle, got its front wheels caught in the trolley tracks, and then lost control in the wet snow on the ground. It careened directly into the squatting man, smashing him against the tire he was trying to replace.

Another man, on his moped, died when he failed to stop at an intersection. He struck a truck on its side and wound up under the wheels of the truck.

As I look back, scenes like that did not affect me too much. Is it possible a child can be exposed to such things often enough that you get used to it? Pondering about those days, I realize Munich had a strange and somewhat morbid policy at the time. Whenever there was a traffic fatality, a road sign at that spot was erected that showed a black skull and crossbones on a white background. It was about the size of a bus stop sign. The sign was placed at the curb of the sidewalk. Some intersections had six or more of such signs. The most horrifying of this awareness program was a mangled motorcycle and its sidecar which were mounted on a concrete abutment as the traffic entered an underpass. There, on that very spot, a family of four had died in the displayed wreck.

One snowy day, a couple of us boys were throwing snowballs at the traffic rolling by. We were trying to hit the rims of cars and trucks while they were moving. We were a bit up on a bank where the fresh snow was and were throwing downhill. While solely concentrating on my moving target, I failed to see a man on a bicycle enter my field of fire. After a mighty heave, I saw my projectile knock off the man's hat, which straight away sailed right into the path of an oncoming car which completely flattened it. I had but a split second to rejoice at that feat because the bare-headed man had jumped off his bike and was coming at me in a great lunge. Fortunately, the snow was deep; and I was already half way up the bank. Had that man gotten ahold of me, there would have been nothing left of me but a greasy spot.

As I've gotten older, I often think on things that seemed to have been just perfect the time they happened. I made paper airplanes over the years secretly wishing they would fly forever. I especially remember a day after school when my friend and I made a great big paper plane out of old newspaper. That day our hopes were sky high because we knew the chances of this flimsy and awkward fabrication actually flying were practically zero. But we carefully folded the paper together anyway making sure that the folds were symmetric. At last it was time to launch that thing. With a few strides into the breeze and a long follow through with my arm, the paper craft was on its way. To our surprise, the wings of that plane caught an upward draft, and it began to circle higher and higher. We gleefully watched as it finally disappeared behind a tall building. We searched for a while the next block over, figuring it must have struck something and crashed back to the ground; but we never did find it. It was hard to give up something that soon that had worked so well. Maybe that is why this memory is still with me.

If you keep your eyes open in a big city, you can witness many crazy and interesting things. Fruit wholesalers went scooting around in three wheeled trucks. One wheel was in the front, driven by a motorcycle engine; the other two were in the rear supporting the cargo bed. Almost directly over the single wheel were two narrow seats covered with a cab and windshield. Usually these small trucks were heaped with apples or heads of cabbage and the like. One day, a careless driver of such a contraption was coming out of a side street too fast. In the process, he lost control and flipped the vehicle on its side. The wreck scraped off the paint of this goofy looking vehicle as it scrubbed across the cobble stones, all the while spilling cabbage in wild profusion over the entire inter-section. It was kind of funny to watch, but I decided to help the bedraggled fellow pick up his cherished goods. A few pedestrians and bicyclists helped to right the truck. All other vehicles kept on whizzing around us and the spilled cabbage as best they could.

One day walking home, I noticed a crowd of people all staring into a store window. I could not imagine what could be so interesting to look at. Wriggling through the people, I worked my way to the front. In the middle of the display window was a large box sitting on a cabinet. The highly polished wooden box had a small oval window that looked like it had snow swirling in it. Mesmerized, all the folks watched and waited for an occasional flicker of an image to come on. I guess people are still mesmerized looking at a tube.

Non of us had ever heard of a school bus. Sister walked to the same school, but she had her own friends whom she met up with on the way. My buddy and I most-ly stayed together. The closer you got to school, the more kids were walking. One girl in our class, named Monika, was a pretty fifth grader. She had large eyes and curly dark hair. We both must have been struck on her and were quite interested in the showing of her early develop-ment to womanhood. We walked near her, often teasing her a bit to get her to respond, so we could better ogle her. As brave as we were, we actually asked her one day if she stuffed sox in her bra just to show off. Well, that did not set very well with her. She got so upset at this insinua-tion that she went to the teacher and told of the comment we made. The teacher called us to his desk and asked if the story was true. We confessed thinking for sure we were going to get punished. But, he just told us not to let it happen again. Monika was not mad at us; she just wanted to set the record straight.

Walking home, we often trailed Monika. We knew we would not be able to keep up a lengthy conversation with the girl that was messing with our mind, so we stayed about five paces behind. This made us think we were with our girl, and it kept us from making fools of ourselves. When you are infatuated, you just can't talk of sports and trucks. The conversations we had in our minds, we would not dare reveal to the one for whom we had a longing. She was aware of us as we followed her and most likely felt very important to have two sprouts interested in her. After she entered her building, we stayed across the street staring at her fourth floor window until she waved at us. Then we went home.

A STERN TEACHER

Mr. Kurtz was a tough teacher. He had to be. With so many schools bombed out, the class sizes were over forty kids. Two kids sat on a bench that was part of the desk.

Class photo, Munich 1953 - 45 students present.
Young Franz standing in the doorway to right of teacher.

Each desk had two ink wells with a little pot of ink in each. The aisles between went from front to back and were just wide enough for the teacher to walk through. Mr. Kurtz often went to the back of the room to observe us during dictation or quiz time. If anyone whispered or even turned their head, he would approach from behind and grab the person by the short hair behind the ears. He pulled quietly and steadily up until you were in a standing position, plus a little higher. The thin hardwood cane was a formidable disciplinarian. To get this prize of correction for your misdeeds, you had to stand before the class, stand erect, hold out your right hand horizontally, and receive a minimum of six lashes. The fingers smarted mightily after such a licking. They always swelled up and the whole hand trembled, but that was no excuse for poor writing. Penmanship was always graded, and proper spelling was always expected whenever we wrote anything at school, including notes and homework.

During a test one day, I wanted to get a boy's attention in the next row, for what reason I do not remember. Mr. Kurtz saw me reach over with my foot to touch the other fellow. He called me to the front and with the back of his right hand, gave me a wicked blow across the face. This started my nose bleeding profusely. I walked to the corner sink, with blood pouring out of my nose. I stood there dripping while the rest of the class finished the test. I was still bent over the sink after the lunch bell rang, and everybody had left the class. I do not recall when the bleeding finally subsided, but my mother and the school's headmaster came to the classroom and called Mr. Kurtz out into the hall. As Mom and I exchanged quick glances, I could tell she would have liked to mete out a lashing herself, not at me, but at the teacher. That evening at home, I asked Mom how she knew I had been struck across the face. As it turned out, one of my friends gave up her lunch period to run home to tell my mother. That friend was Monika.

All subjects were taught in the same classroom by the same teacher from eight in the morning until five in the afternoon. Although there was talk that school would be closed if the temperature reached over thirty-five degrees Celsius; that day never happened. Even if someone had a thermometer, who would confront the school's decision maker with such an astonishing fact? For that matter, school was never closed–snow and ice made no difference. When it got daylight, you went to school. So, when the room got hot, the day sure seemed to last forever.

On one such hot day in the sixth grade, everyone sat kind of droopy headed. I was sitting next to a boy in the back row. While I was trying to listen to the teacher, I also watched the boy out of the corner of my eye as he slowly took apart a small firecracker. It was the size of a pea and wrapped in paper. He dumped the contents onto a piece of writing paper. He fiddled with the makings that mostly looked like white sand. He then examined a little closer some black looking grains. That was when the whole mess blew up in our faces. Well, that sure got everyone's attention. All eyes were on us, including Mr. Kurtz's. Luckily most of the smoke was not in front of my face. The young man next to me was promptly invited to take the long walk to the front of the class.

THE STRANGE BULLY

There were no organized sports in school. After all, a little free play during lunch time was enough to blow off a bit of energy—even off the fifth and sixth graders. My favorite was the sand pit in the school's courtyard. The sand was a little below ground level; this made for easy jumping and some good distances. Any time a kid is good at something, life is sure easier; and friendships develop for him. However, the kid from the country still had some adversaries. An older fellow–I did not know where he came from–confronted me on a day off from school while I was alone playing in a rubble pile. He wrestled me to the ground, pushed me onto my back, and sat on my chest.

While pinning my arms above my head, he placed his knees on my upper arm muscles and began to roll back and forth on them. This was very painful. I remember him grinning as he did this for a while. Then he deliberately let a generous glob of spit fall on my face. I never met the fellow before, and I never saw him again.

A SCARY MOVE

Forgetfulness was never an excuse. Kids were suppose to remember their tasks and when to do them. That included being prepared and knowing where the pots, the shoe brushes, and the cleaning materials were when a task was assigned. When I got back to our apartment

The dumb adventure along the roof.

building from school one day, sister was waiting for me in the hall outside our apartment. Both Mom and Dad were at work that day, and neither of us remembered to carry the key to the apartment. We had to get in. Mom most likely had written a note to get supper started. The only way Dagmar and I were going to get in was through the windows which we knew were open. The windows were five stories high above the street below.

The attic with our commode and clothes line was unlocked. The attic vent, just a little square window, was propped open. I could see the sky through it. Climbing through that vent could get me on the roof, I reasoned. So, I climed up and out the vent and onto the roof. I slid down about three feet to the snow guard which was anchored to the tin roof. This guard went the length of the building facing the road below. Lying on the steep roof outside, I stuck my head and arms back through the vent. With a little coaxing, I helped little sister out onto the roof. About seventy feet above the sidewalk below, we inched our way along the snow guard over to the kitchen window. After clambering over the herb and flower boxes, we jumped into the kitchen.–Simple? The plan was good as long as we did not look down. I must admit, that day I did not get any sass out of Dagmar. We both were scared to death out there on that roof, high above the concrete, holding our breath, hoping our rubber legs would not give out. (Mom, if you read this forty-seven years later, please forgive us.)

MORE STUPID THINGS

One maneuver I took part in surely takes the cake. In the early fifties, some delivery trucks and all parcel post trucks were battery powered. Lots of the old battery powered vehicles had wooden-spoked wheels with solid rubber tires. A big chain led to the rear drive wheels. The operator sat up front. The many Gasthauses closest to the brewery received their barrels of brew from a wagon drawn by a pair of Clydesdale horses. The battery powered trucks served the more distant ones. On level ground the electric trucks easily outran the horse drawn ones. But going up an incline, the battery powered vehicles really labored. They slowed down to a point where our walking was as fast.

My buddy and I had long observed that the battery powered postal trucks had a pull-out step in the back for the postman to use to step up into his truck. We figured if we could run out into traffic, pull out that step as it crawled up an incline, we could get a ride home. Oh boy! As a kid, things always make so much sense. After all, how in the world could an inquisitive kid think things through if he never partook in any such wonderful experiences?

Then, guess what? Everything fell into place. We were walking home from school, moseying up an incline, when a postal truck was holding up traffic as it slowed down to master the slight hill. The postman cometh! We ran out into traffic, pulled out the step, sat down on it, and grinned. Just the perfect size for two boys with school satchels on their backs.

We sat there looking kind of proud and worthy of praise as we faced the cars that followed behind the truck. The truck had gained considerable speed after the hill levelled out but was still slowing down traffic. We were doing so good that in no time my pal realized he had to get off. There was no need to contemplate, so he just jumped off the moving truck. I did not know a twelve-year old could be so acrobatic. When his feet touched the pavement, he immediately went tumbling like a frantic rag doll.

Well, I was still sitting there; and the vehicle was gaining speed. Soon I, too, had to get off; or stay on for lord knows how many miles. The word inertia was never explained to me. Even if it had, what could I have done about it. I was moving backward. I've seen people jump off still moving trolley cars, but they were facing in the right direction when they jumped.

Well, there I went.—I also made the jump. It was a good thing the cars that followed kept considerably more distance since the first chap's sprawl. I hit the pavement so hard that every bone in me rattled. Flopping around and rolling with the traffic, I came to rest at the edge of the bicycle path. I am sure the cars following blew their horns and hollered at me, but I did not hear a thing. I crawled up onto the sidewalk with my head in a spin. After a spell, I got up, pulled my shirt around so the buttons were again in the front, straightened out my breeches, gathered up my satchel, and slowly dragged myself home.

HEAT

When we set out the ashes to be picked up, it was exactly that—ashes. There simply was no trash. We, as a family, bought nothing that was boxed or bottled. When we went to the store, it was to a specific one that specialized in either dairy products, produce, meats, or breads. There were even places like a Konditorei, a pastry shop which sold torte and other scrumptious goodies. As for us, we always brought our own containers such as cloth bags or a can for milk. Some staples were wrapped by the grocer or butcher in paper, which was coveted as a fire starter. Even the potato peels were either composted if you had a garden spot, or otherwise they were left to dry to be burned with many other scraps. When we lived in the country, we had access to sticks and pine cones. Now, in the city, the competition for burnables was even greater. We cooked with wood and heated water on the back of the stove. When the cooking was done, so was the heating of the room. It took more than a month to fill one of the ash containers the city provided.

The sanitation truck amazed me with its efficiency. It rolled up to the curb, a worker latched the container to the truck, pulled a lever, and the can went up and over to dump the ashes into the open truck on top.

Everyone knows that with sticks and potato peels you can't get a very hot fire. Dad, working for a trucking and hauling business, frequented the rail yards. Where there are locomotives, there is coal. He often brought home a few chunks of coal that had fallen off the coal cars. One evening, the three of us were waiting for him to come home when suddenly we heard this awful commotion. We rushed to open the door to the stairway. There, we saw Dad, half grumbling, half grinning, going after a huge lump of coal that had rolled down a flight of stairs. Looking over the banister to the landings below, I saw several apartment dwellers looking up at us on the top floor wondering if hell really had broken loose. Dad explained to us that he had this large heavy lump folded into a square burlap wrap. Holding the four corners in one hand, he had slung the makeshift sack over his shoulders. A few steps after he started to climb the stairs, he felt one of the corners of that wrap start to slip. He thought he could hold on tight long enough to make it all the way up the 110 steps. Two steps before reaching our place, the wrap slipped loose, sending the boulder bouncing down the stairs. We were all a bit embarrassed at having disturbed our neighbors down below; however, that lump of coal needed to be busted up anyway.

WASHDAY

Each tenant was assigned a half day a week to wash clothes. The wash house was in back of the tenement at the rear of the courtyard, which was paved with old bricks. These courtyards were not a thing of beauty, just a space between the buildings. At times, they had a tree growing, not one to enjoy and congregate under, for people did not do this sort of thing. All the time we lived in the building, we never got to know anyone by name.

The wash house was not big, just one room. It had a tub sink against the tiled wall with a shelf to each side. In the far corner was a large copper caldron that was sitting on a brick firebox. A cast iron door, about two feet off the tiled floor, kept the heat shut up under the kettle. Mom had to start the fire and keep it going until all the clothes were boiled and rinsed. To the left, where the laundry was boiled was an oak wash table about eight feet long and three feet deep. The wood on top was bleached and worn from many scrubbings. While the laundry boiled in the kettle, Mom occasionally stirred it with a long wooden spoon. After a time, she dipped that spoon in; and she'd sling out a piece of clothing onto the scrubbing table. She rubbed a block of soap over the areas to be scrubbed. The soap was home made, dark ochre in color, and looking and smelling just like good old G.I. soap. Using a sturdy brush, about a foot long, with bristles made from small roots, Mom scrubbed both sides of the sheets, pillow cases, dish linens, towels, shirts and work pants. She laid out the sheets lengthwise, scrubbed a section, then folded a new section over it and scrubbed that portion until all the sheet got a treatment of that brush. I can still see Mom giving the collars and other soiled areas an extra scrubbing. After the clothes were scrubbed, they were put back into the boiling water for a while. We rinsed them in the sink then wrung them out by hand. My hands were not big enough to get a good grip to wring much water out, but the smaller pieces were mine to wring. We owned a portable washer that looked like a butter churn. The plunger that was pushed down and up through a hole in the cover looked like a toilet plunger with air holes. This device was quite adequate to wash small garments. It forced air and water through the wash, thus cleaning it.

Managing a fire in the kitchen stove was not much of a problem. Two or three sticks plus a handful of coal, got a good fire going to cook and bake with; but to boil a kettle of cold water on washday was a different story. Our wood supply was scarce. Coal was hoarded for cold weather and then only used a few nuggets at a time. So, what did we burn on washday? Well, Dad was, like I said, in the trucking business. Where there are trucks, there are tires. Dad brought home worn out tires and chopped them into manageable chunks with a hand ax the evening before washday. He sometimes even started the fire for Mom before he went to work. Each chunk of rubber burned hot and long. Thick black smoke came from that chimney on the wash house. Long flecks of soot floated everywhere. People who had their clothes hanging to dry may have grumbled some, but no one ever openly complained. Smoke and soot was part of life. If you could stay out of it, you did; if not, you smelled it. So what? At least there were no bureaucrats getting paid to say there was smoke in the air.

THE COURTYARD

Most city blocks were wide enough for their row houses to have courtyards, providing space between the buildings. In cases like that, the rear of the buildings faced each other. The courtyards backed up to each other and were bordered all around by a six foot high brick wall. I guess that old cities did this to keep people from crossing through other's backyards. It also added somewhat of a community feeling to your own tenement, although, there was very little community sentiment going on during those years. Most likely, the distrust that was in the air was ingrained during Hitler's time. With many displaced people around and the many who suffered through a death or loss of property, joviality was not something I sensed. When I think about it, even the children did not congregate in the courtyards. Maybe it was or is indicative of city life, but we as a family sure stayed to ourselves as did everybody else. To enter the courtyard from the street, one had to enter through the front door of the building, find his way through the ground level, then exit through the back door into the open. No stranger was ever seen there just hanging around.

Times were still rough in Munich in the early fifties. I do not remember seeing beggars or bums, but I remember many men with one arm or one leg hobbling about on crutches. Men with both legs missing pulled themselves along on a dolly. Some amputees backed themselves into a shallow nook off the sidewalk, sitting there on a pallet selling pencils. They sat there, no legs, unable to even pull themselves over curbs and cobblestone. Every day, with despair in their eyes, they hoped to sell a pencil. Some men, fortunate to have their limbs, as well as musical talent, often entered the courtyards. Some would sing famous arias or folksongs. Others played the violin; all hoped that someone would throw a few pennies at their feet, from the window. They all sang or played sad tunes, tunes that swelled the heart with melancholy. The sweet sadness reverberated between the buildings. Even on the top floor, one could understand every word sung.

In those years, everyone was poor. How poor, no one knew. There were different degrees of indigence, but none had lost his or her dignity.

MORE FAMILY

Beisser Opa was over eighty years old and lived in an old age home. It was managed by the church and operat-

Beisser Opa on his 92nd birthday.

ed by nuns. We went to visit occasionally. It took three trolley car switches to get to his place which was on the other side of the city. Opa had a narrow room that opened to a richly planted backyard. Most of his life's possessions were in the night stand. His gold watch was in his vest pocket. He wore it proudly. After I bugged him a little, he would show it to me and let me listen to its faint ticking. Then he'd slip it back into its pocket, leaving the gold chain hanging from one of the button holes.

Beisser Opa had been bombed out twice. Each time he was not home, and each time he lost all of his belongings. He never lost, however, his spirit of going on and his zest for life. I watched him, at his advanced age, do knee bends and back stretches and take two steps at a time going up the stairs. He ate one clove of garlic every day, which he chopped up with his pocket knife on a tiny wooden cutting board, using his nightstand as the table. He also drank a glass of red wine every evening. He lived to be ninety-six.

We also met our new Dad's mother and her husband. Two of Mom's sisters and their families also lived in Munich. Very rarely did we go visiting and rarely did anyone come to see us. Our own little family unit grew even closer together. Mom was determined that we were going to make it on our own.

Dad got me a bicycle and taught me how to ride it. It was a heavy old Schwinn with fat tires, so heavy, in fact, that I could not carry it up the 110 stair steps to our place. Dad just put it on his shoulder, along with his. Mom usually carried her own bike up the five flights of stairs.

A MOUNTAIN VACATION

The workweek in Germany in 1952 was forty-eight hours. When Dad had inter-city driving assignments, he worked lots of overtime. In addition, when some extra hours were left on weekends, he'd borrow a motorcycle and take off to help farmers get in hay and other crops. A couple of times he took me along. I got to ride on the seat behind and hold on to him for dear life. After a day of raking and pitching hay, I got fifty pennies for my labor.

I learned to ride my bike just in time for our planned vacation. Dad got a week off, and he and Mom decided to take a trip to the mountains. They bought a one-way train ticket to take us about fifty kilometers toward the Alps. It was drizzling rain when we got on and raining when we got off. After picking up our three bicycles from the boxcar at the rear of the train, we were anxious to get on with our vacation. We had hopes the rain would stop soon.

Dagmar sat facing forward in a basket mounted to the front of the handlebar on Dad's bike. All three of us had a bundle of clothes and other stuff strapped to a rack behind our seat. Our first stop was at a hydro electric power plant at the edge of a lake called Kochelsee. We all went inside the facility for some sightseeing and a short lecture on the physics of generating electricity. The next leg of our journey took us steadily uphill. This meant that for several hours we had to push our wheels up and up the winding mountain road. All of us huffed and puffed as we pushed on in the steady rain. It paid off as we came to a beautiful new lake called Walchensee. From there the water came roaring down inside a large pipe to drive the turbine below at the electric generating station.

When evening came, we were all soaked to the skin and chilled to the bone. Mom and Dad rented a room at someone's house. The tight room was in the attic directly under the shingles of the roof. The space where I was to sleep was not even tall enough for me to stand up. We hung all of our soaked clothes about the room on nails and over the back of chairs and beds, hoping they would dry overnight. But the rain kept coming down. The dampness was creeping in. With just a single blanket on me, I was trying to relax and go to sleep; but I was too cold. The rest of the family had long dozed off. The rain kept on. The night air got much colder. My body ached from exhaustion, but sleep did not come. I did not want to wake up Mom because complaining had never done much good, so I just laid there in a knot until dawn.

We got up early, put on our still damp garments, and hit the trail. It was still raining. As we pedaled, the body heat kept the muscles loose; but the hands and fingers that gripped the handlebars stayed achy and cold. Dagmar did not have the benefit of exercise to stay warm. She just sat there in that basket with her feet hanging down on both sides of the front wheel. When we left the mountain cabin that morning, Mom asked for some old newspaper. She wrapped it around sister's legs and tied it down with some strings around her knees and ankles. We each had a rain hat and a parka; but, with the wind driving the rain and the dampness in the air, nothing we did kept us from getting wet and cold. Often, when we were able to coast down a hill, Dad would come up behind me, and, just as he passed in the dale of the road, he'd grab my arm and catapult me half way up the next incline. We ate our lunch in the rain and then pushed on again. The view and the beauty of the mountains we never did get to see, but we were together.

Dad must have decided to shorten the trip. Most of the riding seemed to be down hill, Sure enough, when darkness came, we were at the home of one of Dad's uncles in Holzleitern.

Deep down, I sure was glad the vacation was over. I finally did get warm and was able to rest my sore body.

All in all, it was a memorable family outing. No one got fussy or angry or whined. Looking back, it was group therapy. Dad proved he had the mettle and strength, and Mom had the fortitude to stick it out. Dagmar became a zombie and went with the flow because she well knew there was no other choice. I learned that, where there is leadership it is easy to follow. Dad was my hero.

DISCIPLINE

Beisser Opa told stories of long ago when he was a boy. He was born in 1870. The school's teachers and headmaster back then not only handed out corporal punishment on the spot but also went a step further. Each school had a dungeon where a kid could spend some time after committing crimes against the community. The young Beisser Opa apparently got into trouble and was punished at school for stealing apples from a neighbor's tree. He, however, decided to get even. He told me of wrapping fresh manure in paper, then sneaking up to the man's front door, where he placed the package on the front stoop. After setting the wrap on fire, he quickly pulled the cord that rang the doorbell and ran off. He did not stick around to find out how the fire was put out. A quick getaway was more important. Well, he was identified anyway and was brought before the headmaster to be sentenced. The punishment was three days and nights in the school's dungeon. The pit was under some loose floorboards. With no windows, it was always dark. The menu was bread and water. Roaches and rats were vying for the bread. He had to curl-up to sleep, because it was not long enough to stretch out. That was seventy years prior to my going to school.

Discipline in the early fifties was every grown person's responsibility. Any man, whether he was a father or not, was liable to give a kid a wallop for deeds that he thought needed to be corrected. Kids were at all times under scrutiny by adults, and a helping hand was never far from fact. One time, I dashed around a corner, not slowing down to look, and crashed into a baby carriage. No one got hurt. I sort of bounced off the front of the carriage. When out of the corner of my eye I saw a massive hand swiping at my head, luckily I had the mind instinctively to duck. If I hadn't ducked, my head would have been rolling yet.

Mom was still the one to fear as the family disciplinarian. When I displayed bad posture and was hunched over at the dinner table, she'd get the large washtub spoon, make me sit erect, and stick the handle in front of the elbows and behind my back. That sat me up straight. She would then emphatically tell me that I must grow up tall and straight. Eating my dinner in that position was a bit difficult, but I was dexterous enough to still bring the fork to my mouth.

My sister did most of the rebelling and had her share of correction. It was natural then, in order to keep peace in the family, that the one who least complained was privileged to get to do most of the chores. I had been shining the family's shoes for many years, but at age twelve I stood up to my mother stating that I thought it was time for sister at least to polish her own shoes. Guardedly watching Mom, expecting the worst, she thought for a moment then agreed with me. Of course, that cut into Dagmar's quality time, so she did what all siblings do, found a way to get to me by being a bit more difficult in cooperating in everything else.

School was the place where most of the discipline was handed out. A couple of my classmates were caught smoking in the boys' room. Our teacher was informed of the infraction. He was ready and had the means to deal with just such a situation. He gave us all a written assignment and then left the room with the two accused. Fifteen minutes later the three came back to the classroom. The two boys, barely able to walk, were slumped over and very pale, almost looking green. The teacher then showed the rest of the class a fat cigar that he had lit and allowed the fellows to smoke to their heart's content, and then some. The teacher had them dragging on that cigar generating great amounts of smoke. He made them inhale as much and as often as they could. The small bathroom filled up thicker and thicker with the permeating aroma of cigar smoke. He did not give those chaps, who were choking, spitting, and even vomiting, a chance to get away from it. We all could smell the smoke when they came back to the room. Quietly, they sat down in their chairs, eyes red and mouths gaping.

That episode certainly squashed any notion anyone else might have had about taking up smoking.

I was punished once, not wrongfully, but maybe a little excessively. Even I thought so at the time. I recall the teacher was lecturing. With thirty or more students in the class, order was paramount. Every child was sitting erect, arms folded, looking at the instructor. He had everyone's undivided attention, which he insisted upon. Out of the corner of my eye, I spotted a small sliver of paper, about the size of an aspirin. It was laying there on the front edge of my desk. Arms folded and erect, I leaned ever so little forward; and with a soft blow, blew that sliver of paper off the desk. That atrocity did not escape the teacher. Promptly, he stopped his talk, got his oak whipping stick and called me to the front. I knew what the procedure was, and so did the rest of the class. I stuck my hand out, nice and flat, and promptly received six good lashes across the tips of my fingers.

AN AMERICAN VISITOR

In 1951, Baumann Opa, my Mother's father, passed away. The oldest of his children was Uncle Hans, then Uncle Max, Tante Hilde, and Tante Dora, with Mom being the youngest. After word reached Uncle Max, who lived in America, he decided to make a visit back to his home country. I imagine some family affairs had to be settled as well. While he was in Germany, he got to meet all his nephews and nieces as well as Mom's husband, the new brother-in-law, Alfons. A weekend trip was planned to the Alps. None of the family had a car. Alfons, being a truck driver, was the natural choice to chauffeur the rented car. I recall when Uncle Max first laid eyes on the car Dad rented. "What is that thing?" he blurted out when he gazed at the Volkswagen parked there bashfully awaiting to be loved. He went on to yell in amazement, "How are we all going to get into that thing?" After all there were four adults and two good sized kids all planning to go along. Uncle Max had brought his high school-age daughter, Dorothy, with him—Squeeze in, we did.

Dad was driving, Uncle Max in front, and Mom and Dorothy in the back seat. My sister and I had to take turns sitting between the ladies and being stuffed under the rear window. It was my first car ride, although, as a long legged eleven-year-old, I was not comfortable; it was still exciting. Again, one could whine himself right out of having a memorable time. The motto always was: Kids may be seen but not heard.

The culminating highlight of the trip, at least for my uncle, was our getting caught in a cattle drive. While driving through a small Alpine village, we were slowly being engulfed by hundreds of cows as they were driven from the higher elevations down to the still green pastures of the valley. Instead of pulling to the side, Dad sort of inched his way along among the cows. Uncle Max had a habit of saying "Holy Cow" as an expression, but he got to laughing hard as he said it over and over as our little car was being smothered by cows. When two milk cows directly in front of the Volkswagen just waddled along, their udders swaying from left to right and their soiled taillights barely being covered by their switching tails, he laughed almost uncontrollably as he observed this marvel of nature.

TO PLAY

The memory of bombs was part of life. Although bombs no longer fell from the sky, the remains and reminder of these terrible beasts were everywhere. With lots of reconstruction going on, undetonated bombs were unearthed frequently. A full alert was given to the neighborhood, and residents were asked to temporarily evacuate. The evacuations took place not only at the sight where the dud was found but all along the route the flatbed truck would take, carrying the thing out of town to be defused. At times, a few citizens were not so lucky when, while looking for usable or burnable material among the ruins, a sleeping monster went off.

During the war, when a bomb struck an open area, it formed a great crater in the ground. The crater usually had an elevated rim of dirt around the outer edge which made it look even deeper. Often a footpath led over part of the rim. This packed-down path made a great entrance for our bikes when we wanted to ride the rim. The game was to hit the inner slope of the crater as fast as possible, circle the crater, and pedal back out where you entered. If you stayed too high around the rim, you'd get sucked down to the bottom before you could make the complete circle. If you shot into the hole and traveled too deep to gain the extra speed, you might well not have enough oomph to get back out. So, we learned the correct combination of both. Full speed entry, a little dip down to get speed, then use all you had to pedal back out. It was very difficult to accomplish. All of us sure felt mighty stupid having to, at times, push our bikes out of the depth of the crater.

Our cycling escapades often took us several miles away from home. One time, on the first day of April, wonder of wonders, the great olympic runner Zatopek was to train at the city stadium. My friend and I decided to go and watch. We got there in the morning at the time listed in the newspaper, but no one else did. After looking around and asking a few dumb questions, we came to the conclusion that we had fallen for an April fool's joke. The day, however, was not a complete loss because we decided to investigate the origin of a roaring noise. We knew, because we had heard it before, that the noise came from military jets. Our search brought us to a tall, chain-link fence that crossed the end of a runway of an American Air Force Base. In absolute awe, we watched as fighter jets soared directly over our heads as they took off. Now, that was real excitement for a twelve year old. The trip was worth while after all.

One hot spring day, we rode our bikes along the river's edge. The river Isar, with its beautiful pale-green water, flows through Munich. It originates in the Alps and was quite full and fast flowing that early spring day. Being hot, it sure was an enticing sight. Our desire to cool off got the best of us, so we jumped in. The water was pure ice, nothing but melted snow out of the mountains. The swift force of the water snatched us up and carried us away. All I, as well as my friend, could do, was muster up two good strokes toward the edge. Thank God, that was enough to grab hold of a rock near the edge. Because such cold quickly stiffened our muscles, we both knew that if we had jumped out a little farther, we would have drowned. (That was another dumb move I never told Mom or Dad.)

Munich's river, the Isar, with Dad and Dagmar.

THE DRINK OF CHOICE

Beer was the national drink. If you were old enough to carry it, you could buy it. Many a young chap, getting a stein of beer for his parents, tasted a sip or two before he got home. The elders would grumble and blame the bartender for cheating them out of a full stein of brew. When the keg was fresh, the mug had to be filled slowly so the head did not take up too much of the volume. Felsner Oma knew a way to keep the head of foam to a minimum on her stein of brew. She greased the stein on the top inside rim with a thin coat of lard. She always got a full mug of beer.

A wire basket with a handle was made just for carrying beer. It held two Mass, or two one liter steins. Most men drank the light colored brew while the women often drank the dark brew. I liked the dark beer, it was sweeter. When sister or I were feeling sick or just getting over an illness, Mom fed us a raw egg yolk, mixed with a spoon full of sugar, that was blended into a cup of dark beer. Warmed up a little, the yolk gave us strength, and the beer put us to sleep. A lot of women also heated their brew. Felsner Oma had a beer warmer. It was heated on the stove, then stuck into the beer and clipped to the mug. A heavy spoon, after it lay on the hot kitchen stove, worked just as well. People nodded and dozed a lot. As a kid, I heard little about drunkenness. City people did not mix much. No harm was done when a satisfied patron sat in the corner, listening to some zither tunes in a Gasthaus, having dozed off to a trouble free world, with his chin on his chest.

I don't really know why nobody drank water. Could be that the water was not quite safe, but most likely the reason was beer tasted so much better. At home we had a lot of soup. We drank some milk, but it had to be boiled first. At times, with a little sweetener in it, we'd drink it hot. I gagged when Mom made me drink milk that had formed a skin on top after it was heated. She'd get angry when I dipped out the skin and hung it over the side of the cup. Often she stirred the contents before she gave them to me. The bits of milk skin floated around the cup; and when I drank from it, I became nauseated. All that was sheer nonsense to Mom, just a fetish I had to get over. Generally that was her rule for many things. There was no use of questioning, and certainly we were not to argue.

We also drank what we called coffee. It was just a

brew made from ground roasted grain. Various kinds of tea were sipped in the evenings with cookies or cake. We drank rose hip tea, also tea made from the blooms of the Linden tree. Camomile tea was the cure-all drink to settle an upset stomach, loosen congestion, and calm other ailments of mind and body. Soft drinks we never had. The only soda one could buy was a carbonated lemon drink. When the family went on an outing, Dad and Mom at times stopped at a Gasthaus and asked for a Radler Mass. It simply was a measure (liter) for bicyclers. This drink was half beer and half lemon soda. It tasted real good and was refreshing. It diluted the alcohol by half and kept us going straight along the cycling path.

On one of my outings, my friend and I got really thirsty. The sun was beating down, and we had nothing to drink. We pedaled to the nearest beer garden, checking out the cost of a bottle of soda. We found that between the two of us we did not have enough money. However, we had just enough coins for a liter of cold dark beer. With thirst quenched, we pedaled on, so to speak.

GAMES WE PLAYED

Evening play was often just the communal effort of cleaning up the pots and dishes after which followed stories of the day and maybe tea and cookies. When days were shorter and more time in the evening was left, we either played cards or a table game. Dad was an avid chess player, and he taught me well. At first he would set up his side without the queen and one rook. When I got good enough and beat him a few times, he'd play with both rooks but without the queen. Again, as I became a stronger player, he'd remove just one rook from his initial set-up. Soon he lost most of the time with one figure short, after which we played each at full strength. Then I lost most of the time. I hated to lose, but the desire to win brought out a new person in me, a competitive spirit had emerged that soon made me realize that manhood was just around the corner.

I was somewhat of a collector. Collecting information about other countries and their cultures I did for extra school credit. However, collecting stamps was a great challenge for me, as it was for several of my friends. We did lots of swapping and consequently stayed busy many hours during the evening. Felsner Opa worked at a bank which conducted business internationally. He requested the discarded envelopes from all over the world so I could soak loose the various stamps and add them to my collection. My fancy, duplicate stamps were a big hit on the trading block. They brought me many stamps in swaps to round out a series of certain issues in my collection.

On weekends my buddy and I rode our bikes over half of Munich, digging in every public trash basket, looking for coupons. One particular cigarette brand offered coupons we could trade for a series of pictures. The waste baskets at every trolley stop became a magnet for us to hunt for certain empty cigarette packs which had such coupons in them. By mail, we traded the coupons for pictures which were then mounted into albums. I was allowed to bring all of these albums, the Kosmos Zigarettenbilder sets, five total, to this country. Each album contained hundreds of photo-like pictures, showing the birds of the world, a history of transportation and aviation, as well as all the flags of every nation in full color. My, my, I must have been a busy fellow.

We also played games so that Dagmar and I could sharpen our minds. One was a verbal math game. Dad or Mom would make it up either on sister's level or mine. They simply called out in a slow, steady sequence a series of mathematical functions. We worked the series of instructions in our heads as they were called out in a continuous string of little math problems. Mom or Dad would stop the string after they had called out about ten or more functions and ask for the answer. Here is a sample: $6 \div 2x3 + 3 \div 6x8 \div 4x5 + 1 \div 7 + 2x11 - 15 \div 8x2 = ?$ (answer is 10). It was obvious if you got lost along the way there was no answer. So, actually, it was a pretty good way to teach children how to sit still, listen, use their brain, and chal-

Diamonds Are Forever

AND NOW you can be too. LifeGem extracts carbon from the cremated remains of the dearly departed, and with heat and pressure makes them into real diamonds. "It isn't in memory of a loved one, it *is* the loved one," says CEO Greg Herro. You may wonder who wants a ring made from Grandpa, but LifeGem's business has been brisk, thanks to the popularity of cremation. In 2001, 27% of those who died were cremated, up from 18% a decade before, and loved ones want more than an urn of ashes on the mantel, says Herro. LifeGems aren't valuable on the diamond market, but they're still pricey. A .25 carat costs $2,300; a .75 carat costs a hefty $10,000.

© LARRY WILLIAMS/CORBIS

THE RD HIT LIST

5 Summer Camps That Miss the Point

What happened to just swimming and making lanyards?

1. YoungBiz Better Investing campers learn to become savvy stock pickers. Daily fun: reading *The Wall Street Journal*.

2. Skit night on steroids: Camp Broadway kids rehearse eight hours a day, every day, to perfect their big finale numbers.

3. An SAT *class*, fine. But College Admission Prep Camp? Daily fun: vocab flashcards.

4. Young Einsteins toil for a month at NASA's robotics camp to build their own droids.

5. Etiquette Camp teaches little devils the 65 dining manners. Hmm. There are more than two?

over heard

It's sort of the American way to go **up and down the ladder,** maybe several times in a lifetime.

MARTHA STEWART in The New Yorker

© ROBERT RISKO

250 square feet
+ 724 lemons

1 definitive style
statement

thank goodness for **Kleenex** tissues™
BRAND
Whatever your décor, we've got a box for you. Kleenex® Expressions®
offers 18 designs to satisfy the frustrated decorator in all of us.

lenge them to get the correct answer. Of course, the whole family cheered at a correct answer.

We played another game where the entire family participated. It was an all-around subject game. We were each given a sheet of paper, and we sat around the kitchen table and decided on the subjects in the game. We usually chose five categories which we each wrote across the top of our sheets of paper. At random, a letter of the alphabet was called, at which time every one began to write an answer into each column, beginning with the called letter. As a sample:

Letter	Country	Food	Animal	Plant	Body of Water	Score
B	Belgium	Bread	Bear	Birch	Baltic	--

The first to place an answer in every column said STOP. If you had the only answer in any given column, it was worth 20 points. If you and any other player had different answers in the same column, each got ten points. If all or anyone else had the same answer in a given column, each got five points. We played the game as long as there was interest or until all the alphabet was used. If no one completed a round, for example with the letter X, time was called; and the partial scores were added. Naturally, the high score won.

When everyone was doing things and I was left alone, I often went back to my first love, artwork. By going to art class in the evenings, I was introduced to several new techniques of creativity. Dipping a small, cubed piece of potato into watercolor paint, pressing it onto paper, much like a rubber stamp, was an interesting way of assembling a painting. Linoleum block cutting and printing was another new art form. In the art of creating silhouettes of objects by Scherenschnitt, black paper with a dry gum backing was cut with a small pair of scissors, snip by snip, until a delicate shape of an subject was silhouetted. The dry gum was dampened then usually glued to a white board to set off the art. Silhouette art must have been pop-

Scherenschnitt, silhouette cut with scissors, 1953

ular for my father had created such paintings on glass,
along with other bits of art, to sell during the great
depression before I was born. It was told that he and his
brother Alfons went on the 'Walz', meaning they bummed
their way from town to town playing the violin and selling

Silhouette painted on glass by my father. Circa 1934

handmade postcards and other art.

At times Mom brought out her concertina. Dad liked to listen to her play. We would all sing a few songs and generally feel good about life.

THE GOOD IS GONE

In late summer of '52 on a warm crisp day, I strolled to the edge of the rail yard to play. All by myself, I settled down at an abutment at the end of a rail track. It was an elevated area about two meters square. This new spot of play was rimmed with rail ties which made a perfect ledge to play on. I must have summoned all the imaginations of my childhood as I settled into a wonderful and deeply enjoyable time of play. All was perfect. I looked around that small area and found everything my imagination sought. Every nail, chunk of metal, rock, and fragment of wood held the fulfillment of my needs of the moment. I built and manufactured, and I dreamed and imagined. It was a play time within and all to myself. I distinctly remember it as a truly perfect day. For days after, I cherished the feeling and the good I felt in my young heart. Chores, homework, and running errands soon led me back to reality. However, that perfect day stayed etched in my mind and soul.

A month or two later, I found that the previous wonderful experience drew me back to that personal paradise at the edge of the tracks. Ah, I had great expectations that day. The weather was sunny and crisp. I found the place, but the world was not still and quiet. The toy wonders were still laying where I had left them, meaningless and totally useless as they really were. It was a sooty place, a place of rotten timbers and dust. Who had stolen the glee, the power, and magic?–It was time. Time itself was the thief. All the good had gone...along with the boy in me.

NEW RELATIVES

Dad's mother lived in Munich with her husband. They had a son named Willie, Dad's half brother. Dad had lots of family scattered around the countryside. Mom somehow arranged for me to stay with a few of the new uncles and aunts for a week or two in the summer.

One such stay was in a cute little house in a town called Tann in lower Bavaria. The house was on a really small lot. Their garden was across the street because the little land surrounding the house was totally used for raising animals. They raised them exclusively for food. They had rabbits and guinea pigs, hens, roosters, and a good-sized hog.

All the animals were caged except for the hog. It got the run of the side yard which was about six feet wide and thirty feet long. The rabbits and the small guinea pigs were in cages hanging above the pig run on the outer wall of the house. Of course, the chickens were wherever there was a morsel to be had.

Attached to the back of the house was a hay and feed shed. One side of it was the chicken house. The neighbor's hay barn shared a common wall with uncle's shed. A small window on top of that common wall kept some air flowing between the two barns.

I met the neighbor's young daughter there. We whispered and told stories. We were the same age. We both knew what could happen between a boy and girl, but each of us was too scared to take the lead. We both dreamed, and our eyes sparkled with anticipation of our next meeting.

One day we heard the pig squealing like it had been stuck with a knife. She had gotten her head stuck in the picket fence. She forced her way through the pickets which closed in on her behind her jaws. I never heard such carrying on in my life. It sounded like a middle-of-the-day killing. Uncle Sepp was not home, so it was left to me to rescue the hog. I strained with all I had trying to pull the pickets apart. Finally the hog backed out, snorting and shaking its head.

The outhouse was a study in itself. It was at the back of the house at the end of a covered hallway. A single seater shared the rear and one side wall with the feed barn. The other side wall was along the side road. Through its cracks, you could watch the goings-on on the outside. After the door was closed and you had assumed the posture of contemplation, you could study the home-made barometer. Uncle Sepp had nailed a root to the door. When the humidity increased, the root bent toward the spot marked "Rain." When the air got dry, the root bent to the mark that said "Sunny." It worked.

At that tiny farm I saw bacon frying for breakfast, and I got to eat that and more than one egg. Times were good.

ANOTHER UNCLE

An uncle that we met on our ill fated cycling trip to the mountains allowed me to stay at his small place. He only had one arm but still was able to build a house for the family out of cement blocks. Adding on seemed to be an ongoing thing, and that is what he was doing when I was there. Every evening after work, he'd mix a wheelbarrow of cement and pour the batch into the block mold. After mixing a new batch, he laid the blocks he poured the evening before.

He was an amazing man. He played cards with one arm, holding the cards in a folded-up yard stick that he placed on its edge on the table in front of him. I saw him catch a chicken one time, lay it on the chopping block, hold it down with his foot, and then, with one sure whack, cut its head off with a hatchet. I remember the chicken ran around the yard without a head until it finally keeled over.

My uncle had a wife and three children, including a son my age. The son and I tried to earn a little money. We picked potato bugs by the jar full for five pfennig each jar. He had his own little enterprise of collecting mole tails. He told me he trapped them then cut their tails off with his pocket knife. The tails were bringing five pennies each. He never showed me any. I guess it was a good business to be in.

On a bright sunny day, I got an offer from a neighboring farmer to ride on his tractor. The farmer had just finished pumping the Odel, which was the seepage from the dung pile, into a great wooden cask. This brown gold had been collected all winter and spring, and it was now being put to use. The liquid fertilizer cask sat on a wagon, with four large wooden wheels, and the farmer used the tractor to pull the wagon and cask to the fields.

I had never seen a tractor before, thinking all farming was done with horses. Delighted to get to ride on a real machine, I climbed up and held on tight to the seat the farmer sat on. Slowly we drove out of town along a country road, then onto a field. The farmer had explained all the knobs and handles to me as we bounced along. I could hear the sloshing of the juice in the huge keg on wheels. I felt quite important to get to be doing this and even more so when the farmer asked me to help.

When we reached our destination, he stopped the tractor and told me to jump down and open the lever to start spraying the field. I saw a rope that ran through loops along the side of the barrel and around the corner leading to the rear. I saw it was tied to the top of the lever handle, but it never sank into my head that the rope was meant to be pulled. Being all excited and anxious, I stood in front of the spray mechanism at the rear of the wagon, reached up, grabbed the lever, and pulled the valve open. A tremendous rush of concentrated brown liquid hit my face, hair, and chest. Before I even realized what was happening, I was soaked.

After I walked back to the tractor and climbed back up, the farmer said little. He just grinned. I wished I could have jumped into a creek somewhere, but work came first. The farmer slowly pulled the wagon around and around the field, the spray from that wagon covered an eight foot swath.–Time dragged on. The sun was beating down. My clothes were drying, and my skin was baking. Yet, we circled that field until the liquid was spent.

Eventually, when I got back to my uncle's house, I had no trouble convincing his wife and her older daughter that I needed a bath. They ushered me into the washroom and showed me a laundry tub, brushes, and soap. With a little help from my new cousins, we poured water into the washtub. After they rounded up a pile of borrowed clothes, they left me alone. I stripped, got into the tub of water, and commenced to soaping and scrubbing. From the hair on my head to the bottoms of my feet, I scrubbed. I was a guest in this house, and I sure did not want to be a smelly one. I cleaned myself with the scrubbing brush until my skin felt raw.

Later that evening, all cleaned up and hair combed, I sat down with the family at the supper table. My uncle had just gotten home from work and was not aware of the happenings of the afternoon. He sat down to eat. He children were quiet. Before he took the first bite of his supper, he twitched his nose and said, "what stinks?" Owning up to being plain stupid is never easy, but I had no choice but to confess. I was the brunt of many jokes for the rest of my stay.

A NEW SCHOOL

Great progress was being made in reconstruction of the city. Dagmar and I were transferred to a new school which was closer to home. New shiny wood floors had been installed in the three-story school, which had been heavily damaged during the air raids of the war. The students who wore shoes had to remove them inside the entrance and go in stocking feet. Most of us went barefoot in warm weather. In the winter when all of us had on wool socks, the waxed floors and stairs were very slippery. If you fell down you got in trouble instead of getting sympathy. When a kid fell down, he was either running in the hall or was not holding on to the hand rail.

The new school had a visiting doctor who came periodically. I remember him checking our ears and throat as well as our eyes to see if we were sickly. The good doctor was a curiosity among the kids. He had one blue and one brown eye.

Either some of the students smelled or it was part of a new way of teaching. However, we learned a lot of

School picture of Dagmar in 1954.

new stuff about personal hygiene. The classroom teacher went as far as to tell us where and what to wash. Most of us knew all that. The difference was in the suggestion of frequency. I had been with Dad to the public bath house. There, for fifty pennies, you got five minutes of warm water to take your shower in a stall of your own. The teacher also introduced us to proper oral hygiene. I recall an all-student assembly that showed a cartoon-style movie on how to brush one's teeth and perform other recommended daily cleaning measures. I was thirteen years old before I really knew, or even cared, about germs. As a result of all this, I was found to have several large cavities. I did not know much about dentistry, or I would never have had the gumption to see the dentist.

The medieval looking gears, belts, and wheels were sure interesting. I tried to analyze their function before the good dentist told me to open my mouth. When he started to poke around and hit a few nerves, my toes curled up. When he cranked up his hi-tech rig and started to drill, smoke came out of my mouth and probably out of my ears as well. I thought I had been cast to hell where there is weeping and gnashing of teeth.

Growing up was not much fun any longer. The demands of school were getting so great that no one even wanted to talk in class for fear that he or she might miss something. We were deep into fractions, ratios and percentages, geometry, and some trigonometry. We had to remember formulas for seemingly dozens of mathemati-

School picture of Franz, 1954.

cal functions. There were no text books. The blackboard was it. There were no copiers. The hand-written notes were all you had to help you do your assignments. I pitied the disorganized person. All problems given were hypothetical and related to an everyday situation that we as students could understand. For instance: A swimming pool is ten meters wide and thirty meters long. It is one meter deep on one end and gradually deepened to three meters on the other end. Question: How much water could it hold? How much could it hold being ten centimeters shy of full? When empty, how much inside area of the pool is there? How much paint will it take if one liter of paint covers three square meters? How much would the water weigh if full to the top? With the metric system, this was all fairly easy. We were encouraged to solve all problems in our head first. We were taught to attack the tasks a step at a time. By rounding off all numbers and jotting down subtotals, we could come up with a good, educated guess at the answer. With this in mind, we then had a reference to check the final answer to see if by accident we had misplaced the decimal point during our actual calculations. Always, the point was to think and get sharp.

Prior to working the pool problem, we learned to work with all shapes. With ruler, protractor, and compass, we laid out the surface areas of shapes such as cubes, cylinders, cones, and three- and four-sided pyramids on paper. The drawn surfaces had to be connected, tops and bottoms to the sides, so when we cut them out in one piece, the desired shape assigned could be folded into an actual three-dimensional sample. This taught spatial relations and forced us to plan and think, then do and verify.

We had daily dictations. The teacher spoke, and we wrote it down, just a short story, usually a page long. We used a pencil. None of our pencils had an eraser on the end of it. The block eraser we had was used more in geometry and was not recommended to be used during dictations. At the end of the dictation, we handed in our page to be graded for spelling, proper use of punctuation, and penmanship. The first thing the teacher did with each page handed in was to hold it up to the light. If any thin spots in the paper were found, that indicated an eraser was used, and the spot was circled in red. This simply meant that it was impossible for anyone who had used an eraser to get an A, even if there were no other mistakes. This was true also of homework.

At the new school, we all learned shorthand. Certainly not all of us were going to be secretaries, but listening and quick thinking skills were the name of the game. Shorthand was taught just one hour a week, first the basics, then the shortcuts and an ever-faster pace at taking dictations. For additional edification, such as music, art, or a foreign language, we were encouraged to take these subjects in the evening for personal enrichment. When we went to school, we received eight hours worth of meat. The fine arts were offered in the evenings. There were few libraries in those years. A curious lad like me had to scrounge and dig for information.

A couple of evenings during the week, I took evening courses in art and English for "personal" fulfillment. Actually, I was interested in a girl that signed-up for the same "personal" evening studies.

PEELS, PEELS EVERYWHERE

In 1952 Mom read in the newspaper about a woman from Denmark who set a world record for peeling potatoes. The lady peeled one kilogram of raw potatoes in just over two minutes. Mom had strong quick hands, this I knew. She was accustomed to carrying three or four full beer steins in each hand as she served the thirsty folks in the beer gardens. She decided to find out if she could beat that so-called world record. We measured out one kilo of potatoes, so Mom could give it a try. The very first practice Mom shaved fifteen seconds off the record. Wow, we were on to something. Mom knew she could beat that record. All she needed was a stage, a forum where she could get the reporters out and get some recognition. Sometime later, Mom got her day at a convention hall during a large trade show. With thousands of visitors

Frau Friedl bricht den Kartoffelschälrekord

„Das kann ich auch", rief Frau Friedl Pfisterhammer, als sie im „Münchner Merkur" las: „Als beste Kartoffelschälerin erwies sich Fräulein Herdis Larsen aus Kopenhagen. Sie verteidigte ihren Titel erfolgreich, indem sie ein Kilo in der Rekordzeit von zwei Minuten und einer Sekunde schälte." Das war am 12. September dieses Jahres. Fräulein Larsens Rekord ließ Frau Pfisterhammer keine Ruhe: schon am nächsten Mittag setzte sie sich mit dem Wecker in die Küche und stoppte ihre Kartoffelschälzeit. Tatsächlich: Eine Minute 50 Sekunden.

Weltrekord war fällig

Bei Pfisterhammers gab es in den folgenden Tagen fast nur noch Kartoffelknödel. Die junge Frau, die immer bessere Zeiten stoppte, meinte, wenn es in unserer Zeit schon um Rekorde auf allen Gebieten geht, warum nicht auch im Kartoffelschälen.

Dazu gab ihr die Ausstellung „Schalten und Walten der Hausfrau" die ersehnte Gelegenheit: auf Rücksprache mit der Messeleitung wurde ein offizielles „Rekordschälen" festgesetzt. Friedl Pfisterhammer erschien im Vortragsraum in Halle I, mit ihrem Kartoffelschälmesser — Preis 15 Pfennige — bewaffnet, aus der gläsernen Fischküche wurde ein Kilo Kartoffeln geholt und auf ging's! Der ganze Zuschauerraum war g'steckt voll, während die junge Frau in Windeseile die dicken, braunen Erdäpfel schälte. „Fertig", rief sie, und hatte ihr Kilo in einer Minute 30 Sekunden bewältigt und damit sowohl die Kopenhagener als auch ihre eigenen Rekordzeiten gebrochen. Als Belohnung bekam sie von der Messeleitung eine Fruchtpresse geschenkt. „Ich bin ganz außer mir vor Freude!" strahlt die Münchner Kartoffelschälchampionin.

(Partial translation of news article).

"I can do it" she said, after reading of the new record for potato peeling. The next day, using her alarm clock, she found out she can beat it by 10 seconds. Everyday following, the family ate potato dumplings. The convention hall exhibit "Ways and Methods of the housewife" gave her the opportunity and the Press. Armed with her 15 penny peeler, she attacked the potatoes. The showroom was full. Can she do it? ...."Finished" she cried out. One minute and 30 seconds! She broke the record of the lady from Kopenhagen, also bettering her own time. Her prize was a fruit-juicer. "I'm beside myself," said the potato-peeling-champion from Munich.

World record article as it appeared in the Munich newspaper.

from all over milling around the convention floor, Mom was introduced. She was up on a platform in front of a table with a washtub on it. It was supposed to catch the peels. Armed with a potato peeler in one hand, a bowl of potatoes to her left, and a large stop clock above her head, all was ready. A bell rang, and within a second the peels were flying. Most of them sailing way past the washtub. At first the crowd was in awe; then when she picked up her last potato, the cheering began. When the last peel landed on the floor, the stop watch said one minute and thirty seconds. A huge cheer went up, and all the people clapped. Mom's picture was in the paper the next day with all the statistics of a new world record set by one of our own, a housewife from Munich. That was all there was to it, a brief moment of glory, a picture in the paper. Mom was still going to work every day, and we all came home to an attic apartment of a little more than 200 square feet. The record, however, was a lift to our family; we had a feeling things were going to change for the better.

Three or four days later, Mom received a letter from the City of Munich. It was from the mayor himself. He wrote about how proud and happy he was of her achievement. He also stated that if in the future he could be of help, please let him know. How about that! Mom did not waste much time in letting the mayor know the conditions of our small living space. Sincerely, she asked him if he could help her find a better apartment. Not long after that, we were offered, and accepted, a new place to live.

The new apartment was on the second floor, had nice big windows, and was roomy. We now had a living room, two good-sized bedrooms, kitchen with eat-in area, and even a private toilet. The bedrooms and living room had their own coke or coal burning heaters with just a regular cookstove in the kitchen. We still took baths in our washtub, but that was all right, too. We were so happy. Mom was able to set up her bedroom furniture the way it was meant to be. Dagmar and I got our own room, a room where we argued and also whispered secrets after the lights were out.

Our happy family in the new apartment in 1954.

A WEB OF TROUBLE

Our new place was just across the street from Felsner Oma and Opa and two blocks away from Oma's sister, Tante Zenta. Aunt Zenta and her husband managed a kiosk at a busy intersection. During the summer, when school was out, we often whiled the day away at the kiosk. They sold newspapers and magazines, comic books, maps, candy, cigarettes, and chewing gum. The German version of gum was about one third the size of a piece of Bazooka gum. It was hard to start with and hard to continue to chew. Not often did we chew gum, only on special occasions like a birthday, and, of course, when we were of help to Tante Zenta. The sweet in that German gum left really soon, but we kept on chewing because the prestige of chewing had to be relished much longer. So, after a day of chomping at the thing, we stuck it behind our ear while eating and then on the bedpost overnight. We heard that this was the American way. We also found out that after a day or two of giving that piece of hard rubber a good going over, it suddenly fell apart into a thousand crumbs. This phenomenon I could never figure out.

American chewing gum was much rarer. If it was available to be purchased, it was very expensive. Somehow, my sister and I each got a piece. The softness and flavor were just great. We were really up-town. I'll never forget how amazed I was at the elasticity when I pulled it outward from my mouth. The arms were never too long to break the stretch of gum. Even when sister grabbed one end of it, she could walk clear across the room and the other end in my mouth would still be connected. This truly intrigued us. Promptly, we devised a test to see how far this American gum actually would stretch. We pulled the gum from the bedpost to the curtain rod, to the wardrobe, to the doorjamb, to the nightstand, back to the wardrobe, to sister's bed, to our work desk, back to the other bedpost, to the ceiling light, back down to the stovepipe, to her dresser. The possibilities were endless, and so was the stretchability of the great American gum. We were just viewing our handiwork, which we so lovingly strung, when Mother stepped into the room and let the air out of us—not to mention the assortment of other instant reprimands that came with it.

A NICE BREAK

At the beginning of eighth grade, we got to apply the math and physics we had learned. Part of the new school was dedicated to vocational training. I do not know what the girls got to do, but the boys were put into two groups. One group worked with steel, the other with wood. Six weeks were set aside to let us get some hands-on experience. Every day we spent several hours at the shop. First we made a coat hook that mounted to a door. The crowning piece we made was a double candle holder.

As we all expected, none of us was allowed to jump into these projects headlong. First things first. We had to draw a blueprint. Even before that, we had to learn how to

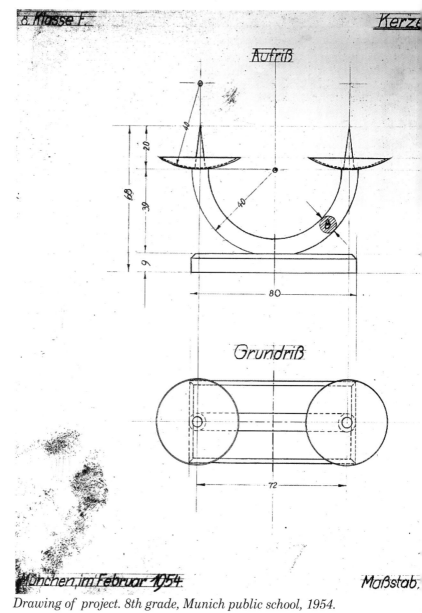

8. Klasse F.

Kerz

Aufriß

Grundriß

München, im Februar 1954

Maßstab

Drawing of project. 8th grade, Munich public school, 1954.

draw a blueprint. Strict attention was given to learning to write in a precise way that was to drafting standards. The height of letters above the baseline were to be seven

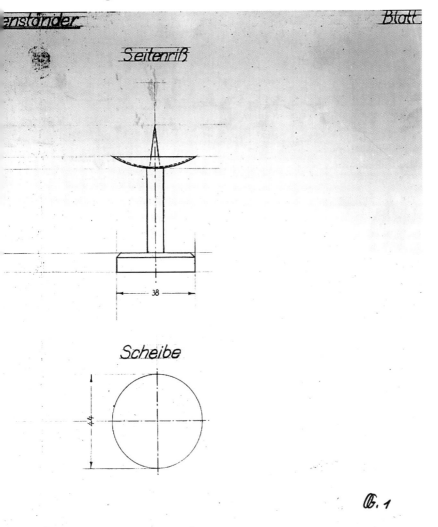

millimeters. Lower case letters were to be exactly four millimeters tall with the descenders dropping two millimeters below the baseline. All lettering was to be non cursive and written at an angle of seventy degrees leaning to the right. There was no use grumbling. If you did not pass that part, you were not allowed to start drawing the blueprint for the project. As for the lines on the blueprint, we had to learn to draw the proper thicknesses of lines and learn their purposes. A number two pencil was for the main lines of the object depicted. The harder lead pencils were for guide lines and lines that showed dimensions and such. Finally, we were assigned a work area. We each had a mounted vise and also were given a ruler, a file, a hacksaw, and a ballpeen hammer. We had to cut our steel from bar stock with the hacksaw, shape it with the ballpeen hammer, and dress it with the file. We got to polish parts with steel wool, and some we blackened over the open fire which we also used to soften the steel before bending. We used a brace-and-bit to drill a hole for a rivet. We made our own

Candle holder fashioned by hand in eighth grade.

rivet. Then we riveted the project together. I still have the blueprint and the end product. I am grateful to Mom and Dad for letting me bring some of my treasured things to America.

A NEW DAY IN THE WORLD OF SPORTS

At the beginning of the eighth grade, I was officially allowed to participate in sports for the first time in all my school years. I had been excused from strenuous, physical exercise since I was five years old due to an enlarged heart from childhood diseases. Schools at that time had no team sports but had gymnastics and track and field events for their students. All previous years, I did extra assignments or homework while all the other kids were in the gym or on the field. For the first time now, I coul run and jump with my friends.

One day while doing some warm-up running, I pulled something in my lower, groin area. A sharp, little sting was present as I jogged. After the warm-up, I went over to the physical education instructor and explained the pain to him. He told me not to worry about it. I had already signed up for the broad jump which was my favorite event. I was waiting for my turn to get to fly way into the sand pit and make a mark for myself. My spirit was ready when my turn came up. Approaching the sand pit, I was running as fast as I could, concentrating on the white board at the end of the narrow track from which I would take off to jump. At full speed, I had timed the jump so my right leg would be the one to push off. As I stepped on the white take-off marker and strained with everything in me to achieve the optimum thrust, something cracked. Instead of sailing through the air, I crashed into the sand face first. Somebody helped me up and half dragged me over to the side and out of the way. They placed me on the ground and propped me up against a building. From there I could have watched the event, but my pain was too great to see anything. Silently crying, I sat there waiting for the school day to end and be dismissed. No one came to check up on me that afternoon as I leaned against the wall.

It was only a quarter of a mile home, but that was the longest walk I ever took. I was dragging my injured leg and hopping on the other one slowly as I steadied myself along the buildings on the way. At the intersections, I had to muster extra strength to hobble across quickly. When I finally got to the door of our building, exhaustion and pain made me lose it all. I must have collapsed and passed out, because the only thing I remembered was some stranger carrying me up the stairs to our apartment.

While lying on my bed, I recall gripping the bedstead, agonizing with every jolt of pain as the torn muscle twitched. Mom had gone to get an ambulance. I do not know how this was done since no one I knew had a telephone. In any case, the paramedics arrived. They took one look and promptly gave me an injection. With the needle still in me, I passed out again. I remember hearing the sirens of the ambulance, but I do not remember being admitted to the hospital. When I woke up, I was in a room, in bed, lying on my back with a sand bag under my right knee. I was to lie there in that same position for the better part of five weeks. The doctor came to see me and showed me an x-ray of my injury. Apparently, when I took off to jump, the strained muscle gave way and snapped loose. That in turn put pressure on my femur. As the torso twisted for the take-off, the bone broke the socket in my hip. I'm sure my folks visited me once or twice while I lay there for weeks on end. It was too far for them to walk to the hospital. Anyway, I was in good hands. As far as the school and its physical education staff was concerned, they never mentioned my injury and probably really did not care.

The hospital I stayed in was known to be a very progressive one. It was a practice of the doctors and nurses there to force patients up and out of bed as soon as possible after an operation or childbirth. Patients who had an appendectomy or a hernia operation were seen walking the hall within two to three days. As for me, the exact opposite was true. I lay in bed absolutely motionless. Every time I moved my arms or even took a deep breath, the injured muscle jerked and sent out a sharp pain, which in turn made me stiffen my body, and that made the muscle twitch even more. It was awful the first couple of weeks on my back. The doctors decided that no corrective procedures were necessary, just to lie still was the order. I was told the bone and the hip socket would settle back to their proper position, and the fracture would fill in and heal given the right time. All in all, between crutches and rehabilitation, I missed six weeks of school.

During my stay at the hospital, several roommates occupied the other bed in the room. One man, about thirty-five years of age, was admitted one afternoon to have a hernia operation the next morning. The nurses, who were nuns, strictly warned the fellow not to drink anything after the evening meal. To a young chap like me, he was the perfect example of a person not doing as told. After a light meal that evening, he disobeyed the strict orders, left the room, and went to the nearest tavern for a couple of liters of beer. His operation went on the next morning as scheduled. While still under sedation, he was wheeled back to the room and put to bed. I watched all this. As he came to, he must have felt some extra discomfort for he called for a nurse. When she came, she asked him if he had drunk any liquid after supper the night before. He sheepishly admitted to doing so. She knew then what his problem was and promptly walked out of the room. Well, his belly was swelling; and the expansion was very visible to me. The day before he looked like a normal guy, but, looking over at him, I could see that he looked more pronounced around the mid section then a pregnant lady about to give birth. The man was in terrible pain. The gas on the inside of him was causing him to moan and writhe in agony. The nurses propped up his legs and put hot towels on his belly. Finally, the natural pressure valve let loose. Normally, sounds of that magnitude would have tickled me; but the nightmare I was witnessing just made me more resolute to follow orders from anyone, at all times, and to the letter.

WIESEN

The Octoberfest grounds were called The Wiesen, or pasture, by the inhabitants because, other than during the Octoberfest, it was nothing but a large grassy meadow with a few roads crossing it. For the most part, the Wiesen was encircled with a tree lined avenue. On one side of this vast open space was a grassy bank that led up to a portion of the city called the Schwanthaler Heights. On that side of the Wiesen was a large bronze statue, the Bavaria, that overlooked the grounds below. We lived just a few blocks behind the statue. In the winter, thousands of kids used the sloped banks leading to the flat area below as a sled-riding hill. I did the same. Keeping up with the other boys on the slope was often hard on me.

The Bavaria overlooking the Octoberfest grounds.

My chest would ache, and the pressure in it felt like it was ready to explode. So, I sat awhile on my sled until the pain subsided.

Being close to the Alps, there seemed to always be plenty of snow in Munich. We built snowmen and snow bunkers on the Wiesen and spent half the day making snowballs in case we were attacked.

I expressed to Dad the desire to learn to ski. Within a short period of time, he managed, somehow, to get me a pair of skis. For some reason, my skis were much longer and wider than anyone else's. Not only that, they had three grooves along the bottom instead of one. Once I got going down the slope, there was no stopping me; and nobody had better get in my path, because I sure could not swerve. I could do nothing but go straight and I could stop only when the hill flattened out. Later I found out that my skis were made for ski jumping only.

When mid-September came, even the natives' hearts welled up with excitement when the humongous tents started to be set up for the Octoberfest. The beginning of the festivities was started when the colorful, highly-decorated beer wagons, drawn by large teams of Clydesdale horses, rolled into the grounds. To me, it always was a big event just to see so many people in one place. There were food vendors, shooting galleries, and rides for all ages, from the carousel to bumper cars, Ferris wheels, and roller coasters. As kids, we seldom had any money to spend; but on occasion, Mom and Dad would buy a mug of beer, just to get to sit in one of those big tents and listen to the oom-pa-pah band. Each local brewery was represented with a huge tent which held tens of thousands of people. The Löwenbräu tent had a great big lion mounted in front over the massive entrance. The mechanical mascot said in a slow, low voice, "Lö - wen - bräu," after which the lion drank from the mug he held in one of his paws. In a different beer tent, a whole, full-grown steer was roasted on a spit. Visitors went to the front and had the butcher cut off the slice of meat they desired. The huge carcass slowly turned on the spit as it roasted over an open charcoal fire. Those days, barbecued meat was foreign to me. Now, in America, I know what I was seeing then. I can only imagine sitting there, eating German potato salad and a fresh roll with that roasted meat.

Another delicacy, I'm sure, was the charbroiled trout. The vendor simply had dug a trench in the ground in which a red hot charcoal fire was burning. Walking by, one could see and smell dozens of fresh trout, each on a spit, and stuck into the hot coals. They were called Steckerlfisch, or fish-on-a-stick.

My saliva really started to run when I walked past the roasting chickens. Great racks of hens on long spits were slowly roasting on a rotisserie over hot coals. I stood there watching those golden brown birds going round and round trying to get my fill on the smell. I guess the whole family agreed that we should treat ourselves to one of the roasted chickens. However, the ones on the spit were too expensive. So, Mom went to the local butcher and bought a hen. The best she could do was to brown it in a roasting pan in the oven. She fixed the best trimmings to go along. It was the first chicken I ever ate. It tasted good but was somewhat tough. We had a good feast that day. All of us placed the bones, after we chewed the good off, in a bowl. The next day Mom cooked a pot of soup with them.

BIG ENOUGH

Mom always had her chives growing on the window sill. The delicate, onion flavor made a great snack. Finely chopped, we sprinkled it on buttered, rye bread. If we had no butter, chives on bread, spread with lard, was just as tasty.

The beer radish was Munich's symbol of relaxation and home grown friendliness. The beer radish grew big, even to the size of a good-sized turnip. There were two varieties. Both grew to the same size and tasted the same, but one was white, and the other black-skinned. Radishes were always eaten raw. At times, we grated one to serve as a side dish with pork roast. Most of the time after it was peeled, the radish was sliced from the top to the root. Special care was taken not to slice all the way through. The slices were left attached at the root end. Carefully then, every slice was spread apart and salted. With salt between each slice, the radish was left to "cry" for five or ten minutes. The salt drew out some liquid, thus the term crying. After it cried, most of the pungent heat had soaked out. The radish was now ready to eat. Again, a real delicacy when eaten with buttered, rye bread.

Dad built a storage rack in the hall, just inside our entry door. On the floor, it had a box filled with sand that stored carrots, beets, radishes, and other root vegetables. The racks above the sand box were designed by Dad to hold and keep apples. He made the racks out of wood slats. We placed on it apples and such fruit as tomatoes, which were picked green just before the frost. The pieces of fruit were carefully placed so they did not touch each other. If one of the apples rotted, at least it did not contaminate the one next to it.

Once, Mom got a deal to buy one hundred fresh eggs at a good price. Eggs were a valued food, and we used them sparingly. Not having any refrigeration, we followed the advice and placed them in a pail of waterglass. I remember sticking my arm in that milky slush to get an egg. After the first month or so, the eggs started to taste and smell not too fresh. I do not know whether the so-called preservative penetrated the eggs' shells, or the eggs themselves started to decay naturally. In any case, we ate every last one of them.

The apartment had terrazzo floors throughout. For the cold times, Mom made rag rugs to put under the kitchen table and in front of the chairs and the sofa in the living room. We never started a fire in the bedroom heaters, just in the kitchen wood stove and in the living room stove. The heater in the living room was fired with a combination of fuel depending upon how fast and how hot we wanted it. Torf, dried slabs of peat moss, was used for a light, quick fire. Briquettes, which were coal dust molded and pressed to the shape of a brick, were the cheapest and were what we mostly burned. The heater in the living room was also designed to burn coal and even coke. Dad always had some coke stashed, and we burned it when company came on cold nights. It was truly amazing how much hotter coke burned than all other fuel.

A funny little story was told about a fuel wagon driver in those days. His horse, as well as all other horses, followed three basic commands. "Hüst" meant for the horse to turn left. "Hott" meant to turn right. "Brrrrr" meant to stop. As the fuel wagon rolled into your neighborhood, the driver would shout, as loud as he could, the items he was selling. "Kohlen - Torf - Briquettes." One poor man driving the wagon apparently did not sell many briquettes since he was afflicted with occasional bouts of stuttering. As he hollered to sell his wares and got to the word briquettes, the stammering of the br -br -br- would make his horse stop.

When my parents noticed that I had no trouble lugging home ten kilos of potatoes, they figured I was also big enough to get a hundred kilos of briquettes. The challenge made me strut. With money in hand, I walked to the coal yard. There I borrowed a two-wheeled cart. The wheels were as tall as I was, and the two legs on it were just under the two handlebars. When the cart was properly loaded, with most of the load being directly over the wheels, and a little extra weight on the handle side to keep the cart from flipping forward, I was ready to hit the road. Hey, this was a breeze. Once I got the cart rolling, it chattered along the cobblestones with ease. The real challenge came when I had to stop for traffic at the intersections. To keep from rolling right in front of an oncoming truck, I had to let myself be dragged by the cart to make it slow down. The two legs of the cart were wrought with iron straps, and they just slid over the cobblestones like they were greased. I was it, all ninety pounds of me, trying to slow down a contraption loaded down with over two hundred pounds of briquettes. My heart was pounding in my throat as I barely had gotten the thing stopped and escaped being hit by the truck. After that experience, the admiration of my own strength became suddenly second to the wisdom I had just obtained.

A SOLDIER'S SOLDIER

Dad was a truck driver. He hauled bulk goods, but often he also trucked kegs of beer and bar ice to cities other than Munich. Although every town in Bavaria had its own brewery, some of the major brands of brew out of Munich were sought after in other cities. The ice bars, about one meter long and twenty centimeters thick, were loaded in rows of ten, or so, with burlap in between the layers. The ice would always freeze together while being trucked, in which case Dad used an ice pick to separate the large bars of ice. The ice pick was long and sharp-pointed with a good sized wooden handle.

One day, Dad, with his massive arms and shoulders, was chopping when the wooden handle came off. The pick remained stuck in the ice. He did not notice this. While vigorously in the chopping motion, he slammed his fist, holding but the handle, down onto the rusted spike sticking out of the ice. The spike went in his palm on one side and came out near his thumb. The hospital gave him a tetanus injection and took x-rays to see if any bones in his hand were damaged.

To the surprise of the doctors, Dad's right hand had oversized knuckles and was full of shrapnel. Dad also showed me his neck, which was full of scars and shrapnel as well. On his back, likewise, was a large lump. All of the scarred areas had fragments of exploded metal shells imbedded in them. The large lump of steel on his back was lodged very close to his spine. The scar, the size of a hen egg, indicated where the fragment entered. It entered about ten centimeters away from where it was now lodged.

Dad told me stories of his days in the military. He had joined the Luftwaffe in 1939 when he was eighteen. He was soon transferred to the army. Like in all military

Alfons Pfisterhammer in 1939, a soldier's soldier.

training around the world, Germany was no different. The first thing a soldier must learn is to understand that by himself he is nothing. He is to depend on leadership and follow orders. While in the German army's basic training, he was told, after doing something wrong, to climb a tree and shout at the top of his lungs: "I am the dumbest jackass of the 20th century." To be reminded where a trainee stands in the chain of command, all recruits had to go through such humbling experiences at times. Another ego dismantling tactic that was used was to have a recruit, with hands behind his back and feet together, fall face first into a mud puddle.

Dad told of a story at boot camp where he slept in the top bunk. He woke up one night really thirsty. The fellow below him always kept a glass of water on his night stand. Not wanting to make the trip to the water spigot, Dad reached for the glass below. He took a good slug and then felt something bump his lips. Not giving it much thought, he pitched the remaining water out the window. Early next morning he heard a despairing cry, "Where are my teeth?–Where are my teeth?" "Look out the window," Dad said, as he left the room.

Apparently, during his brief stay in France, Dad had a sergeant in charge who was particularly gung-ho and obnoxious. Several members of his troop planned retribution against this fellow. A couple of men, one of them Dad, were set to ship out the next morning. The evening before, as was determined earlier, they intercepted the sergeant's daily routine, and covered him with a blanket as he stepped around a dark corner on his way back from the beer hall. While one or the other made sure the blanket kept his head covered, the men thoroughly worked him over.

Dad was shipped to the eastern front. On one of his earlier assignments in combat, he almost got killed. He was ordered to slither into a river unnoticed, swim under water to the other side, and sneak back into the shadows of trees at water's edge. His assignment was to ease his way to the enemy lines, stake out the enemy's position, and if possible, destroy their main gun. Having done the spying while it was still daylight, he decided to crawl into a wheat field and take a nap until it was dark enough to take care of the artillery piece. Laying there asleep, (I wonder if he snored even then) he was pounced on by a Russian officer. The man jumped astride Dad and clamped both hands around his throat. The only thing Dad could do at that instant was to reach up and begin choking the man on top of him as well. They were locked in a life and death struggle, and only a few seconds determined who was to black out first. When the Russian did, Dad completed the struggle by using the Teller mine (a round mine with a handle like on a skillet) for the final blow. Later, he used the same mine to blow up the big, Russian gun.

Hand-to-hand combat was when the antagonists could see the whites of each other's eyes. To be in physical combat with the enemy for one day is demanding enough. Dad had one stretch of hand-to-hand combat that lasted nine straight days.

The trenches that were to fortify a stronghold never ran in straight lines. Overwhelming, a Russian position often included clearing of trenches and eliminating foxholes and other obstacles. A foxhole with a machine gunner was wiped out by running a tank over the hole and doing a 360 degree turn right over it. It was swift, and the poor occupant simply was buried alive. Conquering the trenches was equally hazardous for the aggressor as well as the defendant. Around every bend, potential death was always lurking. A long rifle during trench battles was a bit awkward, so Dad left it behind at camp. Maneuvering with only his revolver was much easier. On one occasion, with his pistol drawn, he jumped into a trench and moved around the first corner, and heard the metallic click of a rifle. A Russian soldier was squatting there waiting for him. His weapon had misfired. Dad quickly pulled the trigger of his pistol–click–also a misfire. In a mere split second, the Russian came up out of his crouch-

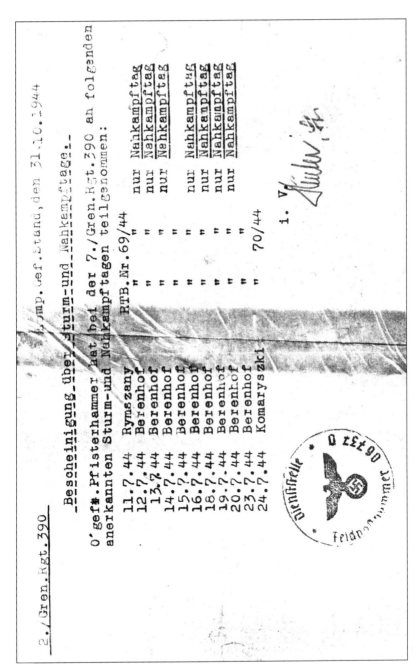

Hand to hand combat days. Compare to days wounded.

ing position, thrusting his bayonet at Dad's body. Instinctively, Dad lunged forward and to his side, barely missing being gored. All in the same motion, he reached for his spade, which he said he kept razor sharp, and with a mighty swipe dispatched the soldier, striking him just below the helmet.....

BESITZZEUGNIS

DEM .... Obergefreiten ....
(DIENSTGRAD)

.... , fisterhammer
(VOR- UND ZUNAME)

7./G.R. 390
(TRUPPENTEIL)

VERLEIHE ICH DAS

INFANTERIE-STURMABZEICHEN

IN SILBER

Rgts.Gef.Std., den 22.August 1944
(ORT UND DATUM)

Tauur
(UNTERSCHRIFT)

Oberstleutnant u. Rgts.Kommandeur
(DIENSTGRAD UND DIENSTSTELLUNG)

The medal received for Hand-to-Hand combat.

Dad was a machine gunner. The Germans had fought their way deep into Russia. The German fighting force was spending much time near the city of Leningrad, now St. Petersburg. Dad spoke of Lake Ladoga and the eventual push toward Moscow. The German forces must have had plenty of resistance at times because Dad's company had been practically annihilated four times. Each time he was one of a handful of men out of two hundred or more who survived the combat.

At times, his company had to retreat, marching daily from sunup till dark. The marching made the feet and toes bleed and soaked with blood whatever was left of the socks.

The German troops were getting their regular monthly stipend, but, other than cigarettes, they really had no way to spend their money in Russia. He told a story of a time when his sparse squad, on such a retreat, negotiated to purchase a pig from a Russian farmer. That evening they quickly killed the pig, dressed it out, and cooked it in a wash kettle over an open fire. Since there was not enough bread to go around during this feast, they ate the lean meat as bread and the fat of the hog as meat.

After a short night of sleep, the forced march continued. Dad said that morning that everyone who had participated in the devouring of the pig had gotten a bad case of diarrhea. A forced march is just what it is called. There was no stopping or falling out of formation for any reason other than one ordered by the commander. Dad recalled that the day after the feast, all he and many others could do was march and answer the call of nature at the same time. With belt unbuckled, the left hand held the breeches above the waist while the right hand held the rifle resting on the right shoulder. Every couple hundred steps or so, he just yanked his pants down, did a quick kneebend to relieve the urge, then jumped back up and in the same motion pulled his pants back up. No more than one or two extra strides, and he was back in formation with the rest of the men. This scene continued on until one of two things stopped: the urge or the march.

The region of Leningrad is on about the sixtieth latitude. It has the same length of Arctic days and nights as has Anchorage, Alaska. In the summer you can watch the sun go down, and in a short time watch it come up again. In the dead of winter, it is almost always dark and bitterly cold.

The envy of many German foot soldiers was the boots of Russian officers. Dad found a pair of these boots still on the frozen, mostly buried, body in the snow. Desperate for better shoes, he cut the legs off. This he could not have done were it not for the everlasting cloak of ice and snow that had covered that poor soul. Dad thawed the flesh and pulled it from the boots.

A machine gunner was the key to keeping the front line secure. Dad had been dug in on top of a knoll in a hole deep enough to stand in. The eyes were just at the correct level to enable him to peer over the rim of earth all around his machine gun nest. His hole was big enough to sit and eat in as well as curl up and sleep. The body waste was pitched out with the trenching spade. A machine gun nest was a wicked instrument of war, highly valued by the defender and terribly feared by those attacking. A German machine gun was much superior to the enemy's. The sound of one was a rapid rrrrrrrrrrrrrrrrrr rather than that of a Russian gun that fired much fewer rounds per burst. During an attack by the Russians, Dad always had at least one private with him to keep a continuous feed of ammunition going into the gun. The barrel of the machine gun would get so hot it glowed red. At that point, a new barrel was popped in place and hardly a round was missed. An ironic fact of life was that my real Father was not drafted into the Army until 1943 because he helped design and build these top secret trigger mechanisms that were now being used to keep the man alive who was later to become my stepfather.

The Russians counter-attacked by the thousands. Rows of hundreds of men, armed with rifle and bayonet, came up the hill charging toward the machine gunner.

Dad had no choice but to mow them all down. Minutes later, a new wave of soldiers crawled to the dead and wounded and gathered up their rifles. At a command, they all jumped up with rifle in hand to charge a little closer. Dad sawed them down again. This scene happened again and again until all available men that day were spent. Truly, there is no beauty in war.

Runners brought food and ammunition to the gunner. These runners were the only connection to the rest of the company. When one who brings food gets killed, dire acts of reprisal are needed. An enemy tank had been stationed on a railroad embankment straddling the tracks. It had its guns trained on anything and anybody who ventured across the rails as well as on all else that moved. Evidently the man who brought Dad's provisions must have wandered within range of the tank. Food had stopped coming to the front for the second day. This was not the first time the tank had wreaked havoc. Some revenge was needed, not only to honor the men who had been killed by the tank but, perhaps more importantly, so Dad could survive.

It does not surprise me that Dad took it upon himself to eliminate the menace. He spied on the tank, its men, and all their activities with his field glasses. After several days, he set out to destroy. He encountered a guard in a culvert under the rail track. No shots were fired. In silence, one more young and inexperienced life had to be eliminated. When Dad told this story, he always mentioned that at all times he carried one additional hand grenade on his belt. It was not for use on the enemy, but for Dad to do away with himself in case he got captured by the Russians. He swore he would never be taken alive and be subjected to torture and starvation. During this mission, he must have thought there was a good chance he was not going to make it. However, with the guard gone, the rest of the mission was capped off after dark. Dad snuck onto the tank and dropped a bundle of four grenades through the top of the turret, jumped off quickly, and rolled down the railroad embankment.

What the foot soldiers and the tank were unable to do,

a sharp shooter, who entered into this drama of life and death, was now trying to do. Another one of Dad's runners had been shot. Dad could not pinpoint where the shots were coming from. He knew it was a Russian sharpshooter nested somewhere about five-hundred meters away. Never once did Dad forget that he was the machine gunner, at all times one of the prized and primary targets himself. The German helmet, which he wore at all times, had a lip protruding around the lower edge, perhaps to divert the rain from running down the soldier's neck. However, one morning, standing up in his foxhole, looking to the rear, perhaps all the way back to his home land, Dad experienced a sharp tap on his helmet. Immediately, he felt a burning in his neck. Reaching up with his hand, he discovered blood. Upon inspecting his helmet, he found that an explosive bullet had hit the very tip of the lip on his helmet. One half of the fragments went over the top of the helmet, the other into his neck.

I saw the many scars on Dad's neck and also knew the fragments were still imbedded. I thank God today that life and death is not only called by inches, but death even comes as close as a millimeter. If that bullet had hit just a bit lower, I would have never had a Hero in my life. . . .

A fierce cat and mouse game ensued after that. The sharp shooter was constantly popping shots at Dad and his runners. Dad spoke of how good and very careful the sharp shooter was in not disclosing his position. It took the last glimmer of sunlight one day to reflect off his scope as he, most likely, was leaving his post in the trees. With that small flicker, Dad now had a target. He immediately pumped an unrelenting volley of machine gun rounds into the tree and below it. He knew his weapon was not a long range rifle but hoped one of the thousands of bullets would get the culprit. It did.

But, was that the end of the war? What will the enemy try next? With desperation mounting on both sides, the Germans mined the fields in front of their main encampment. The mine field was behind and around the machine gunners who were about a thousand meters apart forming the German front. Only the food and ammo runners knew their way through the mines.

The Russians now were bringing up heavy artillery. They began to lob shells all around Dad's dugout. Things were getting tougher. A lot of heat was being applied. Believing in God's ultimate wisdom, I know this was the beginning of the end of Dad's life as an animal. After three or more years on the Russian front, he had been reduced to living like an animal. Killing became routine. Human dignity had been shattered and backed into the deepest corner of his mind. Only the keen awareness of death, creeping ever closer, was the reality.

Then it came. A big gun shell hit so close to him that he was knocked unconscious. When he regained his awareness, he found himself in utter darkness, almost buried in loose dirt. In his torn right hand, he could feel only the wooden stock of his weapon. Dad was blind. Lying there with mortar shells going off all around, he assessed his plight. He must make a run for it. He did not want to lie in that hole and wait for a Russian tank to do

Wounded by grenade in the buttocks, neck, back, and right hand.

a 360° on him. Not being able to see, he had to orient himself by the sounds of the weapons around him. He crawled out of the hole and started running toward friendly fire. The Russians had him now. Stumbling, rolling, and falling into mortar pits, Dad braved his way toward his friends. Shells were going off all around him,

BESITZZEUGNIS

DEM

Obergefreiten Alfons M i s t e r h a m m e r

(NAME, DIENSTGRAD)

7./Gren.Rgt. 39o

(TRUPPENTEIL, DIENSTSTELLE)

IST AUF GRUND

SEINER AM 12. 7.44, 13. 7.44 **ERLITTENEN**

drei MALIGEN VERWUNDUNG – BESCHÄDIGUNG
23. 7.44

DAS

VERWUNDETENABZEICHEN

IN S i l b e r

VERLIEHEN WORDEN.

Dresden , DEN 21. 9. 1944

(UNTERSCHRIFT)

(DIENSTGRAD UND DIENSTSTELLE)

Oberſtabsarzt u. Chefarzt

The medal received for being wounded.

202

and several times he was knocked flat with shrapnel in his back and buttocks.

The next thing he remembered, he was propped up in a side car of a motorcycle, going across the Russian plains. His head, backside and hands all bandaged-up. The driver was making a mad dash over the country side which had no roads. Dad was in pain beyond description. He spoke of trying to brace himself, planting his feet and grasping the handle grips in an effort to relieve the agony that the pounding caused in his bottom that was full of bits of metal. By the time they got to the train station, his knees were raw from the jarring ride.

A Lazaretzug, a train full of wounded and dying men, finally headed west. The cattle cars were full of the wounded lying on straw. After many hours, the train stopped just outside of Dresden. When another Lazaret train passed them and went on into the city, the men were dismayed and began grumbling. After all, they had arrived first. Once again, I know that the Good Shepherd took care of Dad and that train he was on, because the train that passed them and went on into the city was totally wiped out during a bombing raid on Dresden.

Dad spent the good part of two months in the hospital. The doctors removed shrapnel from one eye. The other eye had suffered shock from the explosion and flying earth. During the stay in the hospital, a violinist came to soothe and cheer up the wounded. Dad was lying there in darkness. He recalled a tune played by the violinist, which haunted him the rest of his life. The melody was "La Paloma." His encrusted heart must have softened that day. It must have brought him out of the long nightmare of killing and surviving, a period where humanity was gone, and evil was warring in him.

Over the years I witnessed so much love and tenderness in him, and I know the touching melodies of the violinist must have started his road back to compassion. I can still see a tear in Dad's eyes when Mom played "La Paloma" on her concertina. Life is not fair, but God is gracious, Dad's eyesight slowly returned during the stay at the hospital in Dresden. He was awarded an extra stripe and three citations, one for hand-to-hand combat, one for being wounded three times, and the Iron Cross. Was it worth it? Looking back–war is madness!

Dad liked to listen to music. He spoke of a Christmas Eve, on the front line in Russia, when all fighting sudden-

IM NAMEN DES FÜHRERS

VERLEIHE ICH
DEM

Obergefreiten Alfons Pfisterham····,

7./Gren.Rgt.390

DAS
EISERNE KREUZ
2. KLASSE

Div.Gef.St., 31. Juli 19 44

Generalleutnant u. Div.-Kommandeur.

(DIENSTGRAD UND DIENSTSTELLUNG)

"In the name of the Führer" (translated), Iron Cross presented to Dad.

ly stopped while a trumpeter played "Silent Night, Holy Night." For one hour after that, neither side fired a single shot. What a time-out!

Dad was given a two-week vacation which he spent with his mother in Munich. His half-brother Willi and he took on the job of stealing potatoes for their mother. They rode bicycles, with solid rubber tires, to the outskirts of the city. There in the moonlight they crawled into a potato field to fill their sacks. This stealing business was not just a one-day affair because their sacks never were filled. It seemed like, no sooner did they get started stealing than someone else came to do the same. Not knowing who it was, the owner or the police, they always had to get out of there in a hurry. One night, after hurriedly leaving the potato patch, Uncle Willi realized his ring was missing. Digging in the dirt for potatoes was actually a good way to lose a ring. Waiting until the wee hours of the morning, they returned to the field and tried to find the ring. Entering the field in about the area where they were grobbling earlier, they started their search. While walking between the potato vines in the very first row, Uncle Willi saw in the moonlight a small sparkle on the ground. It was his ring.

A DIFFERENT BATTLE

After he reported back to duty, Dad was shipped to the western front near Aachen. He witnessed a troop of German soldiers using a team of oxen to pull a tank into firing position. The tank's guns were needed at the front, but diesel fuel was no longer available. He also witnessed the overwhelming superiority of fire power of the American forces.

As sergeant, he summoned his men and spoke to them of the end of the war, which was surely to come soon. He reminded them that they still had their arms and legs and that resisting any longer could be all of their doom. He warned them that when on guard duty they should absolutely not fire their weapon.

Dad warned some of his younger recruits that at night, looking at an object too intently, will make it come alive. He said fear in your heart will play tricks on your eyes. That very night, one of the guards, a sixteen-year old boy, was assigned to guard some of the equipment and the dug-in men. For whatever reason, the boy fired one shot. This single shot was followed by a four-hour artillery barrage which leveled at least a twenty-five acre forest. The sixteen year old never returned. The rest of the men stayed dug-in. Soon they all were captured by the Americans.

When Dad was ordered out of the trench by the captors, it was raining. They searched all his pockets and took everything in them. In addition to his offensive weapons, they took his pocket knife, his medals, and even a wet cigar. Taking the wet cigar really irked Dad. He could see them taking his weapons, even his pocket knife, the medals as a souvenir, but the wet cigar?

The prisoner-of-war camp was very crowded. Being caged up and surrounded by barbed wire worked on all of them. Many had acquired a smoking habit and were now feeling the effects of their missing nicotine. I guess many stories were exchanged, and Dad soon became known as a man with guts. One prisoner approached him to make a deal with the GI guards to trade the man's watch for cigarettes. Dad was adamant about the man keeping his watch. Knowing the time of day was one of the last luxuries they had. Desire prevailed, so Dad secretly devised a plan. He picked a place in the compound where the building came closest to the rolls of barbed wire that encircled the camp. Dad removed the band from the watch, then placed the watch in an empty matchbox. He walked outside and waited for the guard to come by making his rounds. After getting the guard's attention, he slid the matchbox open to show the watch and said, "Cigarettes?" It just took a few gestures in improvised sign language to come to an agreement of two cartons of cigarettes for the watch. Not long after, the guard returned with his part of the deal. Dad walked to the wire, showed the man the box, shook it to his ear to make sure it had its content, and held it over the fence for the fellow to take while he grabbed the two cartons. Very quickly Dad dashed around the corner of the barracks. The men inside heard some furious cursing going on outside after the gullible guard discovered that he just swapped a bunch of cigarettes for a rock. Hot water and shaving cream were waiting for Dad. In an ensuing line-up, the culprit was never identified.

All soldiers are taught, whether in the German or American Army, that upon capture, a plan of escape must be devised. Usually the chance of escape is greatest when first captured and when the facilities of encampment are more primitive. Soon after the watch caper, Dad was approached by a fellow prisoner to cut the fence that encircled the camp. This proposal and consequent deal were kept secret between Dad and the dealer. Apparently, the fellow had somehow obtained the tools to escape, but had not the guts to actually try it. The proposition to Dad was, that if he would cut the fence, he would be given a civilian suit and new identification papers. Dad weighed the proposal at length. How was it possible for this captive to come into possession of not only the suit and papers but also the wire cutters? Finally, Dad agreed to do the job. He had one condition–that he was to be the first through the fence. This act could cost him his life. Much planning and calculation on his part alone was mulled over and over. The moon had to be right. The lighting of the compound had to be in his favor. The clothes he wore while cutting had to be as camouflaged as possible. The guards and their habits and demeanor had to be studied. It was the hope that one of the several easygoing guards would be on duty that night. After the job, his suit had to be laid out and close to the hole in the fence. Dad calculated that one round of the walking guard did not give him enough time to complete the task and escape before the cut fence was discovered. His plan was to cut through most of the many layers of spiral and other strands of barbed wire and place them back into their original position, all the while inching himself further through the fence, ready to lie flat and fool the passing guard.

The night came. The guard had just passed and was out of earshot, snipping began, muffled with a rag. The cutting was easy, but getting his muscular body through, and keeping the wire looking like nothing was going on was difficult. All too soon, Dad again heard the whistling of the guard as he slowly approached the spot where Dad now lay. Wearing layers of pure tattered rags, Dad prostrated himself as low as he could go, hiding his hands and face in the dirt. The guard stopped his whistling. He walked closer to the dark, strange mass lying between the rolls of barbed wire. Dad had seen him take his rifle off his shoulder as he came near. He could hear the guard's breath in the still of the night as the man stood contemplating where that strange large bundle, in the middle of the fence, had come from. Dad could sense the question he asked himself: "Was this here before?" After several long moments, the guard turned and continued on his round. When the whistling began again, he snipped in earnest. Using his supplied leather glove, he bent back the clipped strands to create a large hole. After all, he did not want to tear his new suit or get it dirty. That night, ninety-five men escaped.

None of us ever asked Dad how many days he was free after the escape. What those still in the prison had to say about the escape reached Dad's ears in a round about way. He was told that the fellow responsible for cutting the fence was a spy and that he was shot for his crime. Dad's new ID and his civilian clothes served him well but not for long. One night in Holland he was arrested for breaking curfew. He did not know that a curfew was imposed. A young American soldier, with rifle in hand, ordered Dad to follow him to his commander for further action. The young man walked ahead of Dad to lead the way. How easy it would have been for a seasoned fighting man to subdue this civil person. But why? The war surely would be over soon. I guess Dad was tired of blood and death.

The U.S. commander he was introduced to that night was a naturalized U.S. citizen from Bavaria. The American spoke to him in perfect dialect. It was determined however, that Dad was a German soldier. He was soon sent to England as a prisoner of war. While there, he worked on a farm until 1947. He brought nothing back from England except a dislike for potatoes. Dad came home to rubble and despair. He had given eight years of his life to a cause that he did not devise but had to endure if he was to survive.

THE REST OF THE MAN

There were few other tales Dad told about his life before the war. As a child, born out of wedlock and raised by his aunt, he did little but work on a farm. The education he received was haphazard since he had a penchant for playing hooky. He told me he used to like to sit on a hill overlooking the school. He and his pal enjoyed throwing turnips onto the school's roof.

Dad loved eggs. As an indentured farm hand, he found himself stealing an egg daily. You see, initially the missing egg was questioned, but, thereafter it was assumed that one hen had quit laying. So, he simply had to keep sucking an egg each day.

GETTING READY FOR LIFE

Being a child was fun at times, but being thrown into the life of adulthood in such a seemingly sudden way was pretty rough on a kid.

Getting ready for the rest of your life was the direction every thirteen year old had to face. In the sixth grade, a few kids departed from basic schooling to enter higher, academic studies. These kids were expected to pursue professional careers. As for the rest of us, our teacher made it clear that this was the last year of school, and after that, all of us had to be learning a skill in the world of work. We were advised, with the help of our parents, to choose a trade or skill we wanted to learn. There was no way out. No just hanging around and mooching off your folks. This was it, a time to get started. In order to get an interview with a prospective employer, we had to have a copy of an employment application, a transcript of

Beißer Franz Xaver, München, den 16. März 1954.
Volksschüler,
München 12,
Gollierstraße 32/III.

Lebenslauf.

Am 12. April 1940 wurde ich in München geboren. Mein Vater Beißer F. X., der gefallen ist, ist am 29.2.1908 in München geboren. Er war Feinmechaniker. Meine Mutter, geborene Frieda Baumann, verwitwete Beißer, seit 1950 verheiratete Pfisterhammer, wurde am 13.9.1915 geboren und ist Kellnerin. Mein Stiefvater heißt Alfons Pfisterhammer, er wurde am 27.5.1921 geboren und ist Fernfahrer. Ich habe eine zehnjährige Schwester. Wir sind alle katholisch.
Am 1. September 1946 begann ich meine Schulzeit. Bis zur vierten Klasse wohnten wir im Rottal. Seitdem gehe ich in eine Münchner Schule. Ferner besuche ich schon drei Jahre den Zentralzeichenkurs, drei Jahre den Englisch- und zwei Jahre den Kurzschriftunterricht.
Die Kinderkrankheiten habe ich schon alle hinter mir. Seit vier Jahren

kenne ich keine schwere Krankheiten
mehr. Auch die Familie ist gesund.
Meine Freizeit gestalte ich im
Sommer durch Schwimmen und Radl=
turen, im Winter durch Skifahren und
Eisstockschießen. Bei schlechten Tagen be=
schäftige ich mich gerne durch Zeichnen
und Bastelarbeiten.

Franz Xaver Beißer.

*Personal history statement. It lists father, mother, stepfather, sister.
It also states that I began school in '46, had all my childhood diseases, the family is healthy, and lists my hobbies.*

the latest report card, and a resume. To make a copy of
these documents meant that they had to be hand copied,
then validated. We were on our own with this project. It
was understood that clear, crisp lettering was expected by
a prospective employer and that the presentation of documents was a direct reflection upon character. I made
about six hand-written copies of each document. Some I
sent by mail. With the others in hand, I simply jumped on
my bike and personally delivered them to the personnel
officers of prospective employers. One firm I was hoping to
impress was F. Bruckmann, Verlag, a company that printed high quality books and full color catalogs. I was particularly interested in obtaining an apprenticeship position
in the four-color engraving department. There I could
develop my artistic ability. The personnel director, Herr
Daschner, asked to see my portfolio of drawings. I was
ecstatic to get this opportunity to show off my stuff. Having a feel for proportions and color, I could make any
painting look fairly good. Mr. Daschner, however, pointed
out many flaws, thereby helping me improve my drawing
skills. I strongly felt that his interest in my drawings
would have a positive effect. He suggested that I sketch
objects around the house, things like scissors, shoes, hats,
cups, utensils, and the like. For the next half year, I was

Abschrift

Schuljahr 1953/54
8. Schülerjahrgang

Zeugnis

für   Beißer Franz Xaver

1. Halbjahr				
Der anständige Junge könnte bei noch größerem Einsatz nach bessere Leistungen aufweisen.				

2. Halbjahr					
Benotung	1. Halbjahr	2. Halbjahr		1. Halbjahr	2. Halbjahr
Religionslehre	3		Rechnen und Raumlehre	2	
Deutsche Sprache	2		Zeichnen und Werken	1	
Schrift	3		Turnen und Sport	2	
Singen	2		Mädchen - Handarbeit	1	
Heimat - Erdkunde	2		Knaben - Handarbeit	2	
Geschichte - Sozialkunde	3		Englische Sprache	3	
Naturkunde	2		Kurzschrift	2	
Hauswirtschaft	/				
Versäumnisse schuldlos	9		Versäumnisse schuldhaft	/	

Unterschriften: 1. II. 1954

Schulleitung: gez.: Ziegelmaier

Klaßlehrer (in): gez.: M. Kürzl

Erziehungs-
berechtigte(r): gez.: Pfisterhammer

Notenstufen: 1 = sehr gut, 2 = gut, 3 = befriedigend, 4 = ausreichend, 5 = nicht ausreichend.

Den Gleichlaut der Abschrift mit dem Original-
zeugnis bestätigt:
München, den 17. März 1954

Ziegelmaier
Der Rektor der Volksschule
an der Bergmannstraße 36
München 12

Hand copied and notarized report card as part of my resume.

to report to him once a month, on a day I had no school, to show the new drawings. He often pointed out defects in perspective and missing shadows, and he always stressed the awareness of the light source and highlights it created. I was unaware at that time that he was preparing me for an exam.

Beißer Franz Xaver,　München, den 17. März 1954.
　　Volksschüler,
　　München 12,
　　Gollierstraße 32/III.

An die
Chemigraphische
Kunstanstalt,
A. Gässler u. Co,
München 15,
Landwehrstraße 57-59.

Betreff:　Bewerbung um eine Lehrstelle als
　　　　Graphiker.

　　　　　　　　　Am 15. Juli 1954 wer-
　　　　　　　de ich aus der 8. Klas-
Anlagen:　　　se der Volksschule in
　1. Lebenslauf,　München entlassen.
　2. Zeugnisabschrift.　Ich möchte mich bei
　　　　　　　ihrer Firma um eine
　　　　　　　Lehrstelle bewerben, da
　　　　　　　ich gehört habe, daß
　　　　　　　in ihrer Firma die
　　　　　　　Lehrbuben gut aus-

Cover letter and job application

The city of Munich had 4,000 young persons apply for 800 apprenticeship positions in the graphic arts field. The top qualifiers got the positions which required the most skills. The pre-press apprentice programs of top skill requirements were: color photoengraver, color photographer, black and white photoengraver, and proofer.

During this time of job preparation, I was attending eighth grade in full swing. The teacher's warning had proved to be accurate: life was getting tougher. However, in due time, Mr. Daschner recommended me to the city of Munich to be included in their annual testing program. This particular test was the one to see who would enter an apprenticeship program, approved by the city and the printing industry. The test was an all day affair, for which I reported early one morning. The first segment of testing was the study and drawing of objects. There were, perhaps, more than a hundred kids each sitting at a small desk in a large hall. A man carrying a cardboard box walked down the rows of applicants pulling out objects to be drawn. He placed one at the corner of my desk. All of us taking the test were instructed not to touch, just look and draw what was placed before us. My object was the white queen from a chess set. The lighting in the big room was difficult, to say the least. In addition to the overhead lights there was a long row of windows to our right. We were given paper and a pencil and told we had two hours to draw the object placed in front of us. Aside from the basic shape of the piece, I studied the varied castings of shadows the many windows made. I searched the dominant light reflections off the piece as well as the many refractions as they broke up the shadows. I was also aware that, although the object was small, the level of view changed. The top of the figure was almost level to my eyes, while I was looking somewhat down at its base. All these intricacies had been pointed out by Mr. Daschner over the past six months. I was truly grateful for his help as I quietly proceeded to sketch the small figurine.

We had to draw some other basic shapes that morning. The afternoon was devoted to testing our knowledge of math, science, and language.

After that gruelling day, I waited a month to hear the

Sample of drawing for Herr Daschner.

Pencil drawing of my one and only bike.

results. Finally, a letter came in the mail, requesting that I report, on a given day and time, to the city's department of labor. I assumed it was to learn of the outcome. I still had no guarantee of a job. A good enough grade from that all-day exam was the passport to being accepted into a field I had chosen. As I sat in the waiting room, angst almost overwhelmed me, especially when all the boys with names starting lower in the alphabet than mine came out of the office with their heads hung low. Finally, my name was called to enter the room where I just knew I would receive my sentence of failure. I did not know I could go from such a low to an unbelievable high when I was handed my grade. It was almost more than I could take. I was the first that morning to get a qualifying grade to enter the field of photoengraving. Walking as in a cloud, I entered the waiting room again, smiling. I know I gave many still waiting a new hope, a hope in the knowledge that someone had made it, and maybe they would also.

With the new document in hand, Mr. Daschner introduced me to Mr. Hegele.

DO IT AGAIN, FRANZ

Mr. Hegele was the master engraver in charge of all the apprentices, journeymen, and other master engravers. I found out that the firm only hired one color photoengraver per year, and I was the one. At age fourteen, my work week was six days long with Thursday designated as a technical-support and related-chemistry day. We spent that day not at the plant but in a school room. The rest of the week, I was the low man on the totem pole. I was expected to get to work before anyone else and leave in the afternoon after Mr. Hegele had left. It was my duty, at the end of the day, to wait for Mr. Hegele with his coat draped over my arm and his hat in my hand. I remember always holding the coat for him so he could simply slip his arms into it as I pulled the coat up to his shoulders. In the winter time, I did the same with his topcoat but added an extra service to the ritual. After I helped him pull the topcoat to his shoulders, I reached under it from behind and pulled his jacket down in case it had gotten crumpled up while putting on the topcoat.

My pay was eleven marks and fifty-four pennies per week. Most of that went to cover lunch in the cafeteria. The rest, anywhere from fifty cents to a dollar in American money, was hard to spend. After all, I was a high-living fellow. The benefits of the early training in a skill were twofold. One, the company could afford a small stipend for someone who was really non-producing, the other was that, I was young enough not to have much need for money. Just think, if in the U.S. a fellow could learn a skill before he had a girlfriend, a cigarette or beer habit, before he had to make payments on a car and its insurance, before marriage plans and having the need for a place to live, many would not be wandering aimlessly after high school.

I rode my bike to work, riding in good as well as bad weather. A poncho covered me when it rained. Getting the front tire caught in the trolley track was an ever present

Ausgeführte Arbeit	Std.	Muster Skizze Nr.	Ausgeführte Arbeit	Std.	Muster Skizze Nr.
MONTAG			**DONNERSTAG**		
Brotzeit geholt	1 1/2		Schule		
Brotzeit gemacht	1/2		Eine Katze, einen Hahn		
Rot gedeckt und geätzt	5		und ein Pferd gezeich-		
Für Herrn ... schmer	1		net.		
Brot geholt			Rechenprobe		
Putzen und Sauber-	1 1/2		In Bürgerkunde über		
machen			den Lehrvertrag gespro-		
			chen.		
			Fachkunde nachgeschrie-		
			ben		
	9 1/2				
DIENSTAG			**FREITAG**		
Brotzeit geholt	1 1/2		Brotzeit geholt	1 1/2	
Brotzeit gemacht	1/2		Brotzeit gemacht	1/2	
Gelbplatte geätzt	5 1/2		Blauplatte gedeckt	1 1/2	
Altes Klischee erneuert	1/2		Terpentin geholt	1	
Wegen Dämmerung			Alles putzen und sau-	3	
Putzen und Reinigung	1 1/2		bermachen		
			Schwarzplatte gedeckt,	2	
			korrigiert und geätzt		
	9 1/2			**9 1/2**	
MITTWOCH			**SONNABEND**		
Rotplatte gedeckt	1/2		Brotzeit geholt	2 1/2	
Blauplatte eines neuen			Brotzeit gemacht	1/2	
Teppich gedeckt	3 1/2		Schwarzplatte gedeckt	2 1/2	
Brotzeit geholt	1 1/2		Putzkammer vertreten	1 1/2	
Brotzeit gemacht	1/2				
Altes Klischee erneuert	2				
Benzin geholt.	1/2				
Putzen und reinigen	1				
	9 1/2			**7**	

Sample of weekly log shows 9 1/2 hour days, 45 hours at work, plus a full day at a trade school for related subjects, for a total of 53 hours per week at age 14.

danger. Once a tire got into that rut, it was always a sure thing to have a wreck trying to get out of it. It was better just to slow down, jump off the bike, and get on safer ground.

Mr. Daschner had his own private office where he was free to snack at his leisure. Often he would send for me to get him a fresh baked loaf of rye bread. His favorite bakery was a few kilometers from work. I was happy to jump on my bike and do that for him, and I'm sure he also sensed that I did not mind.

To make a photoengraving, several skillful steps had to be taken. Ink colors of yellow, magenta, cyan, and black were used to print on white paper. The tiny dots that make up a picture in the printing of a photo had to be shaped to reproduce the proper tone. This was done by subjecting the engraving to an acid bath. For instance, if an area was not quite green enough, I had to remove some tone from the red plate. To do that, all the other areas that had the proper dot size were covered with staging ink (an acid resisting liquid). Only the areas that had to have a correction were subjected to the acid. The time in the iron chloride bath had to be controlled, depending on how much of the dot size had to be etched and reduced in size. As you can imagine, it was a highly-skilled and specialized trade.

In the beginning, the primary focus was to have the new apprentices learn the use of a fine brush with the staging liquid. The German way was not much of the "shooting from the hip" variety. There was always just one way of doing things, and it was never your way. It was the tried and proven way.

The very first day on the job, I was given a copper plate, three millimeters thick, about the size of a book page. It had thin lines etched into it, much like a writing tablet. I was told to draw hair lines with a camelhair brush using the staging fluid. The lines had to be one millimeter apart. Starting on the upper left hand corner, I could fit around 150 little, painted lines per row. With

| Schilderung wesentlicher Arbeitsvorgänge, Skizzen usw. | Woche vom *13.12.* bis *18.12* |

Tetex-Teppich (habe ich geätzt)

München , den *18.12.54*	*K. Hegele*	
	Unterschrift des Ausbilders	Unterschrift des Erziehungsberechtigten
Bißer F.X.	Bemerkungen	Bemerkungen
Unterschrift des Lehrlings		

Proof of first set of engravings as referred to on the weekly progress report.

twenty or more rows on the copper tablet, I could easily paint 3,000 lines with that fine haired brush to fill the tablet. At first I had to show Mr. Hegele the progress after just a couple of rows. He looked at each tiny hairline painted. Some, he said, were not straight. Some were fat on top and faded toward the bottom. Some were too shaky. Some were too weak and would not repel acid. Some were too thick, slanted, or spaced too far apart. Pretty soon I got the hint. Those little lines that were required of me had to be perfect. Of course, I never questioned Mr. Hegele's motive. All I knew, I was going to learn a skill....some day. If it took drawing tens of thousands of thin lines, well, that was my job. It took almost a week to fill the first tablet full of lines. With a couple of wipes of the solvent rag, I was ready to start on a new set of lines on the same shiny copper plate. As I became accustomed to the fluid and the brush and knew what was expected, I filled up the tablet much faster. Mr. Hegele, however, always found some lines, among the thousands, that did not satisfy him. After several weeks of drawing lines, he did not find much wrong any longer, but I had to keep doing lines–plate after plate full. After six weeks and tens of thousand of lines later, I was given my first real job. I had to create a set of four-color photoengravings: yellow, magenta, cyan, and black. This set of plates was to reproduce a Persian rug in a color catalog. Thank God that I had gotten good at drawing lines.

WHAT ENTERTAINMENT

Since entertainment in the fifties was nonexistent for a fourteen-year old, lots of activities within the family pertained to learning and discovering. Frequently, parents took their kids to such places as the zoo or to the various museums in the city. I always found it very stimulating to see such things as early patents and how they evolved to their current use. Museums of Natural History and museums of science and technology were a real drawing card for any kid. Anyone with a spoonful of sense would want to witness where we had been and then get excited where mankind may go from here. Personally, I also loved to go to the Museum of Art.

Dad took Dagmar and me one weekend. I was fascinated with the paintings of many old masters. I remember viewing a large painting by Rubens. It was a massive painting. As I backed away from the painting to get a more comprehensive look, I had to work my way around an artist who was meticulously creating a same-size copy of that Rubens' masterpiece titled "Rape of the Daughters of Leucippus." It was immediately very apparent that this artist was exceptional and was there only by exclusive permission from the museum. This master painter, copying one of the great master's work, was Mr. Hegele, the master engraver to whom I was indentured.

A NEW TURN

Just as I was getting settled in and was really loving my job, a bombshell was dropped into the midst of our life.

The family received a letter from Uncle Max, who lived in the United States. He had visited Germany in 1951 after his father had passed away. He and Mom had some communications by letter over the past several years; however, the suggestion to come to America was never made before. Neither did we ever dream of such a possibility. The mere mention in that latest letter for us to think about emigrating was enough not only to rattle us but actually shake us to the core of our being. After all, Mom now had an apartment where she could set up her beloved bedroom furniture. The kids had their own room. We were settled. All the pieces were in place. What now?

Once the mere thought of moving to America entered

our mind, it was impossible ever to think clearly again. Oh, we planned and discussed. We debated the pros and cons. America, not Yugoslavia or England or some exotic place like Egypt, but America. Once the possibility was given, there was never again a waking moment the thought left us until its fruition. America–where everyone chewed gum–where everyone drove a car–a country with canned bread pudding and where all men showed their handkerchiefs hanging from their back pockets.

GETTING READY

The American consulate was far enough away that we had to take a trolley there. All four of us were present to apply for visas to emigrate. There was a period of time the idea of my staying behind to finish my trade was considered. I was not ready to have my balloon punctured. My new job was the greatest personal achievement in my life. The idea that I might be going with my family to an unknown world was like being stripped of warm blankets in an icy cold room while blissfully asleep.

As our lives unravelled during the next several months. We had many mixed emotions. On the one hand, was the selling of our household goods; on the other the gradual filling of the shipping crates with the precious few things we were allowed to take to the new land. Dad had built, out of used wooden shipping containers, four crates. It was often agonizingly hard to give up the things we considered part of the family as we slowly decided on what to pack. Dad's few tools, Mom's Blaupunkt radio, her sewing machine, bedroom set and many other things now had a price tag. Our bicycles, the kitchen hutch with its secret compartment, our pots and pans, dishes, homemade rag rugs and curtains, all had to be sold. What did we have left at the time other then a few German Marks –just hope. The only thing that surpassed our sadness and turmoil was a dream, a dream and a profound knowledge that, as long as we all stayed together as a family, we would be all right.

Several months after the application to emigrate, the consulate summoned us for questioning and physical exams, including chest X-rays. While we were there waiting for the results, we met other families who intended to move to America. We exchanged future addresses with one family; and to this day, we are still in touch with them here in the States. Finally, the examining doctor came to the waiting room. He called for Dad to be re-X-rayed because of some questionable area that showed up. Not only was this new event embarrassing, but it also had the prospect of shattering all that had transpired to this point. After an agonizing half hour of wait, Dad and the doctor came back to the room, the doctor full of apologies to the rest of us for having misread Dad's X-ray. As it turned out, as the doctor showed us on the viewer, Dad had a large chunk of iron embedded next to his spine, shrapnel from the war. This chunk of jagged metal, the size of a quarter, sure looked like something was badly wrong with Dad's lungs. With the apology, the doctor promised that he would place our application near the top to be considered. He assured us that our waiting period of the normal six to ten months would be shorter. It was.

Uncle Max, who was going to sponsor us, agreed to pay for the voyage from Bremerhaven to New York. It was up to us to get ourselves and four trunks to the boat. Everything had been sold except what fit into two of the trunks. The other two trunks were filled with gifts. After we purchased train tickets to Bremen, we had just enough money left to buy a bus ticket to the dock. With the little savings our family had, along with the proceeds from the sale, Mom bought two complete sets of Rosenthal china. One set was for uncle Max's daughter Dorothy, who was engaged to be married, and the other for Tante Lisa, uncle Max's wife. The four trunks were stenciled with our new address, and all pertinent cargo labels attached. The shipping company Dad worked for saw to it that our precious cargo wound up on the ship with us. Mom made herself a travel bag with many pockets on the inside. This bag had a few secret compartments to hide valuables like the silver coins left over from before the war. Mom's travel bag also had a little pocket for a vase. She wanted to bring something that was alive from the old country. In that vase she nurtured a sprig of a house plant called "Wandering Jew." I had my own travel bag, the one I always took to camp. Dad carried a black wooden suitcase with personal stuff for all of us on the trip.

WELL - GOODBYE NOW

Whether our relatives did not care or did not know when we were leaving for America is a mystery. I never did ask Mom about it; but when it came time to board the train to leave Munich, no one except Beisser Opa showed up to wish us farewell. To a boy almost fifteen years old, this was a great blow. I'm sure my mother was the one who would have announced such news, why she did not is a mystery even to this day. I thought that we were a fine family and that surely everyone hated to see us go. I figured there would be lots of hugging and goodbyes with tears all around, but the only solemn figure standing there on the platform was Opa, eighty-five years old. I know he was crushed. The only thing he had left in life was just pulling out of sight.

THE LAST TOUCH

It was evening when we left the train station. The four of us were seated on two, facing, wooden benches. Not much was said as the train rocked along, rolling through the countryside. We all knew that regrets were pointless. I felt so torn. If it were just me alone, I could never have left. It was Dad, the rock, that kept us silently glued together as the train pushed ahead into the dark of night. Every minute, everything we ever knew and saw was falling further away, and we were racing toward the unknown.

The benches we were sitting on had no arm rests. Having talked all we wanted to, sitting there staring soon had its effect. As the hours slipped deeper into the night, we all became weary and sleepy. Our bodies began to slump as we nodded, but none of us found sleep. Dagmar was especially exhausted and was desperately trying to recline to get a little rest. Way after midnight, Mom let sister lay on the bench with her legs hanging over the edge of the seat into the center walkway. Even I could sense the relief she felt. It seemed we all relaxed a little more.

Around three in the morning, the door to our rail car opened and in stepped the conductor, a tall gentleman, in proper uniform and cap, carrying a cane. This cane was not some aid to support his stature, but an object with which to point or poke. This he did in the course of performing his job. Upon seeing little sister's legs hanging over the edge of the bench, and lo and behold into the center aisle, he tapped them with his stick. "Move–move, sit up straight, nothing is allowed to obstruct the center aisle," he said with a correcting voice. There certainly was very little stirring around at this hour of the night by the other passengers. However, as we understood, a law is a law. Little sister absolutely had no right to invade an area to which she was not assigned. – what a pity.

That was the last memorable occasion I had in the old country as a boy. The impact of this late night drama never meant anything to my Mom and Dad. They were part of that mentality. To sister, she just obeyed and never thought anything else about it. To me at the time, it was getting caught doing something bad. Later, as I became more aware of the American principle of liberty and self-worth, I realized I had lived in another "Time and Place."

BOOK FOUR

AUTHOR'S NOTE

The sea could not shake us, neither could the challenges of the New World.

This portion of the book sets in motion the energies that epitomize the American spirit. The small, colorful tiles of life keep emerging as they continue to put together the mosaic that is called the immigrant. Though this segment of the book only spans a little more than two years, the pieces shall continue to reveal themselves until the Lord requires the soul.

ALL ABOARD

We arrived in Bremen early in the morning. After taking a couple of pictures, we boarded a bus to Bremerhaven. The seaport seemed crowded with warehouses, cranes, and other structures. I never saw our ship from a distance; consequently I could not gauge its size. Not until I was along side of it, could I really comprehend its awesome presence, sitting there in the water. The sound of gulls and the smell of seawater added a new dimension to my ever growing experiences.

The look of a seaport.

The first step onto the gangplank caused my heart to drop. Something in me disconnected when I stepped off my homeland. It finally sank in that we were leaving. Boarding a ship, any ship, was totally new to me. However, I felt at ease in a sense. Having seen travel brochures of our passenger ship, I had imagined long beforehand what it would be like. The ship was named S.S. America, the sister ship to the S.S. United States.

When the large ropes were loosed and the tug boats struggled to maneuver the massive dead weight, my adrenaline was screaming, "Let's get on with it!" The fog horn of our ship blasted one final long sound, a sound that droned over the early morning harbor. Others may say it was a dreadful mourning sound; but to me, it was a blast that let the world know that the "big mama" was about to move.

The afternoon of the same day, we docked at Southampton, England, to pick up passengers and freight. The next day, foggy and cold, we slowed to a halt

The S.S. America, the ship that brought us to America.

and dropped anchor. Something was going on here. In the distance, I could see land, but I knew it was not America. What were we doing here? This great ship, was it stuck? What were we waiting for? I was sure this modern piece of machinery had the newest navigational systems to find its way through a little fog. Then I spotted a little black spot, a boat, approaching us. Slowly it pulled up close to our ship, bobbing up and down, while we sat still in the water. Slinging out some ropes, it pulled itself as close as it could. The boat had come from Cork, Ireland, and several folks and families entered our ship after walking across a rickety and shaky gangplank. I guess some were immigrants also, full of hope and dreams. Peddlers were sell-

The boat from Cork, Ireland.

Mom and Dad reflecting on the days ahead in our ship's cabin

ing large, wooden clubs called shillelaghs. It looked like a fat stick with a knot on the end. The peddlers actually convinced some of our passengers to buy one. They were stretching up from their boat while the buyers were practically falling overboard to exchange money for the goods.

Loading goods and passengers from Ireland.

I know no Germans on board were buying an Irish souvenir. Neither were any Englishman having just boarded, nor any Irishman on his way to the New World. I guess, even in 1955, the Americans were already known to be suckers for memorabilia.

Our cabin was on the lower level. We could hear the hum of the engines. The cabin was small, a dresser, two sets of bunk beds, and a small bathroom. One port hole revealed daylight. It was just above water level. We had to climb several flights of stairs to the spacious and modern dining hall. I was amazed that such a big room was on board. We had an assigned table and an assigned time to eat our meals. Our waiter was a native of Puerto Rico. The only word Dad could read on the menu was eggs. Of course, that was right up his alley. He ate dozens of them. We could not read the rest of the menu, and the waiter spoke not a word of German. We just ate what he brought us, and loved it, strange as some things were.

Living like kings for a week, on board ship with our waiter.

We met people from many walks of life as we strolled along the deck and lay in the sun. To my surprise, the lounge chairs were for all passengers, even for us, not only for the rich.

I often wondered about a German lady we met and how she was received when she got to her destination. She was married to a black man and was going to her husband's homeplace in Mississippi. He was back in Germany, finishing out his tour in the American military. The lady had four, small children. As I look back, she obviously had not, nor had we, ever heard the word discrimination, much less felt its meaning. The time we met was a happy time for her as it was an exciting time for us.

ROUGH SAILING

Several days into our voyage, the skies darkened, the winds increased, and the waves started to swell. The ocean seemed to puff up its might. Instead of our ship moving on top of the water, it now was among the water. Sleeping became a bit of a struggle as the ship rolled. I felt I had to hold on to keep from falling off the top bunk. We noticed that in addition to the stair rails, heavy ropes were strung so one could hold on with both hands. The stairs to the upper decks had become a real obstacle course. As the ship yawed and listed, the stairs became like ladders, at times almost straight up, then the next moment like corrugated steel boxes that were laying flat. Ropes were stretched everywhere, especially on the open decks. The storm was getting more violent. Dense sheets of rain were blowing sideways. The waves were churning,

Foul weather drill

looking like fluid mountains that threatened to open up and swallow our ship. Amazingly, this massive machine, that I had admired earlier, seemed like a cork bobbing in a wind-blown lake. However, we were not worried or scared. Our minds were so set on what we were doing that the threat of doom never entered our thoughts. As one might say, we simply cast our fate to the wind.

Wearing life jackets was highly recommended while walking on deck. The dining room tables, still covered with linens, all had a curious lip around their edges. This lip was to keep the dishes from sliding off during rough weather. I noticed fewer people showed up at each meal. My stomach became a little unsettled as well but not enough to keep me from checking things out.

I had enjoyed some frolicking in the ship's indoor swimming pool earlier, so, with not much else going on outdoors, I figured I'd go for a swim. Staggering like a drunken man, I made my way to the pool. No one was around. I saw no sign saying the pool was closed. The water looked inviting enough. Although it sloshed around a bit, but it did not hinder me from jumping in. I soon realized that even the pool had turbulence in it. I could not stand up even in the shallow section. The water became a mass that controlled me. It washed over the edges, and I bounded along the tile walls. All the walls and the ceiling were tiled. Apparently they got wet at times. Being sloshed around was kind of fun until all of a sudden the momentum sent most of the pool's water toward the deep end. With a massive slap, all the water smacked against the wall, curled up unto the ceiling, and came crashing down on me. Fortunately it happened on the deep end. Surely I would have gotten smashed or worse had it been on the shallow end. Terrified, I got out of there. I knew then why no one else was swimming that day.

The storm continued. Our ship, not small by any means (35,000 tons of water displacement), was beginning to feel like a matchbox. The mountainous waves sprayed sea water onto the vacated decks. Most people had turned green, they were so seasick. Just a few folks were in the dining hall. None could walk the decks. All the lounge chairs were folded up and strapped down. I venture to say that more people held on to toilet bowls than each other. All four of us had lost our appetites, and each of us struggled to keep our stomachs from turning inside out. The only relief I found was to stand on deck at the rail, looking into the water. That way I could anticipate the up and down motion of the waves and suppress the urge to vomit.

During the height of the storm, our ship was tossed so much that the screws, the propellers which are deep in the water normally, came out of the water and caused the entire ship to shake. This shaking was accompanied by a loud grinding sound that could be heard all over the ship.

Every time I hear people refer to March as the windy month, I think of the week we spent on the Atlantic in March of 1955.

THE FIRST DAY

The ghostly skyline of New York in 1955.

The Statue of Liberty, as seen the morning we entered the mouth of the Hudson river

The morning of March 21, we entered the mouth of the Hudson River. I knew exactly where I was. As we prepared for our trip, I had checked out all the relative geographical points on various maps and atlases. The anticipation of seeing the Statue of Liberty had been bottled up in me. At last, it would be for real.

It was a dreary morning. All four of us were on deck; and through the mist, we were beginning to see the skyscrapers. My eyes were focused on them. Then I heard someone say something—something "liberty." I looked to where they were pointing; and lo, way over to our left was the tiniest little statue, sticking out of the water, with her arm raised to the sky. I knew that was her but was saddened that we did not get to see her close up. Oh, how the immigrants of years passed must have been overwhelmed by her awesomeness as they passed ever so close when they approached Ellis Island. We came the year after Ellis Island was closed. We, as a family, made a pact that day that if the Lord was willing, we would visit her one day. And we did.

The tug boats slipped us into a pier on the West side of lower Manhattan. It was cold and damp. As I looked about, everybody was doing something. There was a drone in the air that somehow tied all things together. No eye contact was detected between anyone. There was no song in the air, no brightness in the sky, no color anywhere. After disembarking, we looked around for Uncle

Dad and young Franz
seeing glimpses of the New World
March 21, 1955

Max. There were people milling all around us trying to locate the cargo they had brought with them. We did the same, but mostly we looked for Max. Some people had found each other and were hugging. Then we located our four crates. Still no Uncle Max. After Dad had searched the entire pier, he finally spotted Max standing on the other side of the rails separating the pier from the sidewalk. We landed as we left, with no fanfare, no hugging and kissing. Again, just one person showed up, and he did not find it necessary to pay the fifty cents to get onto the pier to meet us as we stepped off the ship.

After Uncle Max arranged for our cargo to be delivered to his house, he led us to his car for the drive home. I remember driving through the Holland Tunnel and, finally, as we maneuvered through a lot of traffic lights, onto a long stretch of Route 22 south. I can recall the strange rhythmic sound the tires made as the car rolled on and passed over the cracks of the concrete road. Conversation was casual but business-like. Uncle Max suggested a break and pulled off the highway to treat us to ice cream. We all had exited the car except Dagmar, when the car door slammed shut trapping her fingers. The poor thing was screaming inside the car, as her little fingers were sticking through to the outside of the closed door. No bones were broken; and I'm sure the ice cream, which was wonderfully smooth and sweet, soothed her spirits.

Uncle Max lived with his wife Lisa and daughter Dorothy in a large Dutch-roofed house. He owned twenty acres which was mostly behind the house and his shop. The neighboring houses were within five hundred feet along the same county road.

Tante Lisa, being from Brazil, spoke no German, and neither did our cousin, Dorothy. After smiles, handshakes, and other awkward gestures of greeting, we were shown to the dining room. On the dining room table was a beautifully prepared meal. The center piece was a huge turkey, roasted golden-brown. The ladies had prepared a wonderful feast with lots of trimmings. The food and the thoughtfulness warmed us toward each other. The strangeness of it all vanished somewhat as we all sat down to partake. Just minutes into our meal, however, the shipment of our cargo arrived. Uncle Max got up and met the man on the front stoop. We all sort of quit eating, figuring we'd wait for him to return. As we sat there, hopelessly trying to make small talk, the conversation out on the porch became more and more heated. It was evident that Uncle Max did not agree to the fee being charged and was in the process of whittling the man down to an agreeable sum. All the while, Tante Lisa became more and more embarrassed as the dinner was getting cold.

Finally Uncle Max came back to the table. By that time, however, what little joviality was beginning to gel earlier had completely vanished. A distinct cold and stiffness had overtaken the gathering as we ate the rest of the meal in awkward silence. The most memorable statement of that first meal in the United States was when Uncle Max requested, with a low and solemn tone in his voice, "Salt, please."

A GOOD START

Our accommodations were in uncle Max's basement. Dagmar's bed and mine were set up on either side of the oil furnace in the middle of the basement. Mom and Dad's bedroom was curtained off in one corner of the basement. We all had to get used to the furnace kicking on and off during the night.

Dad soon converted the four shipping crates he built into usable furniture. We were given some toiletries, and, all in all, things started out on an even keel.

The first couple of weeks were nothing but work. Mom and Dad worked long hours in Uncle's shop, where they helped make brass lamps, which were his specialty. During the first weeks, Dad also planted a dozen or more fruit trees, cut enough firewood for next year's winter, and cleared a half acre of land of trees and stumps along the road. This was to be the spot for our house.

MANNERS

Next door to my uncle lived a family with two teenage daughters. Curiosity on both sides sort of drew the two girls and me together to share some cultural highlights. I had studied a little English in the evening back in Germany. That so-called study was only for personal edification, and fooling around a bit seemed more important than learning a new language.

My English speaking skills were very limited. I distinctly remember the girls next door having a giggling-good time trying to teach me manners. They were not laughing at me and my broken English but simply got the giggles when they tested my skill in giving the proper reply to common courtesy statements. When they had me respond to the term "thank you," and I would innocently answer with "you're excused," they would just about fall over laughing. I'd respond to "excuse me" with a "you're welcome" or a "very well thank you." All three of us were laughing until our sides hurt. Since none of the phrases made much sense to me, I was just mimicking their words. We all agreed that the learning curve had to be a bit longer than a few jolly hours.

HEAVEN

My cousin Dorothy was a typical young lady. Being engaged to be married, she spent little time at home during evening hours. Mom and Dad also spent long hours at Max's shop. Sometimes on the weekends, I had a chance to spend time with her. On occasion, she'd fix herself a snack and make me one as well. Her favorite was scrambled eggs with green peas. She drained the water off canned peas, stirring them into the eggs while they cooked. She then popped a couple of pieces of bread in the toaster and took her plate to the living room where she ate with great enjoyment, sitting on a large stuffed chair with her feet tucked under.

In those days I was always hungry and welcomed the chance to be part of her treats when offered. Peas and eggs were good, but I thought they lacked a little zest. She did not mess around in the kitchen much except to snack. One evening, she laid out two slices of bread, pure white and square. This bread was amazing stuff. It sure felt like it was meant to be inhaled rather than chewed. I thought of young princesses in gilded castles and guessed they must have always eaten such soft bread. What do I know, I never lived in a castle. Then Dorothy opened a jar containing some light brown matter. She dipped out a large glob of it, plopped it on the white bread, and tenderly swirled it all around, careful not to tear the white fluff. By that time she had all of my attention. Soon appeared a jar of dark blue jelly which she spread on the other slice. The kitchen had filled with a wonderful new aroma, a smell that aroused all my taste buds. Carefully, with her slender fingers, she put the two slices together and gave them to me, smiling at me, as if to say, try this! I took a good bite and spread the gooey blends all over my mouth. Aah...I never tasted anything like it before.– Peanut butter.– I thought I had died and gone to heaven!

BACK TO SCHOOL

Twenty-two days after we came to America, I celebrated my fifteenth birthday. I do not recall anything out of the ordinary happening that day except I had found out that I was too young to be working full time and was forced to attend public school.

Mr. Kessler, a man of German descent, was principal of the school that my uncle chose for me to attend. It was an all boy vocational school. The print shop of that school was thought to be the closest to the trade I sought. With just two months left in the school year, I was placed into the sophomore class.

For lunch at school, I often took peanut butter and jelly sandwiches, the new delight my cousin had introduced to me. Sandwiches, in general, were all new to me. In Germany, we covered our bread with various toppings, but they were always open faced. One time, after we had discovered bacon in the store, I took a sandwich of it to school. Thinking it was the beloved Geräuchertes that we ate in the old country, I put it on my bread uncooked. That day I became the laughing stock in the cafeteria when I took a bite of my sandwich and the raw bacon came slithering out from between the slices. As it hung from my mouth, I could neither chew nor cut off with my teeth the dangling raw bacon. I simply stuffed all of the slice in, chewed on it a while, then swallowed it. I knew then what a chicken feels like when it is trying to swallow an earthworm that just won't quit.

Milk at school was three cents for a half pint. I took three pennies to school, given to me by either my uncle or aunt. However, to a growing boy, that was not much to drink. Of course, water was free, but milk was so much better. Usually I bummed a penny here and there throughout the morning, so I could buy at least one or two extra milks.

A lot of boys packed their lunches. I noticed that on several occasions, some of the fellows looked into their packed lunch bags, wrinkled up their noses, grumbled something, then threw their entire lunch into the trash can. I was aghast. After that gesture of insolence and wastefulness, they reached for their wallets, pulled out a dollar, and bought from the cafeteria. Often I'd go over to the trash container, pick out the discarded lunches, and eat what I could, especially the apples and other desserts. A little extra to eat was always welcome.

When I first arrived at school, I was treated with silence and curiosity. After that, there was a gradual increase of picking on me and making fun of me. I did not understand most of what they said, but I realized that the other boys were trying to get me to say, among other things, some nasty words. They even tried to convince me that my name, translated into English, was some perversion. All this bothered me greatly. I felt so much out of place. The constant humiliation and the general mind set of these young men worked on me to a point that I went to see the principal. Teary eyed, I tried to explain what had been going on. Mr. Kessler simply put his arm around me and, with an assuring voice, said something I did not fully understand, but it comforted me. Several days later after history class, I was given a pocket size German - English, English - German dictionary. Apparently the history teacher had been stationed in Germany after the war and used the book there to learn to communicate. This little book became my constant companion for the next two or more years. I very clearly remember the very first word that I looked up was "kindisch", translated it means "childish". It was the most appropriate word that I could think of that described the constant pushing, finger flipping, name calling, chasing, and punching that was going on before my eyes. To my surprise, the harassment I had endured almost completely stopped after I pointedly announced the meaning of the word I had just looked up.

The pocket dictionary I carried for the first couple of years.

Looking back, I can now see that the hand of God directs everything. Just a couple of weeks before summer recess, I accidentally spilled a six-point type case onto the floor of the school's print shop. In 1955, type was often set one lead character at a time. The six-point size was the smallest size used. It was very small, and a case held thousands of individual characters. The type case had fallen upside down on the floor. The spilled type was swept up onto three galleys (trays that normally held set type ready for printing). Mr. Quoin, the teacher, just smiled. I gathered that over his many years of teaching the trade, he had seen countless spills. Mr. Quoin gave me a diagram that showed the layout of the type-storage case and gestured for me to start sorting and refilling the case with all its characters, caps, lower-case letter, punctuations, numbers, ligatures, and spaces into their proper places. It took me nearly the remainder of the school year to complete the task. After that, I knew the layout of the type case inside and out. I was so good at it that I volunteered to straighten out many other cases that were in particularly bad shape.

The first week of the first summer in America, I was offered a job at a local commercial print shop. You guessed it–to distribute type back into their respective cases after the printing had been completed. I have not been unemployed since that day and still work in the printing field as we enter the new century.

ALONE

At times, a person or an immigrant realizes that from deep despair and hopelessness, there is only one direction fate can take, and that is up. King Solomon said, "What has been will be again; what has been done will be done again; there is nothing new under the sun." There comes a time when we, as human beings, have to realize this. Individuals are wrong to think that they are the only ones engulfed in complex confrontations and trials. What is happening now has happened before. Pull up your boot straps and go on! That is the spirit of the immigrant. After all, the immigrant gave up all he had to take a chance on a promise.

Uncle Max kept a tight reign on the purse strings. Not long after we started to live in the basement, we ran out of soap. We had to ask for more. We ran out of tooth paste; we had to ask for more. I was required to have sneakers to participate in gym class. When Mom asked for money for the shoes, the response turned into a debate, the debate into an argument. Asking for three pennies each for sister and me was all right, but tennis shoes were a different matter. I do not know what Uncle Max's financial condition was at the time, but many brass lamps were being shipped weekly. After all, Dad was promised forty-five dollars per week and Mom thirty-five for working in his business. Almost five weeks had passed, and they had not been paid a penny.

Late on the afternoon of the altercation, disgusted and frustrated, Mom and Dad went for a walk along the country road having a mind never to return to that house with a Dutch roof. For the first time, they had stepped off the designated realm that belonged to Uncle Max. For five weeks, they had slaved more than they ever expected, working hard to show their gratitude for the opportunity of an America that they instinctively knew was there. As they walked, the afternoon light fleeting, they walked on to face the unknown, an unknown that could not be addressed for they could not speak the language, an unknown that could not be managed, for neither had they a job nor any money. Yet Mom and Dad kept on walking, to where they did not know. I always thought they must have kept walking because they felt a sense of freedom.

Later that evening, word came to Dagmar and me by way of a stranger who spoke a little German that Mom and Dad would stay at a house nearby and not return to sleep. My sister and I were comforted, though, when we were told that they would send for us at a later time.

THE HUNGARIANS

A week or more had gone by since my sister and I had last seen Mom and Dad. We mostly stayed to ourselves in the evenings and went to school during the day. Aunt Lisa did not say much, but she still was friendly toward us. As for Uncle Max, we saw little of him. When we did see him, he was reclined in his chair intently watching television.

Then the day came. A young man, driving a Jeep, pulled up to the basement door of the house. Dad was with him. They entered the basement where we had our

Our first moving day

meager belongings and quickly piled them into boxes and our precious crates. They carried the first load away, along with my sister. Just a short while later, Dad and the young man returned to get me and the remaining two crates, which I had filled with the rest of our things while they were gone. Dad did not make any attempt to speak with either Lisa or Max. He came unexpectedly and, within a half hour, had pulled up stake and was gone. All contact was broken, just six weeks into our new life. We never stepped foot into Uncle Max's house again.

As it turned out, when Mom and Dad left that late afternoon the week before, they had walked about a half a mile when they saw a lady tending to her flowers in the front yard. They waved. The lady waved back. When the lady said "Hello," my parents felt they should say something back to her. After just a few awkward gestures and trivial words, both my folks and the lady realized they had something in common–both sides of the fence spoke German. The woman was a broad faced and robust Hungarian. She and her husband were immigrants. He could speak a little English and even less German. He was a gruff-looking man, saying little himself, but he readily agreed with his wife. When darkness fell, Mom and Dad were invited to stay the night. They accepted.

Less then five hundred yards from their house was a factory where they both worked. The factory made garden hoses. The next morning Mom and Dad went to the factory with them. After meeting with the bossman, they both were hired. Mom was to separate recycled plastic scraps by color for eighty-five cents an hour. Dad was given a chance to learn the skill of dying molten plastic, then extruding garden hoses. He was paid a little more per hour. Both jobs were very hard work in hot and miserable conditions; but, praise God, they both were able and willing.

Things were moving rather quickly. Now all Mom and Dad had to do was find a permanent place for all of us to live.

A WELCOME OFFER

I do not know how many nights my parents spent with the Hungarians, but one evening they were encouraged to walk about a mile to meet another German family who lived along the same road. The man of the house was from Germany and had come to this country right after the great depression, as had Uncle Max. They lived in an older, farm house on a sizable piece of land of about forty acres. The middle-aged couple showed concern for Mom and Dad's plight and agreed to help. Dad was anxious to have a roof over our heads; any roof would be fine. The man offered one of the farm's out buildings, a cinder-block structure, for us to move in. The building was less than fifty feet from the farm house. It had a concrete floor and one garage door facing the road. The building was about square in layout with half of the structure being used for storage of stuff like rabbit hutches, a surplus of canning jars, animal traps, and chicken feed. It was with renewed excitement that Mom and Dad approached the task of clearing the building. They swept and washed the floor and generally got the place ready for us all to live in.

NO WHERE BUT UP

I don't remember the details, but we got four fold-up, steel beds from somewhere. Four crates, four beds, and four people were now housed in that block building. There was no ceiling under the roof; and, beyond the structural timbers, we could see the sky through the roof's gable vents. A steel framed window was on the wall where we had our beds. The two smaller crates acted as chairs with one of the large crates as a table. The other large one stood upright and acted as a closet. The wind whistled under the garage door, but warm weather was surely around the corner. We were shown where to catch the bus so we could go to town and explore the art of grocery shopping. The bus stop was only half a mile away, which was not bad. When we bought milk, we were allowed to keep it in the refrigerator at the farmhouse. Mom and Dad got up early to go to work. They'd go across the yard and into the farmhouse's kitchen, quietly take out the milk, and use the landlord's cookstove to quickly heat cream of wheat or oatmeal. After that, they would dart back to our building where we'd all sit on the crates to eat breakfast. It was very awkward when we had to go to the bathroom. The minor business we did around and behind the other farm structures and chicken coop. To do the major business, we were allowed to use the toilet at the farm house. This, however, was a very unsettling venture. We had to tiptoe through the master bedroom to get to it. At times, the farmer and his wife were still sleeping when nature called.

All this awkwardness of day-to-day living soon changed for the better. Mom and Dad agreed to pay thirty-five dollars a month rent. The landlord agreed to improve our living quarters. Part of the deal was that Dad, with the help of the rest of us, would furnish the labor while the landlord was to provide and pay for the materials. The first project was to install a septic tank on the outside while we installed a tub, a sink, and a toilet on the inside. We also removed the garage door and filled the opening with cinder block, except for a window which was added. We built a divider wall to separate the bedroom, added a ceiling, and painted everything on the inside. We covered the concrete floor with tile in the living area, and Mom got a kitchen sink and a few old cupboards. Things were looking up. Spring had sprung, and we all had a newness of life. Word got out that Mom would like to do domestic work. Soon she cleaned one house on weekends at the nearby town. As word spread, Mom was offered jobs to clean more houses. Soon she gave up her job of sorting plastic; instead, she now worked six days a week cleaning homes in a very exclusive neighborhood.

NEW JERSEY MOOSE

School was in recess. The work on our bungalow was coming along well. The days became long and hot, hotter and a lot more humid then anything we had ever experienced. Mosquitoes were the menace of the evenings. Dad had mounted a screen door at our side entrance, but mosquitoes were everywhere inside the house. We could do nothing in the evenings but swat them to get ready for sleep at night. They were big mosquitoes, plump and dark. So big, that if three of them a night got hold of you, you had to get a transfusion the next day. We were at war. Surely four, grown people were not going to be taken over by such small beasts. We could not figure out where they all came from. Then one evening sitting down, I happen to look up and saw five or six critters flying single file, about eyeball level, toward us. We decided to make no sudden moves or disturb their pattern. Slowly I got on my knees keeping the beasts highlighted against the white ceiling. I noticed a parade of mosquitoes was coming from the bathroom. Without any air turbulence present, they looked like a steady stream of bombers on a mission—so they were. Finally, stalking them to the point of entry, I realized they all came through a small hole in the screen that covered the tiny vent window over the tub. Quickly and with a sigh of relief, the hole was plugged. With renewed vigor, we hunted down the pests, until every last one was finally destroyed.

IT WAS LOOKING FOR MOISTURE

The night air in Germany was fairly cool in the summer. I knew we were not in the tropics; but to us, it sure felt like it. The night was hot! There was no fly screen on the bedroom window that would allow a breeze to get a cross draft. Nevertheless, sleep always did come.

At times, we were awakened by the thumping of the rabbits cooped up along the outside back wall. At other times, something disturbed the chickens that roosted in the small trees just outside the window. Their squawking, in general, took some getting used to.

I was aroused one night while sleeping on my back with my mouth wide open. Something had crawled over my face and was straddling my open mouth with its legs. Slowly I brought my hand up and quickly snatched the thing with my fingers. While I held on to it, I reached to the floor with my left hand to pick up a sock which I knew I had left there. Then I took the strange critter, now motionless, between my fingers and placed it into the sock. Quickly, with both hands, I mangled the catch inside the sock to make sure it would not crawl out again. I threw the sock on the floor and went back to sleep.

My curiosity was revived the next morning when one sock was not in the usual spot. I remembered the midnight visitor. Carefully, I picked the sock up and turned it inside out. I was stunned to see that it was nothing more than a humongous spider.

I was not so sure we had not moved to the tropics.

The renovated garage the summer of 1955.

MY SHOES FIT FINE

One morning I swung my feet off the bed, put on my socks, and was about to step into my shoes when I noticed that water was sloshing in one. I looked to the ceiling to check for a leak, but then I thought it probably had not even rained during the night. With shoe in hand, I walked to the kitchen where Mom and Dagmar were getting the day started. I showed them the unlikely vessel holding the liquid. They both were baffled. How did that bit of mystery make its way into my shoe? Then, all of a sudden, Dagmar straightened up, her eyes got very large. She covered her mouth with one hand and stepped backward. She began to tell us, looking at the shoe, about a dream she had during the night. After listening to her, we all recalled the conversation we had the evening before. The discussion was about Dagmar's shoes getting too tight. We jokingly suggested she do what they do in the Old Country. It was told around the farm circles that, when a shoe starts to hurt in one area and refuses to mold itself to the wearer's foot, just pee in it before going to bed. By doing that and leaving the liquid in the shoe over night, the leather will soften, having been soaked with the correct combination of magic ingredients. All one had to do is pour out what was left in the morning, slip the shoe on, and wear it the rest of the day. Any pressure point that caused pain the day before was now being molded to conform to the foot.

If my sister was trying to get even with me over something, I do not know; however, the good acting job convinced me that this act of kindness was truly the result of a dream.

A SCHOOL WITH A NEW FLAVOR

As a county Vo-Tech student, I was issued a free pass to ride on public transportation. Every morning I'd walk the half-mile to the bus stop and get on my first bus to the town of Metuchen. From there, I'd board another public bus to downtown New Brunswick. There I waited for a school bus to take me to the technical school which was a good distance from the center of the city.

Smoking was a desirable and hip thing to do. Most fellows smoked like freight trains. Guys were leaning their backs all along the outside wall of the school building, one leg hiked up, foot flat against the wall, just sucking away on the weed. Each strived to achieve a certain image with which they might be identified. All were trying to get pumped full of nicotine before the bell rang. Some guys practiced blowing smoke rings. Others worked on holding their butts with thumb and two fingers, pointing the lit end toward the palm of the hand. This they must have seen their Dads do. It was meant to shield the glow of the burning tobacco from being seen at night by the enemy during World War II. Smoking was a sure-fire way of creating a macho image. Many were adept at holding a cigarette in their mouth, face all scrunched up from trying to avoid smoke burning their eyes, while they worked on something that required two hands.

Flat top haircuts, with the sides long and greased down, were the rage. If you could sport good sideburns, you got respect. "A little dab'll do ya" held the hair in place after it was combed to make a D.A. in the back of the head. (D.A. stood not for District Attorney but for a duck's posterior). Metal taps on boot heels were outlawed in school, but many had them anyway.

A person could get his driver's license at seventeen. That generally meant that only seniors drove cars to school. I noticed that one of the premier achievements of a young man was to be invited to sit in one of the senior's cars while waiting for the bell to ring. Cigarettes were shown off in shirt or leather jacket breast pockets. In warm weather, the boys, some so small they could not look over the top of a car, had their pack of butts rolled up into the short sleeve of their white T-shirt. The arm with the rolled up T-shirt was always hung out the car window. There it was pressed against the outside of the door to create a look of having massive biceps.

Once the school day started, it was hard for the teachers to convince these "technically" oriented boys to do academic studies. I recall that one day in English class when the fellow sitting next to me was asked to read from the book in front of him. He promptly told the instructor that as a pressman he did not have to be able to read. He punctuated his statement by pushing the book off his desk onto the floor. The teacher simply asked someone else to read. I thought of Mr. Kurtz and what he would have done.

In American history class, I had little if any knowledge of the subject matter. What good was it to know about the Egyptian, Greek, and Roman Empires when you are supposed to know about the Constitution of the United States? However, I did learn some of the ways the American government was formed and learned about America's wars and the expansion to the west. I even learned a bit about the functions of the judicial, legislative, and executive branches of government.

When it became known in shop class, and consequently by all other teachers, that I had some skills in art, the
history teacher, who also was an artist, ushered me into
his back room. There on an easel was a partially completed reproduction of a famous Picasso masterpiece. The
teacher challenged me to go ahead and work on the oil
painting while he was teaching the rest of the class. I
could hear him lecturing while I painted. Every day,
instead of sitting in class, I'd paint for an hour in the
back room. The painting was being copied from a printed
page of an art catalog on Picasso. The impressionistic
style was new to me. I soon became enthusiastic and was
excited to be working in the back room. I finished the first

Silk screen art. Stencils cut by hand for each color.

and several more paintings during my junior and senior years. I actually saw my paintings in a store in Metuchen being displayed as incidental pieces to the decor but also with a nifty price tag on them. I did not know what was going on and certainly never received any money for any of them. All I got was a B in history.

Related drafting and math were two other classes required. I asked the teachers if they would let me forge ahead in the assignments laid out for the marking period. I received a permission slip from the shop teacher to come and spend any extra time in the print shop. So, both drafting and math teachers let me go full speed ahead. With my background, drafting was easy, as was the relat-

Middlesex County Vocational School, 1956.

ed math, once I figured out the points and pica system. Within two weeks, I completed all assignments in both subjects. I spent the rest of the semester in the school's print shop.

As the school year progressed, I found myself creating more and more silk screen printed art in the print shop. In place of a normally printed invitation, I'd create an appropriate design, cut the silk screen stencils by hand, and print a colorful piece, rather than a drab few lines in black type only. For such efforts, I was recognized by several, local, civic groups. Of course, their requests never ended.

My senior classmates became more bold in annoying their shop teacher. Mr. Quoin was an older gentleman. He was a bit shorter than some of the other students and I. We had learned long ago that he, in his younger days, was a prizefighter. He often threatened to take any of us into the back room and "bat the hell" out of us. We just grinned, knowing for sure that probably in years past, he did just that. Mr. Quoin's nerves were shot. It did not take much for him to get excited. His voice would rise, and his fleshy hands would begin to tremble. This appearance of weakness of the man in charge prompted the boys to stage some mishaps.

The biggest printing press in the shop was an old Kelly cylinder press. As the printed sheet came out of the press, it passed over a series of gas flames to help dry the ink. Naturally, if one of the sheets got hung up over the open flames, it caught on fire. Normally, there was always one student who watched for just such a mishap and quickly removed the sheet before it went up in flames. Well, on more than one occasion, I witnessed a pretty good bonfire. The boys operating the press conveniently helped the paper get jammed and watched the blaze get started, all the while keeping the press going to add more fuel to the fire. Then with mock surprise, they'd yell for Mr. Quoin. Acting frightened and scampering away from the flames, they let old Mr. Quoin fight the blaze while they watched and snickered.

The shop also had a huge, lever-operated, paper cutter. It easily was able to cut 500 sheets of paper in one slice. Needless to say, it was a dangerous machine. We were often lectured on its dangers and were told always to operate the cutter alone. This way, when you hung onto the cutting lever with two hands, you could not possibly cut your fingers off. One of the boys, always full of mischief, brought a very realistic, severed finger to school. The gag object was in a little box laying on a cotton pad. Just looking at it in that box made me cringe, it looked so real. I reckon that is what it was meant to do. Well, several of the fellows got together and worked up a plan. The gruesome game played itself out as one of the boys was actually cutting some paper. One other chap was mixing a little fake blood out of red ink and solvent. That mixture was dribbled on the cutter bed and on the floor. The artificial finger was laid in front of the blade. Then the boy, known to be the biggest cut-up, let out a fierce scream after the giant blade was loudly dropped to its down position. The supposedly wounded fellow ran around the shop holding his hand while several of the other guys were pointing at the cutter. Mr. Quoin bobbed up from his desk, the pointing fingers guiding him to the cutter. With utter shock, all color left the poor man's face as he stared at the blood and the finger, while the "wounded" one was still howling somewhere in the other corner of the shop. I must admit, I felt sorry for Mr. Quoin. The team work, however, was excellent.

NEW FOOTWEAR

During the summer of 1955 after I had started working at a printing place in Metuchen, I found myself in need of a new pair of shoes. If there were any discount stores at that time, I sure did not know about them. The only shoe store I knew was downtown. My English was very limited at that time. Fortunately, the words Schuh and shoe were pronounced the same way in German as in

English. I had a time trying to tell the salesman that I wanted work boots. Work boots would do fine in summer and winter. I wanted to buy them bigger than my feet measured, so I'd grow into them. This seemed totally new to the man. Several times I got the impression that he wished I had never come into his store. At long last after many gestures, looks, and waving of the arms, I settled for a pair of leather boots. He showed me, using his fingers on both hands, that the selected pair cost twenty-three dollars. I, in turn, showed off my English, with the support of my fingers, that I only had eighteen dollars. He then motioned to me that he would keep them in a corner until next week when I then would pay him the balance. I gestured and stammered back at him that I wanted to take the boots with me. The hardest thing for the sales clerk to understand was that I just offered eighteen dollars, all that I had to my name, and that was all I was going to pay him. He then started to put the deal on a sales ticket. He got out of me where my job was and now was ready for me to sign on the dotted line. When I looked, I saw that he had put the five dollars difference in the deal, listing it separately as a balance due. Well, I was not born yesterday. I pointed at the amount due and shook my head. Taking his pen, I motioned for him to scratch out the five bucks due; and he'd have a deal. In frustration, he raised his arms, then scribbled out the five on the bill-of-sale. He also most likely told me to take the blame shoes and get on out of his store. What he muttered I do not know; but I was out of there, shoes firmly under my arm, and debt free.

VAN VECHTEN PRESS

Actually, it was a blessing in disguise when I dropped that type case in school. It sure forced me to learn the location of all characters and prepared me well for my first job in America. Using the same buses after school, I got off in Metuchen and walked to a small printing plant named Van Vechten Press. Having saved a part of lunch from school, I added a quart of milk that I bought from the grocer across the street and ate supper at the printing place. After that, I distributed hand-set type that was laid out for me. I worked every night until eight or nine o'clock at which time I caught the last bus back to Oak Tree where we lived. Saturdays, I could not use my school pass. I did not mind paying the fare. I was making big bucks now. Working for eighty-five cents per hour was big money that added to the family kitty. In a real work situation at fifteen years old, I was not allowed to operate certain machinery. It did not take my boss long to realize that I could distribute a lot of type in a hurry. The natural step of progression led me to print jobs on the hand press. Pretty soon, I had a galley full of type waiting for me to print, not to distribute. The instructions given to me were simple. All I had to be able to read was the quantity, the color ink, and the type of paper for each job. The hand printing press and the paper cutter were identical to the ones in the school shop. It was a good part-time job. (I kept that job, part time, for the next five years. By then, I had a full time job as well. As a member of the Photoengravers Union, I was asked to drop the moonlighting job being that it was a non-union shop.)

MY GIRL

In the winter of 1955 when I was speeding toward the ripe age of sixteen, I mustered up enough courage to call a girl from the place of work one evening. We did not have a phone at home. I had seen the girl only once–briefly, at a gathering of the folks Mom cleaned for. Of course, I thought she was lovely with blond hair flowing, rosy cheeks, and a coy little smile. I lost sleep over her. I realized that I would never be good enough for her, but maybe. . . we could see each other once and just talk, well, try to talk. I have long forgotten her name, but I clearly remember the ache in my chest whenever I thought of her. One evening, at Van Vechten, I could hardly do my work for thinking about her. I had her phone number in my wallet. Until then, it was that number in my pocket that made me feel close to her. That night a tremendous longing welled up in me. I needed to hear her voice for the first time. I practiced all night the line I would say to her father or mother when they answered the phone. I figured that I could express myself well enough to introduce myself and ask to speak to their daughter.

Van Vechten's lights were on all over the shop, except the front office, which was dark and which I locked up every night. There, sitting in the dark office, in the shadows of the streetlight outside, with a lump in my throat, I stared at the black telephone in front of me. Was I man enough to make the call, a call that might round out my life?–possibly including in it a new part, a part outside my immediate family, a new part in my life that until now had been taken up with nothing but an all-boy school and work.–Yes, I was man enough to make the call! I picked up the phone and dialed. A voice on the other end said "hello." It was a sweet young voice, obviously not the mother. It was her — the girl of my dreams. The shock of her picking up the phone totally scrambled my much rehearsed lines. I was speechless, literally. My heart pounded so hard, and my breathing became so labored as the seconds ticked on. All I could do was hang up, never having uttered a word. Such was the world of a boy in love.

HIGHLIGHTS OF A NEW LIFE

By now Mom was cleaning seven houses a week. People came to know us and where we lived. During the first months in America, folks for whom Mom cleaned stopped by, tapped on the wooden screen door, and handed us bags and boxes full of goods. Even strangers came to the door and brought us things that we might be able to use. We were very thankful for all. Mom managed to make curtains, alter some of the clothes, hem up pants, and take in extra material around the waist. I knew my trousers were altered when the back pockets touched each other. People brought pots and pans, dishes, and utensils. We all loved the toaster that showed up one day. It was the manual, turn-the-bread kind. You had to sit there, watch it get brown, then grab a little knob with which you flipped the half toasted bread to face the other side to the glowing filament. From somewhere, somehow, we even got a refrigerator. You can imagine how we rejoiced when we made ice cubes. Dad loved left over coffee, iced, with milk and sugar, when he got home from work.

Dad loved iced coffee all right. I had gotten a set of watercolor paints and brushes. One afternoon, I was dabbling in my new paints, trying to loosen up to possibly create a new painting. I had mixed many different colors, each time washing out my brush in a tall glass filled with water. During the afternoon, the water in the glass had gotten kind of murky, I'd say a grayish-brown. When Dad came home hot and sweaty from the day's hard work, he grabbed the first refreshing looking liquid he saw to quench his thirst–my rinse water. I was not paying any attention, while Dad was guzzling down the entire glass full of murky rinse water. Setting the empty glass back on the table, he simply shook his head like a wet dog and asked in a shocked voice, "What was that?"

Going to the grocery store became the highlight of our lives. Often all four of us went. We were walking home from the bus stop one day when one of the bags containing groceries broke. The paper bag with the watermelon in it became a little soggy with dew from the cool melon. As the melon started to slip out the bottom of the one bag, Dad struggled trying to catch it. He then inadvertently spilled the other bag he was carrying as well. The melon hit the road and started to roll down the slight hill, gradually wobbling its way toward the ditch on the right. The other bag, which had the canned goods in it, burst when he made the sudden move; and its contents also rolled down the hill, gaining speed as a dozen cans headed for the ditch on the other side of the road. We all thought it was hilarious until we tried to figure out how to carry a water melon and a dozen cans without a bag.

After we got home, we hurriedly cut the cool melon to taste what had been so highly touted. The four of us easily ate the entire watermelon. That evening we all had a bout with the dysentery. We blamed it on the watermelon, being so new to our diet.

Why stop with the watermelon. When in Rome, do as the Romans do. From somewhere, we got an old grill. To save on things like starting fluid, Dad took a stove pipe and cut a few notches in the metal on one end. He stood the pipe up on its end, stuffed it half full with newspaper, then filled the rest of the stovepipe with charcoal. After striking a match, he lit the paper on the bottom through one of the notches. In no time, we had a roaring blaze getting the coals ready for our favorite. We grilled chuck steaks, nineteen cents a pound. The size of those steaks covered the entire dinner plate. We had a time!

Maize (corn) was Schweinefutter–feed for the hogs. We had never eaten corn in our lives in any form. I saw popcorn being sold in the Munich zoo. The vendor was set up just outside the monkey cages. It was the perfect food to be bought for apes. We never purchased any, and even if we had, we would never have tasted it. It was strictly for the animals. So, why are all these American in love with monkey food? Let's find out. We bought a small bag of the kernels. As far as we could decipher, the instructions said to "put in skillet on stove." That is what Mom did. With the corn in the skillet, the heat on, she stood there and nothing happened. As the stove continued to heat the skillet, we all were doing something else. Suddenly, out of the corner in the kitchen came a strange rapid fire–pop, pop, pop. Mom let out a whoop; and before she could find a lid, popcorn was everywhere. So, that is how it is done! Seeing is believing.

The exclamation point of America was neither the toast nor the watermelon. It was not the chuck steaks, roasted chicken, or popcorn. It was the heavenly gift, the gentle touch to mankind. It was the toilet paper!–The white, unprinted roll of small, soft squares of paper, which hung next to the throne of contemplation, just beckoning to comfort. Just think, never again would I have to tear little squares of newsprint and stick them on a wire hanger. Now, that is what I call living!

MAROON WAS ITS COLOR

Dad walked over a mile to work each morning. The rest of us walked the other direction to catch the bus. What made us desire a motorcar was not that we were not used to walking. It was the fact that no one else walked. Getting a car was one of these materialistic objects that was within reach only in America. When we saw the extra cash to buy a car accumulate, since three of our family had income, it became even more important to us to be driving one.

Our landlord at the time was showing off a brand new Buick Special. He told me that the Special model was the biggest and most expensive of all Buicks made. Well, it was easy for a teenager to find out from his buddies at school that the Buick Roadmaster was in reality the fanciest. The Special had three, round holes on each side of the front fender while the Roadmaster had four. What ever reason Mr. Landlord had to mislead a young impressionable kid, I do not know. The falsehood was enough for me to lose total respect for the man.

We all watched our stash in the tin can grow as we counted it periodically. We dipped into it when we all decided to make what we called a "major purchase." This time the family went to the tin can to buy a used car.

Dad and I got on the bus to check out an ad. For seventy-five dollars, we bought a 1948, four-door Chrysler. It did not have the shape of the new Buick; but to us, it was the most beautiful automobile this side of the Passaic River. The paint job on that car was deep and rich. It was a shiny maroon after we washed and shined it for most of the day. We parked it proudly just outside of our front window. Every time any of us got up and walked about in the house, we always were drawn to look out the window and admire our newly purchased treasure. All of us got up during the night, not only to answer nature's call, but to sneak a peek at our wonder outside. From the twilight's last gleaming through the stars' light in the air, we were glad to find in the morning that our car was still there.

Late one evening, sitting in the quiet of our bungalow, we heard a distinct noise coming from the direction where

Our first automobile. Truly the object of adoration.

our car was parked. It sounded like someone had quietly closed the door on it. With adrenaline flowing, Dad snuck out the side door. He inched his way along the building, ready to surprise the culprit. I know Dad was capable of wringing anybody's neck or ring their bell for that matter. He could see no one messing around on the outside of the vehicle. He decided to lunge the last ten feet toward the car, yank the door open, and grab the would-be thief. However, as he darted toward the door handle, a couple of chickens squawked wildly and scattered into the night air from their roosting perch on the roof of the car.

AT ODDS

There were actually very few times when Mom and Dad disagreed. Often the spat was short lived, just an airing of views. Although the world of opportunities was now wide open, being strapped for money brought on new anxieties and pressures. I do not remember the reason, but my parents, one afternoon, had quite a vociferous argument. Seems like Dad rarely got the last word, and this time he did not have it either. He simply went out the door and walked away. He did not take the car, he just headed up the road. Hours passed, and the shadows started to lengthen. I became very upset because he had not returned. We did not know any neighbors well enough to think he would have gone there to cool off. We had no phone to call anyone. I decided to walk up the road to look for him. I always knew Dad had made war and plenty of it. I also knew he wanted to make peace whenever he could. That afternoon he had been cut down with words that he could not match, or didn't want to match. So, he left. I sensed very strongly that Dad was very capable of leaving, never to return. Even worse, he would not think twice about taking his own life. I became very frightened at that thought, especially when I did not find him along the road. I became irrational with fear and was convinced that he had hanged himself. I headed into the woods. Looking at every tree with limbs strong enough to hold a body, I could see in my mind what it would look like. Faster and faster I stumbled through the woods, wanting to find and check out every tree, as the setting sun starkly outlined them against the dimming sky. Frantically I rushed back and forth, combing every acre of land. I told myself a thousand times, do not cry, keep looking, you must find Dad before it is too late.

It was about dark when I returned to the house, exhausted. I did not tell Mom that I had searched out all the trees nearby. I just told her that I could not find him. The three of us sat quietly, waiting, staring, each of us to our own thoughts and worries. At last the door opened, it was Dad. He simply stated that it was a good thing no train had come. With that he went to bed.

I never thought of the train tracks. The woods led right down to and along the tracks. God was watching over us again. He made us all realize how fragile are the webs that hold life together. We are all just hanging in there, hoping none of the strands will break.

HOUSE HUNTING

All of the seven houses that were Mom's to clean were nestled in one neighborhood. I might say it was a bit uppity and well-established. New homes were being built nearby with hopes that one day they might become part of the affluence of the area. Somehow, we had the distinct inner feeling that in America all things were possible. Home ownership was certainly one of them. We already had passed several milestones in the five months of being on our own.

We had bought a car, an important part of feeling good. Mom's new wringer washing machine was a necessity. She was happy being able to reuse the soapy water. After the whites were washed first and the clothes were wrung out, the water was drained back into the tub of the machine. The everyday shirts and pants were washed second, and then finally Dad's grimy work clothes, using the soapy water a third time.

By far the most expensive item we had bought thus far was a three hundred dollar secretary, complete with little pigeon holes and small drawers. It was a beautiful piece of furniture, but it sure stood out, among the much appreciated hand-me-downs, like an Arabian horse at a pig auction.

One Friday night, after payday, we all sat around the table and once more counted the family's stash. It was stored in a special tin and was hidden in our secret hiding place. We counted it periodically as we made plans to save toward our next purchase. That Friday evening we had a total of three hundred and sixty-two dollars and sixty-four cents. I will always remember that number exactly. It was a lot of money, and we probably went to bed that night quite pleased with life and the direction things had taken.

That weekend we took a ride. I do not know whether we made a specific trip, or just wound up there out of nosiness, but we found ourselves looking at one of those brand new homes in the fancy neighborhood. A sign on the front yard beckoned us to come in. Obviously it was a model home because we were greeted by a salesman. After looking around, the desire for such a palace almost got the best of us. The price for the home was $28,000, high dollars in 1955. Seeing that we all liked what we saw, the salesman asked us if we would like to buy it. Sure, we all agreed that we would. The salesman then asked us how much money we had. Dad very innocently replied, "Three hundred and sixty-two dollars." At this simple and truthful statement, the man said not another word, but turned and walked away.

THE BLUE HOUSE

We all worked to improve our bungalow, which had been converted from a garage. Most of the work was done during the first summer. We installed ceilings, laid tile floors, put up trim, and painted the inside. Mom planted flowers along the outside walls. We were even allowed a garden spot for vegetables. Although there was room for a garden just outside our little house, the owner made us dig up a patch of sod about five hundred feet away, over a slight hill and out of sight. Why he insisted on that, we never understood.

The rent was set at thirty-five dollars per month from day one. The extra incentive was, that we supply the labor while the owner supplied the materials to make the garage livable. However, as soon as the last brush stroke of paint had been applied, the landlord raised the rent to fifty-five dollars a month. This really irked Mom and Dad; and since the owner was German, my parents gave the man a piece of their mind in the native tongue. With that spat over, Dad immediately started to look for a new place to live.

We moved into a house in the town of Metuchen. It was a big frame house on a very small lot. In the spring, we dug up the soil for a little garden, just a small spot, between the building and the gravelled area for the car. Dad offered to paint the house in exchange for a month's rent. The rent was seventy-five dollars monthly. We painted the house a bright blue, with white trim — the state colors of Bavaria. I venture to say it was the only blue house in town. When one rounded the corner of our street, all one could see was the bright color of fresh, blue paint. No one said a word. If we liked it, that was all that mattered to the neighbors. We were free.

Painting our new house for a month's rent.

A HOSPITAL STAY

As a youngster in Germany, I noticed many older people, men and women alike, had goiters protruding from their necks. We know now that a lack of iodine is the cause of such growths. Mom's goiter was not as visible as most. It grew more toward the inside. It was slowly cutting off the blood supply to her brain, causing her to have ever more frequent and severe headaches. The diagnosis was easy, and a hospital stay to remove the growth was set up. Having come from a country with socialized medicine, we never gave it a thought that this country was different in that matter. I knew we had no insurance and did not realize we should have. The families Mom worked for recommended the doctors, and, as far as I know, we never received a bill from either the hospital or any of the doctors.

We rented only the ground level apartment at the house in Metuchen. The people who lived upstairs had a different entrance. I slept in the front room, just inside the L-shaped covered front porch. A bathroom and two other bedrooms were in the back of the house. The kitchen was off the living room; it was large and had our eating table in it. When Mom was in the hospital for the goiter surgery, all three of us did the cooking. Since coming to America, we hardly ever skimped on eating. Our tastes were simple, and the food plentiful. Even while Mom was incapacitated, we had wonderful meals. The highlight was a roasted duck dinner. Stuffed duck it was, not one duck, but two. When the three of us went grocery shopping that day, we happened to notice a special on duck. Being hungry all the time was the norm for a sixteen-year old. It did not take much to convince Dad to get two birds, since his eyes also were often bigger than even his belly. Rarely were there any leftovers other than what had been set aside for next day's lunch at work or school. You might say we all were "good eaters." We figured, since the second duck did not cost much, we might as well roast two. The oven would be on anyway, so why not. There was a chance one, plump bird may not be quite enough for the three of us.

I chopped a bowl full of French bread for the stuffing. Added to it were chopped onions and celery. The hearts and livers were quickly fried in a skillet with salt and pepper, and eaten on the spot. This made for a good snack which held us over until the ducks were roasted. The gizzard was also chopped into thin slivers and added to the stuffing mix. Before the stuffing was mixed, a couple of eggs, several cups of heated milk, and salt and pepper were added. I had the privilege of plunging my hands into the mound of ingredients to mix them all together. We had the good feeling that we were getting close to a great event. Dad held open the carcasses, while I stuffed the fattened birds. While the ducks roasted, we grated potatoes to make dumplings. We decided against any other veggies that day. The men of the house were perfectly happy with lots of meat, plenty of gravy, potato dumplings, and stuffing. Dagmar just went with the flow. The mouth-watering smell of the roasting birds permeated the house. We all sat back and reminisced of times we watched chickens broiling on spits over an open fire at the Octoberfest. Then we had just stood there, watching and wishing. Today we would be partakers, not spectators.

We were so famished when the meal was finally cooked–two ducks, stuffing, and potato dumplings–that everything was eaten in one sitting. I clearly remember feeling kind of guilty of having gorged myself while Mom was away in the hospital. We all knew that we would never have gotten by with making total pigs out of ourselves had Mom been home. As the saying goes: "Wenn die Katze aus dem Haus ist, dann spielen die Mäuse." Or in English, "When the cat's away, the mice will play."

1957, THE YEAR OF NEW THINGS

Dad taught me to ride a bicycle in 1951. Six years later, on a different continent, he taught me to drive a car. He had gotten his driver's license by taking an oral exam. Mom did the same a bit later. She took her driver's test the day I took my driving and written exam. We still had the old Chrysler. It had served us well. The day Mom took her driving test, she wore a long-sleeved sweater. In Germany that type of sweater was called a Pulover. During her driving exam, the officer in the car with her asked Mom to pull over. "Ja," she said, and kept on driving. A little louder the officer said, "Pull over." Mom glanced at her sweater and kept on driving. "Pull over, pull over," the policeman yelled, pointing with his finger to the side of the road. She did understand that gesture, but still had no idea what her sweater had to do with it.

In 1957, I graduated from high school, went to the senior prom, and got to borrow the family car to take my date to a fancy restaurant. The tuxedo, the gown, the candle light, and music were all kind of stiff and snobbish. It was a good lesson in culture and manners. The dress of the evening did bring out the gentleman in me, as well as the grace of the lady. Frankly, I'd rather have gone on a picnic.

The principal of the school was instrumental in helping me land a job in New Brunswick with Empire Photoengraving. I started a new six-year apprenticeship with that company. Being the only young fellow among the workers, I soon learned a new English, a language with substance such as politics, world events, and other shared experiences. I realized, having only associated with teenage boys, that I had become as childish in many ways as I had accused them of being two and one-half years earlier.

The group I worked with had several men who were from the country Armenia, then a republic of the Soviet Union. Even in school in Germany, I had never heard of Armenia. Talking to these men on a daily basis was like reading a book about a foreign culture. I seemed not to have acquired enough English to ask the proper questions. I just kept on asking, changing scenarios, trying to absorb more and more. The Armenians with names like

Bedrosian, Santoian, Markarian and Boghosian at times reverted back to their native tongue when the discussions became too heated. What a thing to witness. It sounded like a group of stutterers having a hissy. One of my co-workers was a man from Great Britain. One office lady was from Germany, a survivor of Auschwitz. The boss was from Turkey. The rest were Americans. The Americans were often all ears and ever congenial. Working there made for quite an educational experience.

One day the boss asked the English man why I was always whistling. Chas just told him I was a happy young man– and let him be.

A LESSON LEARNED

The last couple of weeks in my senior year, I pur-chased and got to drive to school my own car, a 1951, four-door Dodge.

The seniors hung out in their cars with their buddies before school started. They also spent the balance of the lunch period sitting in the cars smoking and listening to Chuck Berry, Elvis, and Fats Domino.

One of my buddies was Ray, the one I mentioned who refused to read in English class. He was a good printing press operator, but he also was a speed demon behind the wheel. Before I could drive, Ray picked me up once to go to school. The odometer on his car soared past ninety miles an hour, as he casually steered with one hand. I did not tell him, but I was a little more than worried. Before we both graduated, he had lost his permit to drive because of too many speeding violations.

The summer after graduation, Ray and I got together one weekend. We cruised around in my Dodge and picked up three of his friends along the way. The car was full, the day was hot, and we had nothing to do. Ray suggested that we go swimming in a pond tucked away in the Watchung Mountains. Since he knew were the pond was, he asked me to let him drive. I did. Going up hill on the winding road, with five guys in the car, kept us within the speed limit. It was a different story, though, when we crested the incline and started to head downhill. Ray let the Dodge roll as fast as it would go. Sitting in the middle of the front seat and not behind the wheel, I knew I had made a mistake. Ray, and Ray only, was in control. With left arm out the window, steering with only the right hand, and going ever faster, he nonchalantly whipped the car through every bend in the road. The ditch on either side of the road was cut deep, with no shoulder to pull on to. Everyone was quiet, as the trees whizzed by. Ray was still in control, or was he? Entering into the next curve, we encountered a car coming up the hill. Ray yanked the wheel to the right, barely missing a head-on collision. We, however, went off the pavement; and Ray jerked the car back to the left. He lost control. On two wheels, we shot across the road, hitting an embankment as the car started to flip through the air. The car hit the ground once or twice as it went heads over tails. When the car finally quit flipping, it was on its wheels in a grass covered spot. I very clearly saw the open front door of the car come slamming down within inches of my head, like a giant hatchet, preventing the car from rolling on top of me. I had exited the car somewhere along the jolts and was now partially lying on the front seat cushion on the ground when the car door slammed down and then came to a rest. All the windows of the vehicle were out. All the seats were strewn on the ground, and all of the fellows had been thrown through doors and shattered windows. When I gathered myself together, none of the others were around except Ray. They all had bolted from the scene, either in shock or afraid the car would explode. Ray's face was ashen. His nose was obviously broken. Blood was running from it and from under his hair. Slowly the other three eased their way back to the crash site.

The older man and his wife, the ones in the car coming up the mountain, stopped long enough to say that they would get help.

There on the side of the mountain road, five young men were falling to pieces. We all realized that we had had a brush with death. Much later, I marvelled at the grace of God to pick a spot along that mountain road which had no trees in it. All five of us were walking around. It was truly by grace.

Ray, the macho man, approached me in tears. He said that if the police found out that he was driving, he would lose his license forever. With him having no insurance for such a happening, his mother would have to sell the house to settle the liabilities. His dad, already in a lung sanitarium, would not be able to be supported by his mother any longer. He was a pitiful sight. He begged me to tell the police, when they arrived, that I, not he, was driving the car at the time of the wreck. He mentioned that I had no driving points against me, and he offered to help pay for the car. But please, please, save his mother and his home.

When the police came, I told them that I was the driver of the car. All the other boys agreed to that as well. All of us were taken to the hospital by ambulance. Two of the boys stayed several days with lacerations and internal bleeding. Ray had a broken nose and received stitches, as did one other fellow. I had my arm placed in a sling because of a broken shoulder blade. Up on the mountain, I received a reckless driving ticket, which carried six points and an automatic six-month revocation of driving privileges. The court date was set.

The next day, Dad and I drove to the garage to where they had towed the car. We were shocked to see such a frightful sight. We were very thankful, however, that no one had gotten killed. During the night at the garage, so we were told, the tires, the radio, and the battery had been stolen. Dad expected to get at least fifty dollars from the wreck; but since the car was stripped, we paid for the towing and just signed the title over to the owner of the garage.

Three days later my insurance was cancelled. I was forced, if I wanted to continue to drive, to be placed on assigned risk. That type of insurance was about four times more costly than normal coverage under a family plan.

When the court day came, Dad went with me. My hope was to talk the judge into reducing my reckless dri-

One lesson of the New World.

ving charge to something less of an offense. I took along my various awards and honors I had received in high school and planned to tell the judge that I had been careless that day, but not reckless. It worked. The judge reduced the charge to a careless driving ticket. I still lost my permit but for only ten days.

When I got my license back, it was not the customary piece of paper the size of a Social Security card. It was an official document, a full page in size, hot pink in color. I carried that driver's license for three years, until I got off the assigned-risk policy. Had I been involved in any infractions, speeding or otherwise, during the three years, the police, seeing that hot pink license, surely would have thrown the book at me.

If that was not enough for being a good guy, about a month after the accident, we received notice from a lawyer that we were being sued. The parents of all four boys, including Ray's mother, were trying to collect. This is when my mistake really hit home. Perjury under oath or any time, for whatever reason, is not worth it. The first thing I did was tell Dad the truth. I could just see it on his face, as the hair on his neck stood up. He was angry. He had not lectured or punished me in any way. He knew I was thrashing in my own miseries these past weeks.

We promptly drove to Ray's house. There we told his mother the facts. She was shocked and ashamed of the action she took against me. Ray agreed to come along with us to confront the other three families. We told them the truth also and asked them as well to drop the lawsuit.

A week later we received a letter stating that all four claims were dropped.

What did I learn? The truth will set you free! And, aside from the obvious, I vowed that if I ever had sons and they became of driving age, I would lay down the law to them in simple terms. "You will have your own car. It might not be a thing of beauty, but you shall be in charge. You will at all times do the driving. You will never have an excuse to be hauled around by someone else. You are in control because I trust you."

That law did not fail me. Although each of my three sons has been in a car accident, no one got hurt, and each was driving when the accident occurred.

ONLY IN AMERICA

Given the opportunity, there is hardly a person in the world today who would not come to America. Why is that so? It may be that, world-wide, there is a deep down feeling that in America no one will squelch the drive and determination of its people. America is known to elevate not the lazy, but the honest man, a man striving toward a goal with a dogged zeal. People coming to America do not look for handouts. Most are on a mission to prove to themselves, and their new countrymen, that a goal set was not a goal set in vain.

A lot of good things had come to fruition during the first two years in our new homeland. About a year and one-half earlier, we were shown some disrespect for only having three hundred and sixty-two dollars toward the purchase of a new house. The sting from that experience was the impetus to keep us pushing. Mom consistently found ways to put a few dollars away. She always had been very aware that pennies make dollars. Ever since the war, she'd sewn and mended. In many other ways, she figured out not to waste. She saved the grease from roasts and gravies to use again in frying potatoes and baking cakes and cookies. I remember casually mentioning once that a cake she had baked tasted a bit too much like bacon. Every piece of soap that had gotten too small to use was saved. When a cup full of small chunks were collected, they were shredded on the hand-held vegetable grater, and then used to do a load of wash in Mom's wringer washer.

All Dad did was work, then work some more. For many months, he worked two full time jobs. For eight hours, he loaded trucks, then jumped into his car to go to work at a bakery, making doughnuts for another eight hours. Mom cleaned houses six days a week. I worked full time and all the extra hours I could get at Van Vechten Press, including all day Saturdays. During the various harvest times, Mom and Dad went to a local farm to pick vegetables with the migrant workers, during the few hours they had left in the week.

This had nothing to do with being cheap or greedy. It had all to do with goals. You have heard me talk about whining and complaining. Well, you do not do that when something is achievable. Complaining is not part of getting there.

While taking a shortcut through a residential community, Dad spotted a new house under construction. The style of the house was called a front to back split level. It was constructed on a fifty-foot wide lot, between two larger homes. As it turned out, the owner of the new home was also the builder. We set a date to meet with him and talk about the possibility of buying the house. The finances, we knew, had to be worked out. After looking over the house, we all fell in love with it. It had three bedrooms and a bath upstairs. The elevated front of the house provided the living room, with cathedral ceiling, and a full kitchen with an eat-in area. The ground level in the rear had a recreation room, a sewing room, and a washroom with toilet. A cellar was under half of the house, with more usable space. The lot extended in the back for one hundred feet or more, enough for a good garden, flowers, and fruit trees. It was a dream home in a convenient location. We were ready to buy; but could we borrow enough money, that was the worry. With no credit and not much established work history, Mom and Dad found out that they could not borrow enough. All the pool-

Linoleum block print of our very own first house in America. 1957

ing of our monies did not add up to enough to make the difference between the purchase price and what the bank would loan us. We needed almost four thousand dollars.

We took the sad news to the builder and his brother, who kept on working daily on the house to bring it to completion. Dad negotiated with the contractor for a two thousand dollar discount. For this we would have to paint the house, inside and out, as well as do the backfill of the excavated soil around the foundation. This was normally done by a bulldozer, but we had a shovel and were ready. It took a little longer, but it got done.

My parents also approached a German friend for a loan. The friend, who came to this country about the same time we did, offered to lend us one thousand dollars at ten percent interest. We took him up on it. I took the responsibility of paying back that loan with interest. In addition, the builder was kind enough to prolong the closing date until we had saved, or rounded up, enough to meet the bank's required down payment.

We were so convinced that this house was going to be ours that we started to clean up and do other things to help the builder.

One day Dad and I were shoveling dirt to fill the gaping hole around the house, when a man, in his thirties, stopped his car in the front of the house. He climbed up on the dirt pile and introduced himself. He inquired if we were the owners. Mr. Davis said he was a storm-window salesman and asked if we would like him to measure for combination storm and screen windows for our new house. Dad explained that we were working toward becoming the owners. In his ever present naivete, he told Mr. Davis that we still lacked three hundred dollars before we could buy the house. Graciously acknowledging that we were probably not ready for storm windows, Mr. Davis got back in his car and drove off.

Within the hour, Mr. Davis reappeared at the construction site, walked up to Dad and me, and handed us three hundred dollars. He simply said, "My address is on that slip of paper, pay me back when you can." With that he turned and got back in his car.

I saw an angel when I was six years old. I believe I also saw an angel that day in flesh and blood. — He was an American.   PRAISE GOD!

———— · ————

To read more about Franz, go to: www.fxbiii.com

Emily Anne Giles and Franz Xaver Beisser, III
on their wedding day, April 16, 1966.

The American Dream. All the Beissers in the winter of 1999.

Top left: Chris and Katrina, Top right: Brenda and Alfons, Middle right: Kathryn and Franz IV, Middle left: Franz and Emily, Grand children: Jacob, Megan, Chloe, Rachel and newborn Julia, born Aug. 6, 1999.